# Context and Culture in Language Teaching

Claire Kramsch

Oxford University Press 1993

Oxford University Press
Walton Street, Oxford OX2 6DP

Oxford New York Toronto
Delhi Bombay Calcutta Madras Karachi
Petaling Jaya Singapore Hong Kong Tokyo
Nairobi Dar es Salaam Cape Town
Melbourne Auckland

and associated companies in
Berlin Ibadan

*Oxford* and *Oxford English* are trade marks of
Oxford University Press

ISBN 0 19 437187 5

© Claire Kramsch 1993

Set in 10/12pt Sabon
Typeset by Wyvern Typesetting Ltd., Bristol
Printed in Hong Kong

Mod. Lang.

# Contents

122209 D-79

For Olivier and Christophe

# Acknowledgements

The author and publishers would like to thank the following for permission to reproduce material that falls within their copyright:

Piper and Co Verlag for the poem 'Drei Arten Gedichte zu schreiben' by Hilde Domin.

Athenäum Verlag for the poem 'Lied zur Ermutigung' by Hilde Domin from Domin, Hilde (ed) *Doppelinterpretationen. Das zeitgenössische Gedicht zwischen Autor und Leser.*

Schocken Books Inc for 'Kleine Fabel' by Franz Kafka.

H. Luchterhand for the short story 'Schlittenfahren' by Helga Novak.

Carl Hanser Verlag for the poem 'Die Lorelei' by Heinrich Heine.

Gallimard for the poem 'L'école des beaux-arts' by Jacques Prévert.

Jonathan Cape Ltd. for the poem 'Dust of Snow' by Robert Frost.

Coca-Cola Co. USA, for a transcript of a TV commercial.

National Textbook Company for the chapter from *TIME Magazine— We The People* selected by Linda Schinke-Llano.

Aufbau Verlag for the poem 'Mondnacht' by Josef Freiherr von Eichendorff.

Every effort has been made to trace the owners of copyright material in this book, but we should be pleased to hear from any copyright holder whom we have been unable to contact.

# Preface

This book has grown over many years of teaching foreign languages and training language teachers in the United States and abroad. Its different layers of understanding of what it means to be a language teacher, mediator of a foreign culture, and catalyst of educational change, are the product of many conversations I have had over the years with colleagues, students, friends, and family; they were also inspired by the many multilingual and multicultural people I have come to know and who, like me, live with two or more languages and cultures. To all those who have made this adventure worthwhile and who have clarified my thinking I am deeply indebted.

The idea of this book matured at MIT while I was teaching German to undergraduate students. Chapter 1 captures the questioning that went on during these years, as I attempted to make sense of the sometimes brilliant and quixotic ways MIT students learn foreign languages. The book started to take shape at Cornell University, where I visited in 1989. Chapters 2 and 3 grew out of an 'Introduction to Applied Linguistics' course I gave there and a 1990 TESOL Summer Institute course I gave at Michigan State University on 'Language Teaching as Social Interaction'. Chapters 4 and 5 are a direct outgrowth of the course 'Literature in Language Teaching' that I gave at Cornell and at the 1989 LSA/MLA Summer Institute at the University of Arizona with Yvonne Ozzello. I wish to thank those who invited me to give these courses, and those who thought through the ideas with me — my students, for their probing questions and untiring interest. Special thanks go to Linda Waugh, John Wolff, and Sally McConnell-Ginet at Cornell for their enthusiastic support of my work. I finished the book at the University of California at Berkeley. Chapters 6 and 7 reflect my current concerns as I now train graduate students to become linguistic 'go-betweens' in multicultural classrooms.

I would like to thank all the teachers who welcomed me into their classrooms and gave me valuable insights into their daily encounters with foreign language learners. I am grateful to all those schools and universities in the United States and in Canada, Germany, France, Spain, and Russia, who invited me to give lectures and workshops in which I tried out some of my ideas.

There have been a few persons who have shared with me over the years my interest for problems of language and culture. I am grateful to Catherine Chvany for her wise mentorship, Suzanne Flynn for her companionship in linguistic matters, Michael Geisler for his grasp of popular culture, Jim Noblitt for his insights into computer literacy, Peter Patrikis for his unfailing support. Our long and sometimes impassioned conversations gave me the necessary inspiration to write this book.

My gratitude goes to the careful and critical readers of earlier versions of the manuscript: Brian Harrison and Eberhard Piepho, and, especially, Henry Widdowson, who with his wise understanding and impeccable logic encouraged me to refine my argument and to say what I really wanted to say. I should like to thank also Linda von Hoene for being the ideal empathetic and yet questioning reader and for her help in tracking down references. David Wilson was the most careful and patient editor I could have wished for. Finally, I would like to express my sincere thanks to Cristina Whitecross and Anne Conybeare from Oxford University Press for their encouragement and support during the preparation of the manuscript. If this book can make a modest contribution to the emergence of cross-cultural understanding in a united Europe, it will be thanks to them.

Claire Kramsch
Berkeley, January 1992

# Introduction

By its very nature, foreign language teaching is predicated on the conviction that because we are all humans, we can easily understand each other provided we share the same code; all we have to do is learn that code and use it accurately and appropriately. This view of language teaching values consensus and negotiated understanding. Because we all have the same basic human needs, we only have to agree on how to fulfill these needs in various situations of everyday life. On this shared experiential basis, it is believed that one language is essentially (albeit not easily) translatable into another. In foreign language education, this belief has been most fruitful in promoting functional and pragmatic approaches to the teaching and learning of foreign languages around the world.

Where it has encountered difficulties is in the teaching of culture: for culture is difference, variability, and always a potential source of conflict when one culture enters into contact with another. Culture in language learning is not an expendable fifth skill, tacked on, so to speak, to the teaching of speaking, listening, reading, and writing. It is always in the background, right from day one, ready to unsettle the good language learners when they expect it least, making evident the limitations of their hard won communicative competence, challenging their ability to make sense of the world around them.

Consider, in fact, the differences among people due to such factors as age, race, gender, social class, generation, family history, regional origin, nationality, education, life experiences, linguistic idiosyncrasies, conversational styles, human intentionalities. Given these differences and the enormous complexity of human relations, communication in general and, *a fortiori*, communication in a foreign language should be all but impossible. And yet, more often than not, we do understand one another, however imperfectly, however temporarily.

This book takes a philosophy of conflict as its point of departure, thus reversing the traditional view of language teaching as the teaching of forms to express universal meanings. It takes particular meanings, contextual difference, and learner variability as its core: a rose, maybe, is a rose is a rose, but it is not *une rose*, is not *eine Rose*, but multiple ways of viewing and talking about roses. Such an approach is more interested in fault lines than in smooth landscapes, in the recognition of complexity and in the tolerance of ambiguity, not in the search for clear yardsticks of competence or insurances against pedagogical malpractice. It is convinced that understanding and shared meaning, when it occurs, is a small miracle, brought about by the leap of faith that we call 'communication across cultures'.

Language teachers are well aware of the difficulties of their task. But they often view these difficulties in dichotomous terms that unduly simplify the issues and prevent them from understanding the larger context.

## Dubious dichotomies and deceptive symmetries

With the ebb and flow of educational philosophies and methodologies, themselves reactions to larger social and political events, language teaching has tended to swing between what it views as opposite extremes: grammatical versus functional syllabuses, teacher-centered vs. student-centered classrooms, cognitive vs. experiential learning styles, learning-based vs. acquisition-based pedagogies. These swings have been nurtured by the belief in the linear progressive development of the 'ideal' language learning environment and the disillusion with the betrayal of earlier teaching methods. For example, professional rhetoric views the functional–notional approach as having superseded the audiolingual method and having been superseded itself by a proficiency-oriented curriculum. Such a view is comforting—teachers are given a feeling of progress and achievement—but it is deceptive. Teachers know well the variability inherent in the educational context and the impossibility of capturing this variability in any methodical way. They either compensate in enthusiasm and personal commitment to a new method what they lose in global understanding; or they minimize the conflict between methods, styles, and goals, and settle for the so-called 'eclectic' middle ground.

Not only teachers, but teacher trainers themselves are trying to escape dichotomous thinking. Swaffar *et al.* (1991: 6) describes the traditional disparity found in higher education 'between initial semesters of language training (the remedial work) and later scholarly training (the academic mission)'. Richards (1990) sees a 'dilemma' in the fact that teachers have to master low-inference techniques and teaching behaviors that can be readily learned, and at the same time follow higher-level principles of decision making. He suggests that a balance needs to be struck between holistic and atomistic approaches to teacher preparation. This idea of balance between the polarities in the teaching of foreign languages is expressed by Maley, who strives to help teachers arrive at a personal synthesis or 'balance of opposites' (personal communication). Larsen-Freeman (1990) calls for a theory of language teaching that would help teachers find their own way out of the conflicting recommendations they receive from second language acquisition (SLA) research. Lightbown (1986) encourages teachers to become familiar with SLA research—not to find out what is good and bad teaching, but to understand the nature of language and language learning.

Indeed, classroom teaching is a juggling act that requires instant-by-instant decisions based on both local and global knowledge and on an intuitive grasp of the situation. Many of the decisions teachers make are based on compromises between how they perceive the needs of their students and how they view their role and their responsibility as teachers. These many factors are often in contradiction with one another and call for personal judgment based on as broad and differentiated an understanding as possible about what is going on at that particular moment in the classroom.

Rather than fall prey to attractive but ultimately reductionist dichotomies, this book will explore their possible reformulation within a non-dichotomous perspective. In the following, I examine some of the polarities most often cited by teachers and I attempt to break their symmetry by reformulating the questions within a larger contextual framework.

## Learning by doing versus learning by thinking

One of the more tenacious dichotomies in foreign language education is that of skill versus content (see Kramsch 1988a). Language is viewed as a skill, a tool that is in itself devoid of any intellectual value. As an academic subject, it becomes intellectually respectable only when learners are able to use it to express and discuss abstract ideas. This argument has two aspects that reinforce one another. First, an administrative one. In most Western countries, the teaching of foreign languages made a late appearance on the academic scene that was traditionally reserved for the study of ancient and modern literatures. The language teacher has hence a lower academic status than the professor of literature or even civilization. The interface between upper-level language courses and literature seminars is traditionally a particularly sensitive area of the academic curriculum in terms of staffing and syllabus.

The second aspect of the skill versus content argument is an educational one. Functional approaches to language teaching have been adopted with enthusiasm by educational systems in which educational effectiveness is traditionally measured according to its practical outcomes. For example, as Freed and Bernhardt (1992) have recently pointed out, American foreign language education values action over reflection; it believes that the sole responsibility of language teachers is to get their students to talk and write as well and as fluently as possible. Depth and breadth of thought belong to other subjects. The overall result of both these aspects of the skill versus content dichotomy has often been the trivialization of the teaching of foreign languages; it has made the teaching of culture a particularly controversial issue.

We can get out of this dichotomy by seeing learning by doing and learning by thinking as two sides of the same coin. Learners have to experience new uses of language, but they do not even know how new they are if they do not reflect on their experience. It is a fallacy to believe that students do not acquire content as they learn the forms of the language. To be sure, much of this content is not verbalized, it is the unspoken ideological substratum of the educational system, the community, the peer group, the family. If we consider language learning as the acquisition of new forms of discourse, learners have to first recognize to what extent their discourse is that of their surrounding environment. Chapter 1 offers an in-depth analysis of a segment of classroom discourse and explores the lessons we can draw from it to define the nature of the educational challenge we are faced with.

## Grammar versus communication

If both action and reflection form the basis of the acquisition of a foreign language in educational settings, teachers will no doubt argue that the two processes have to be weighted differently at the beginning and the more advanced stages: do beginning learners not have to *do* things with words before they can *reflect* with words? This was the argument made in the early 1970s against the abuses of grammatical metalanguage and structural analyses at the expense of communicative practice. Unfortunately, in many cases, the argument has been couched again in dichotomous terms as: grammar versus communication, conscious application of rules versus unconscious acquisition of conversational patterns.

Because of this dichotomous thinking, many teachers still believe that students should learn to use the language in communication only *after* they have learned to master its structures in drills and other mechanical exercises. On the one hand, it is a fact that structures have to be broken down and learned, that rules have to be explained, inductively or deductively, and that students have to get the necessary linguistic skills. On the other hand, teachers are now told that learners have to be given the opportunity to use their skills even before they have completely mastered them and that they should focus on the message, not on the form of their utterances. The pedagogical result, however, is often an 'everything-goes' attitude on the part of both learners and teachers, with a concomitant abdication of teacher responsibility.

Rather than an either–or dichotomy, grammar and communication can be seen within a view of language as social semiotic (Halliday 1978, 1989, 1990). The structures which speakers choose to use and hearers choose to listen and respond to construct the very context of communication in which learning takes place. Rather than a dichotomy, then, we have multiple options regarding the way language is used in variable contexts of use. In Chapter 2, drawing on Halliday's work but also on that of anthropological linguists like Hymes (1974), Goffman (1981), psycholinguists like Charaudeau (1983), Edmondson (1983, 1985), Ellis (1987), Long (1983, 1989), and sociolinguists like Saville-Troike (1989), I will examine the notion of context and of language teaching as contextual shaping.

## Teacher-talk versus student-talk

The notion of social interaction itself has often been undermined by the phrases 'teacher-talk' versus 'student-talk' and by the pedagogical principle that students should talk as much as possible, the teacher as little as possible. The metaphor 'teacher-talk/student-talk', coined by Flanders (1960), has no doubt been useful to dramatize the new focus on the learner, but it has limited our understanding of the nature of classroom dialogue. It has encouraged teachers to view these two notions as exclusive of one another and to focus on the amount of 'talking', not on what is being talked about nor what meanings are negotiated.

This dichotomy has become a dilemma in recent years as teachers are now told that learners should be exposed to a lot of comprehensible input (Krashen 1988) but that this input should be 'quality input' (Lightbown 1992). Teacher-talk and student-talk seem to be in competition with one another for which of the two provides the best 'input'. Here, quality input is still seen in structural terms, not in terms of quality of interaction, or in overall gains in cultural understanding.

How can we reframe the question in qualitative, rather than quantitative, terms? The larger psychological issue seems to be the following: teachers have to impart a body of knowledge, but learners have to discover that knowledge for themselves in order to internalize it—how can teachers at the same time give it to them and make them discover it on their own? This question is the fundamental paradox of education. Rather than worry about how much speaking, how much listening students should do, we might want to explore the various ways in which learners learn to learn, both as a cognitive and as a social process with variable individual styles of learning. In Chapter 3, I shall analyze the way in which teachers and learners shape contexts of learning both cognitively and socially during classroom lessons, and how they can become aware of this double process.

## Reading to learn versus learning to read

Learners who become aware of how their interaction as speakers and hearers affects the type of knowledge they gain in the classroom can better understand the interaction between readers and texts. It can help them get out of the dichotomy that is still perceived by many when learning to read a text in a foreign language. Either they view reading as an exercise to reinforce their knowledge of grammar and vocabulary, or they treat written texts only as a source of information about the foreign culture. In the first case, the emphasis is on reading to learn—that is, to decode forms in texts; in the second, the main thing is learning to read—that is, to decode information from texts and to make sense of the text *despite* a deficient knowledge of forms.

This polarity—reading to learn the forms, reading to extract informational content—excludes other sources of meaning. It ignores, for example, the unexpected particularities of a writer's style, the social conventions regarding the use of genres and registers, the fractured symmetries of a literary text, and the special kind of interaction all these features require of the reader. It deceives learners into believing that all they have to do is 'retrieve' a meaning that is already in the text. It does not account for the fact that a text creates its reader through its very structure or form, and that readers in turn create the text as they imbue it with meaning. In Chapter 4, building on the work of linguists like Widdowson (1975), Chafe (1982, 1985), sociolinguists like Becker (1985, 1992), Fowler (1986), Tannen (1982, 1985), and literary scholars like Rosenblatt (1978), I will explore the dimensions of this interaction in its 'orate' and 'literate' modes.

## Language versus literature

As language teachers are encouraged to help their students not only to read texts for information, but to interpret them for their many layers of meaning, it would seem natural to draw on literature as a means of teaching language. Yet some teachers still feel hesitant to use literary texts in the language classroom. Their hesitation is often a reflex of academic self-defense. As language teachers they are told they are competent only to teach language, not literature. The language–literature dichotomy has been institutionalized in departments of foreign languages and literatures at North American universities, but the split can be found in other forms all over the world. Teaching language is consistently viewed as a less sophisticated, hence less difficult, task than teaching literature.

As Widdowson has rightly pointed out (1975), the distinction is one of disciplinary boundaries, not of intellectual content. It serves to maintain a certain academic, political, and economic power structure, where language teachers and literature scholars are careful not to tread on each other's territories. The result in the language classroom is an ambivalent one. Even when literary texts are chosen to teach reading because of their general interest and cultural appeal, language teachers seem constrained to teach these texts for their information value only.

Given that the dichotomy between language and literature has no intellectual justification, we have to reformulate their relation within the language teaching enterprise. Texts can be read on different levels of meaning. Whether they are texts of information or works of literature, language is the stuff they are made of. The pedagogical question may not be whether language teachers should teach literature or not, but, rather: how can language teachers help learners read texts at a variety of levels of meaning? This question will be pursued in greater detail in Chapter 5.

## Language versus culture

The same hesitation about the teaching of literature in language classes can be found with the teaching of culture. One often reads in teachers' guide-lines that language teaching consists of teaching the four skills 'plus culture'. This dichotomy of language and culture is an entrenched feature of language teaching around the world. It is part of the linguistic heritage of the profession. Whether it is called (Fr.) *civilisation*, (G.) *Landeskunde*, or (Eng.) *culture*, culture is often seen as mere information conveyed by the language, not as a feature of language itself; cultural awareness becomes an educational objective in itself, separate from language. If, however, language is seen as social practice, culture becomes the very core of language teaching. Cultural awareness must then be viewed both as enabling language proficiency and as being the outcome of reflection on language proficiency.

Several researchers have recently furthered our thinking about the relation of language and culture in language teaching. Halliday's systemic linguistics gives a unified theoretical framework within which to view this traditional dichotomy. By calling grammar 'a theory of human experience' and text 'the linguistic form of social interaction' (1990), Halliday anchors culture in the very grammar we use, the very vocabulary we choose, the very metaphors we live by. Others approach this problem from a different angle. Quasthoff (1986) and Blum-Kulka, House, and Kasper (1989) have explored the cultural dimensions of speech acts and discourse pragmatics, Keller (1987) and Müller-Jacquier (1986) have examined stereotypes and self- and other-perceptions, and Byram (1989) has reassessed the role of cultural studies in foreign language education. In the United States, scholars like Nostrand (1989) and Kramsch (1988b) are reevaluating the notion of cultural authenticity, while Valdes (1986) gives a fresh look at the 'cultural gap' in language teaching.

The question that concerns us here is the following: given that we want to teach language in such a way that learners are initiated into its social and cultural meanings, how many of these meanings must be made explicit, how many can be understood implicitly? How can a foreign way of viewing the world be taught via an educational culture which is itself the product of native conceptions and values? Once we recognize that language use is indissociable from the creation and transmission of culture, we have to deal with a variety of cultures, some more international than others, some more conventionalized than others. Chapters 6 and 7 will seek to describe the dialectic relationship of language and culture and suggest ways of developing not only the culturally competent learner, but the cross-cultural personality.

## Native speaker versus non-native speaker

For research purposes, it has been customary to view the linguistic development of a learner on an interlanguage continuum whose endpoint is a linguistic construct called the 'native speaker'. Non-native teachers and students alike are intimidated by the native-speaker norm and understandably try to approximate this norm during the course of their work together. If, however, we consider language study as initiation into a kind of social practice that is at the boundary of two or more cultures, such a linear progression makes less sense. In fact what is at stake is the creation, in and through the classroom, of a social, linguistic reality that is born from the L1 speech environment of the learners and the social environment of the L2 native speakers, but is a third culture in its own right. Chapter 8 will sketch the personal and political dimensions of such a 'third place'.

## The importance of context in language education

The polarities mentioned above can be traced to the age-old duality of language as text and language as context—that is, language as expression of an individual's thoughts and intentions, and language as expression of a speech community's knowledge and expectations (Kramsch and McConnell-Ginet 1992a). As Halliday and Hasan (1989: 117) have argued:

> The notions of text and context are inseparable: text is language operative in a context of situation and contexts are ultimately construed by the range of texts produced within a community ... One commonsense conception is ... that our ideas, our knowledge, our thoughts, our culture are all there — almost independent of language and just waiting to be expressed by it. This attitude is so deeply rooted that it finds its expression, for example, in our theoretical writings about language.

The dichotomy between language as an expression of personal meaning and language as a reflection of the social order is already inscribed in the very way we write about 'texts' on the one hand and 'contexts' on the other. It reflects the fundamental polarity of linguistic discourse that describes language use as both the creation of texts and the shaping of contexts. In order to conceptualize these processes we use two different words, but in fact they are, as Halliday and Hasan write, 'inseparable notions'—much like the dichotomies mentioned above are often two sides of the same coin and act as such upon each other.

Teachers eager to apply the findings of recent psycholinguistic research to their teaching often confuse the descriptive language of science and the prescriptive language normally associated with education. For example, research in cognitive science distinguishes between 'bottom-up' and 'top-down' processes to capture the way form and meaning contribute to an understanding of spoken and written texts. Teachers tend to teach these processes separately, at different stages, say, of learning to read. But what needs to be taught is not the one or the other, nor even the one and the other, but the *interaction* between the two.

On the one hand, if we teach language use, we are teaching not only a rule-governed structural system, whose usage is sanctioned by society, but 'the actualization of meaning potential associated with particular situation types' (Halliday 1978: 109). By teaching grammar we are teaching, to use Gregory Bateson's metaphor, 'contextual shaping' (Bateson 1979: 17).

On the other hand, language use has its own social grammar of roles, settings, rules of speaking, and norms of interpretation.

As Saville-Troike (1989: 258) remarks:

> That meaningful context is critical for language learning has been widely recognized. There has not been adequate recognition, however, that this context includes understanding of culturally defined aspects of a communicative event, such as role relationships and norms of interpretations, of holistic scripts for the negotiation of meanings, as well as observable aspects of the setting.

The difficulty of teaching the *interaction* of linguistic and social structures, of bottom-up and top-down processes, is that language and social reality are not coextensive. Researchers can describe the variations in language use but these descriptions are still no blueprint for the language teacher on how to teach the interaction of linguistic forms and social meanings: for this interaction is dependent on the context and the way this context is perceived by the participants. And two participants might see the context quite differently even though they might share the same language.

Given that language teachers have to teach both a normative linguistic system and its variable instances of use, attention to context calls for a type of pedagogy that fosters both direct and indirect ways of transmitting knowledge, that values not only facts but relations between facts, that encourages diversity of experience and reflection on that diversity.

## A discourse perspective

The view of language that best captures the dynamics between the various opposing forces mentioned above is that of *language in discourse*. Between the learner and the language, between the teacher and the learner, and among learners, discourse is 'the process by which we create, relate, organize and realize meaning' (Riley 1985: 2). The classroom as 'coral gardens' (Breen 1985b) draws its impetus from the tension between a multitude of psychological, social, political, moral, and linguistic oppositions in conflict with one another for the construction of meaning. It is on the level of discourse that these tensions find both their justification and their dialectic resolution.[1]

Neither second nor foreign language education have any tradition of dialectic thought. Languages are taught from the perspective of either the L2 or the L1, or L2 forms and discourse patterns are contrasted with those of the L1. There is rarely any attempt at a synthesis that would permit the learner to see these contrasts from a higher ground. This is nowhere more apparent than in the cultural values that are promoted together with the language, be it a second language—such as English as a Second Language, Français Langue Etrangère, and Deutsch als Fremdsprache—or a foreign language, such as those taught in British, French, or German schools as part of the general education curriculum.

Second language instructors, who teach their language to immigrants or visitors in their country, or to adults abroad, have tended to transmit, with the language, a view of the world that reflects only the values and cultural assumptions of the native speaker's society. Even as an international language, English instruction transmits such Anglo-Saxon values as efficiency, pragmatism, and individualism, that superimpose themselves on those of the learners' native culture. Foreign language instructors, on the other hand, who teach a second or a third foreign language to students in educational settings, generally transmit with that language a view of the world that mainly promotes the values and cultural assumptions of the L1 educational system.

Foreign language education has been characterized up to now by the search for a 'middle landscape'. It has usually tried to solve conflicts quantitatively by taking a little bit of this and a little bit of that from several, often opposing, viewpoints—the well-known methodological swings mentioned above. By refusing to be ideological, this approach has in fact espoused a middle-ground conservative ideology, recognizable by its positivistic, pragmatic bent, intent on assimilating conflicts by minimizing them. However, as in other sectors of education, questions are being raised about a purely pragmatic type of foreign language education.

As other fields of inquiry, like cultural studies or literature studies, are redrawing the boundaries of their disciplines, it would be appropriate for foreign language study to reexamine its disciplinary base and its cultural presuppositions. Its main goal can no longer be the one-sided response to national and economic interests, and the pursuit of communicative happiness; it must include the search for an understanding of cultural boundaries and an attempt to come to terms with these boundaries.

To summarize, the contradictions sketched above, rather than being problems that can and should be solved, represent the basic condition of classroom learning—what Yves Châlon calls the 'conflit inhérent à la condition pédagogique' (quoted in Riley 1985: 1). As such, they can only be described and accepted. However, a dialectic perspective can help reframe traditional questions, break their deceptive symmetry and eventually bring about change.

This book, then, is an attempt to redraw the boundaries of foreign language study. Rather than dealing with the teaching of each of the traditional 'four skills' and then with the teaching of 'culture', it takes its impetus from a concrete occurrence of cross-cultural miscommunication in a language class (Chapter 1), and takes *cultural context* as its core. The educational challenge is teaching language 'as context' within a dialogic pedagogy that makes context explicit, thus enabling text and context to interact dialectically in the classroom.[2]

Chapters 2 and 3 define the full dimensions of the here-and-now context of interaction between speakers and hearers in classrooms—what Wells calls the 'sphere of intersubjectivity' (1981: 47). Chapter 3 applies this definition to an examination of concrete foreign language lessons and of the interaction of teacher and learners. Suggestions are made for enriching the spoken discourse of the classroom by taking advantage of its diversity and variability.

Chapters 4 and 5 expand the notion of context to include the more distant interaction between readers and texts in the creation of what could be called a 'sphere of intertextuality'. Chapter 5 applies this definition to the teaching of literary texts in language classes. Here again, the challenge is to exploit the particular voices in the text and the particular responses of its readers.

Chapters 6 and 7 broaden yet again the notion of context to include the creation of a 'sphere of interculturality', through the use of culturally authentic texts. Chapter 7 gives a critical look at some of the cross-cultural approaches currently advocated for teaching texts from the media and other non-pedagogic sources.

The last chapter, Chapter 8, offers a reflection on a critical language pedagogy that values dissent, dialogue, and double-voiced discourse. It shows how learners can use the system for their own purposes, to create a culture of the third kind in which they can express their own meanings without being hostage to the meanings of either their own or the target speech communities.

## Notes

1 I will take here 'dialectic' to mean a dialogue between two opposed or contradictory viewpoints. In the course of this dialogue, each party comes to understand the other's position from a broader, less partial perspective, which does justice to the substance of each point of view, but allows the search for a common ground. It is in the course of this search that understanding between people may emerge, based on a recognition of difference and an acceptance of continued dialogue despite these differences.

2 In his desire to rehabilitate the particular voice of the individual in a totalitarian political system, Bakhtin makes a distinction between 'dialogic' and 'dialectic':

> Dialogue and dialectics. Take a dialogue and remove the voices (the partitioning of voices), remove the intonations (emotional and individualizing voices), carve out abstract concepts and judgments from living words and responses, cram everything into one abstract consciousness—and that's how you get dialectics.
> (Bakhtin 1986: 147)

In this book I will not separate the two, since text and context cannot exist outside the individual voices that create them. I will therefore consider dialectics as being the very essence of dialogue, and dialogue as being intrinsically dialectic. The term 'dialectic' stresses the dynamic relation of text and context, the term 'dialogue' focuses on the relation of both text and context to the individual speaker/hearer.

# 1 Educational challenges

> ... si l'on ne veut pas voir la pédagogie s'enliser dans le conformisme, il faut qu'à tout moment elle enseigne le refus de se conformer. Il n'est de pédagogie constructive que sauvage et la vraie pédagogie se moque de la pédagogie.[1]
> (Yves Châlon, cited in Riley 1985: xix)

Every folktale has its good guys and its bad guys, its winners and its losers, but its real heroes are the tricksters, the naive ones, who stray by the wayside to pick the forbidden flowers, the wilful ones, who trick the powerful into releasing their treasures. Every language class has, too, its 'good' and its 'bad' language learners—but who speaks for the tricksters? For the so-called poor learner of German who, instead of doing the assigned reading, finds a twelve-verse-long poem, memorizes the lot, composes music to it, synthesizes it, records it, and recites it in front of the class with his own background music? For the nonconformist learners of French who, instead of the expected situational role-play, enact a fantastic Ionesco-type dialogue based on the dehydrated sentences of the textbook? It is with those learners in mind, those who use the system but resist it for their own purposes, that I will look at the educational challenges confronting teachers and learners of foreign languages.

## Of challenges and conditions

The class was a fourth semester German class at a prestigious school of engineering in the United States. Undergraduate students there take foreign languages as part of their humanities requirement. The students in this particular class had been asked to learn a poem of their choice and prepare to recite it in class. The next day, Amy brings a copy of a poem by Hilde Domin that she found in the library. It is the third in a group of three poems entitled *Drei Arten Gedichte zu schreiben* (three ways of writing poems). Before reciting the poem, she lists on the board some important words that the students might not know, together with their English equivalent, and a sentence to illustrate their use. Among them is a word that is not in the poem, but that she feels is important to understand the text: *die Herausforderung*—'the challenge'. She writes the following sample sentence on the board: *Ich mag Herausforderungen aber diese Klasse ist lächerlich*, meaning to say 'I like challenges, but this class is ridiculous [in the large amount of work it requires]'. She then proceeds to recite the poem, with deep conviction and obvious pleasure:

Ich will einen Streifen Papier
so groß wie ich
ein Meter sechzig
darauf ein Gedicht
das schreit
sowie einer vorübergeht
schreit in schwarzen Buchstaben
das etwas Unmögliches verlangt
Zivilcourage zum Beispiel
diesen Mut den kein Tier hat
Mit-Schmerz zum Beispiel
Solidarität statt Herde
Fremd-Worte
heimisch zu machen im Tun


Mensch
Tier das Zivilcourage hat
Mensch
Tier das den Mit-Schmerz kennt
Mensch Fremdwort-Tier Wort-Tier
Tier
das Gedichte schreibt
Gedicht
das Unmögliches verlangt
von jedem der vorbeigeht
dringend
unabweisbar
als rufe es
'Trink Coca-Cola'
(Hilde Domin, 'Ich will dich', 1970)

[I want a strip of paper / as tall as I / one meter sixty / on it a poem / that screams / when someone passes by / screams in black letters / demanding something impossible / like for example the courage to dissent / that courage that no animal has / like for example com-passion / solidarity instead of herd / foreign words / to be made your own through doing

Human / animal with the courage to dissent / human / animal that knows compassion / human foreign word-animal word-animal / animal / that writes poems / poem / that demands the impossible / of everyone that passes by / urgently / unavoidably / as if it called out / 'Drink Coca-Cola']

What was Amy resonating to in this poem written in someone else's language, born out of someone else's experience? The poem is not about challenges in the usual American sense—those obstacles that one can overcome if one really wants to; it is, rather, about paradoxical conditions, that both call for action and question the usefulness of action. It appeals to such uniquely human feelings as compassion, solidarity, courage to dissent, and yet proclaims that it demands and will continue to demand 'the impossible'.

The poem, written by the German Jewish writer in 1967–8 upon her return to Germany, is an appeal to question the herd mentality, the conformism, and the brutality that forced her into exile during the Third Reich and that, in her view, still need to be fought against today. The first verse maintains the distinction between humans and 'animals', between rational beings who have noble feelings and write 'foreign' words like 'solidarity', 'compassion', and 'courage to dissent' on big sheets of paper, and proclaim them through the streets—and animals who are known not to do any of these things. In the second verse, the poet slowly, step by step, enacts the last two lines of the first verse: 'making the foreign words your own by doing' (*heimisch machen*: literally, 'making foreign words into your home' or 'making oneself at home in the foreign words'). The text of the poem written on the life-size sheet of paper undergoes a metamorphosis as the poet renames the rational human being an animal, that 'knows compassion', 'has the courage to dissent', and 'writes poems'. At the end of the second verse, human and animal, mind and body fuse together and become one with the poem, as it celebrates the challenge of 'the impossible', with the same urgency as a Coca-Cola advertisement. The turning point, between the two verses is arguably the phrase *Fremd-Worte heimisch zu machen im Tun* (making oneself at home in foreign words through doing). Appropriating for oneself foreign words by reciting them aloud ('screaming' them), rather than reading and analyzing them, is a provocation, something Domin calls in the second of the three poems *das Dennoch jedes Buchstabens* (the spite expressed by each letter). It is one way the poem and its readers can express the paradox of language.

Amy certainly did not analyze the text in any systematic way, nor did the teacher offer any formal analysis. It was Amy's poem and she was asked why she had chosen it. Amy explained that what had caught her interest, was the notion of challenge, of asking the impossible, and the general political message of the poem. Also she liked the idea of a poem that 'screams'. And yet, the sentence on the board, *Ich mag Herausforderungen aber diese Klasse ist lächerlich*, did not seem to be related to that at all. It was a direct translation from the English and as such, it made no sense in German. A native speaker of German, complaining about the amount of homework, would speak of assignments (*Aufgaben*), of duties to fulfill (*Pflichten*); he or she would call an inordinate workload 'unreasonable' (*eine Zumutung*), not 'ridiculous' (*lächerlich*), which in German seems to imply that it is a ridiculously small task and that the student feels underchallenged.

What should the teacher do? She could respond to the surface features of the student's utterance and correct her error as a lexical error, cautioning her against building German sentences from their English dictionary equivalents. However, she notices that in this sentence, Amy is not only trying to express a typically American notion of challenge; she is also complaining publicly, albeit in an indirect manner, about an educational system that abuses the very concept she cherishes. (Note that it is customary for students at that engineering school to complain about the workload, but it is rather unusual to file the complaint publicly on the blackboard in front of the teacher, even under the guise of a vocabulary exercise.) The foreign concept *Herausforderung* as illustrated by Hilde Domin seems to allow her both to adopt and contest, in the same German sentence, an American concept of challenge that overvalues individual competition and hard work over solidarity and compassion. Moreover, Amy seems to have found in this German poem a deep personal vindication of her unique position as a female student in a traditionally male-oriented school of engineering. The fact that the poet is a woman surely adds to the personal resonance which this poem has for her. Hilde Domin enables her both to affirm a notion of challenge that gives equal opportunity to women in higher education and to question a male style of syllabus based on cut-throat competition and quantitative measures of success.

Amy has thus constructed several texts: she has given voice to a German poem which has a specific cultural context of production, and she has put on the blackboard a parallel text that has its own social and personal context of production and reception. At the same time, of course, she has tried to fulfill the lexical and grammatical task required by the teacher.

Her recitation of the poem is at the intersection of what Edmondson (1985) calls the multiple worlds of discourse that coexist in any language class. Under the guise of a vocabulary exercise (pedagogic discourse), she has voiced her discontent with the amount of homework required in this class (everyday non-pedagogic discourse). Beside belonging to a stock of phrases that are representative of American ideological discourse ('I like challenges'), the sentence she wrote on the board belongs also to a stock of phrases frequently uttered by students at that particular school ('This class is ridiculous'). Thus the whole utterance could be taken as a citation of her immediate environment (citational discourse). In addition, her performance of the Domin text gives voice to a type of political discontent that she makes her own (political discourse), while using it as a moral exhortation to her audience in the class (educational discourse). As in all human interactions, the particular voices of the individual mingle with the voices of the social communities from which they draw. And, beyond the social and the particular, stands the attempt by Amy to create an 'intermeaning' that violates German lexical usage. Given the abundance of meanings of the event, how can the teacher help weave all that into an appropriately educational experience?

The teacher decides first to congratulate Amy on her eloquent rendition of Hilde Domin's poem. Then, in simple German, she makes the following remarks. According to Domin the role of poetry is not to change the world but to speak its paradoxes, and so the meaning of *Herausforderung* here is both an appeal for action and a provocation based on an acceptance of the human condition and on the perceived impossibility of change. She observes that, although Hilde Domin's life experience was quite different from Amy's, Amy is doing exactly what the poet had in mind: by selecting and then reciting that poem, she, too, is affirming her demand of the impossible within her own social system. She is, so to speak, re-writing herself through that poem.

The teacher then turns to the sentence on the board and points out that it presents quite an interesting cross-cultural problem. The sentence does not mean what Amy had intended it to mean, because German society does not find this particular use of the word appropriate in this context. When speaking of education (*Bildung*), German speakers do not think in terms of challenges or opportunities—two untranslatable words—but in terms of requirements (*Anforderungen*) and performance (*Leistung*). Amy's statement on the board is perfectly valid in its intention, but it raises the problem of wanting to express one world view through the language normally used to express another society's world view. Amy's face shows disbelief. How can it be that Germans do not have a word for the American notion of challenge?

That summer, Amy went and spent some time with a German family near Heidelberg. She later recounts:

> The most difficult thing to get accustomed to was not the different foods or the fact that the stores close at 1.00 p.m. on Saturday. You get used to that. No, it's the culture. When I told them that what I wanted to do later in life is become a biophysics engineer and build my own company, they laughed! They just laughed and I felt hurt. It seemed inconceivable to them that a woman would have an opportunity to build her own engineering company. And I was suddenly reminded of what we had discussed in my German class about 'challenges', about the uses of the American concept, and about the way Hilde Domin viewed challenges. It helped me understand things a little better. In the United States, I know that I will not be able to do all the things I say I will, but I know it only intellectually—I don't *feel* constrained right now.

The confrontation with another culture gave Amy an outsider's perspective on her personal situation. She was faced with a paradox, incompatible with her own self-image as a successful young woman engineer: the laughter of outsiders shocked her into realizing that for some people she was indeed demanding the impossible; and yet the German poem she had found seemed to legitimate her continued quest for the impossible. Moreover, in the reflective environment of the classroom, the German language had given her a way of critiquing the existing competitive structures of the school. Now it provided her with another way of seeing challenges, namely as paradoxes and food for thought, not only as opportunities for action.

I would like to hold on to this slice of classroom life to reflect on the nexus of forces at work in the teaching of foreign languages in educational settings. For historical and political reasons, the concept of challenge forms the bedrock of American educational ideology, like that of doing your duty is part of a certain German educational tradition.[2]

However, there are two clusters of meanings surrounding the concept of challenge, which are in apparent contradiction with one another, according to whether one views a conflictual situation from the perspective of mainstream politicians and educators, or from that of persons and groups who are not in positions of power, such as women, foreigners, and classroom learners.

## Challenge as action

In the first case, a challenge is a test of strength, a potential measure of oneself against a more powerful obstacle. It is predicated on an adversarial view of humans versus nature or things perceived as natural, and the conviction that humans will eventually overcome the obstacles set by nature. North American settlers met the challenge of the New World by taming (i.e. industrializing) the garden of Eden (Marx 1964); Amy lived up to the challenge of the sex barrier by becoming a woman engineer in a male-dominated field.

A challenge is also an opportunity to show what one can really do. It is assumed that the task is feasible, the solution within reach, otherwise it would be called an 'obstacle' or a 'problem'. Calling it a challenge emphasizes the fact that solutions can be found, even though it might require hard work and perseverance. This meaning of the term includes therefore an 'appeal to action', mostly of the individual kind, an incentive for personal ingenuity and resourcefulness to remove or overcome the obstacle. This is also how politicians use the term. By naming budget cuts, poverty, crime, bad schools, or the lack of foreign language competency 'challenges' rather than 'problems' or 'conditions', people in power remove the discussion from the larger context of causes and origins, conflicts and responsibilities, and focus instead on the engineering of solutions. People are supposed to 'rise to', 'respond to', 'pick up' challenges. These metaphors by which we live reinforce the social order and show our capacity to live up to its demands.

Challenge is predicated upon 'competition'. In political and educational parlance, competing and responding to challenges are frequent collocations. The greatest challenge of all is often not a thing or an event, but one's fellow competitor. American economists prefer to speak of the Japanese challenge rather than of the Japanese threat; the economic superiority of the Japanese sets a challenge for American school children to learn Japanese and other foreign languages; each learner is seen as a challenge to his or her peers on the various achievement tests.

Competition is often legitimized by what has been termed the 'pursuit of excellence'. Within a challenge-oriented ideology, this originally uncontroversial phrase (who could be against excellence?) has come to mean the pursuit of comparative 'superiority', not just the laudable attempts to do one's best and to reach relative mastery in one's area of expertise.

Over the last few years, the meaning of the term 'challenge' has incurred an ideological inflation. It is directly linked to an entrepreneurial view of education that views knowledge as an economic commodity and knowledge of foreign languages as a means of individual advancement on the world market place.[3]

## Challenge as paradox

These uses and abuses of the term 'challenge' are distinct from, but related to its second meaning in education, namely 'paradox'. In this meaning, the focus is on the challenge itself rather than on the person challenged. The emphasis is not on the appeal for action, competition, or superiority like in a sports arena, but, rather, on the implicit 'appeal for reflection' and enlightened understanding. A challenge in this second meaning is a paradox for one's intellect, an invitation to question existing logic and existing world views. Phrases like 'the feminist challenge' call for reflection on the patriarchal conditions under which knowledge is acquired and transmitted. They lead people in subordinate positions to question and problematize existing power structures. The paradoxes that ensue—such as, for example, the conflicting demands of individual freedom and social order—

have to be first thought through before any course of action can be taken. Hilde Domin's poem illustrates that kind of challenge. Whereas the first verse refers to those challenges that can be met by doing, such as political action and humanitarian relief, the second verse does not offer any solutions except the poem itself.

Since this view of challenge accepts irreducible social and cultural differences among people, it is predicated on a permanent confrontation of divergent value systems. Thus it calls for an acceptance of difference and for 'cooperation' (solidarity), rather than for competition and the achievement of a consensus (herd mentality).

Challenge then becomes a call for 'dialogue' between speakers of different languages who struggle to keep the channels of communication open in spite or because of the ideological differences they recognize and maintain between them. In this sense, communication becomes a challenge in the Pascalian sense of *pari*—that is, an act of faith in the willingness and ability of people to bring about change through dialogue (Attinasi and Friedrich, forthcoming). It is on this faith that, I suggest, foreign language teaching should be predicated. To be sure, it requires a new definition of what it means to be a language teacher.

## Challenge as dialogue

Teachers and learners in educational systems are subjected to the ideology of the institution, which itself responds to national and international imperatives. However, as we shall see, learners as well as teachers repeatedly use the system to promote their own local and personal meanings as well as for their own pleasure. In the interstices of the native and the target cultures, they are constantly engaged in creating a culture of the third kind through the give-and-take of classroom dialogue.

The two meanings of the concept of challenge featured above coexist in foreign language education in a dialectic tension between the global needs dictated from above and imposed to teachers via state guide-lines, textbook industry, and the institution's curricular decisions, and the local needs of classroom participants as they struggle with the foreign language and culture.

Up to now, the teaching of culture in the language class has taken two main directions. One has focused on cultural information: statistical information (institutional structures and facts of civilization), highbrow information (the classics of literature and the arts), lowbrow information (the foods, fairs, and folklore of everyday life). This view of culture has favored facts over meanings and has not enabled learners to understand foreign attitudes, values, and mindsets. It has kept learners unaware of the multiple facets of the target group's cultural identity. It has left them blind to their own social and cultural identity, implicitly assuming a consensus between their world and the other (Tajfel 1982).

The other direction taken recently has been to situate culture within an interpretive framework, taken from cross-cultural psychology or cultural anthropology, using universal categories of human behavior and inferencing procedures for making sense of foreign reality. Language learners are given a key to interpret phenomena in the target culture. This culture is usually generalized to mean national culture with slight variations. Not only are learners still considered the passive recipients of cultural knowledge, but it is left up to them to integrate that knowledge with the diversity they encounter when they go to the target country. It is also up to them to integrate it with their own various social and cultural allegiances in their own society. This model too is a consensual model, for, although it does show differences, it does not address the conflicts and the paradoxes that ensue from these differences.

Recently a third direction has begun to emerge, one to which I hope this book will contribute. It, too, sees culture both as facts and as meanings, but it sees it as a place of struggle between the learners' meanings and those of native speakers.

The cultural context of the target society contains enough predictability to ensure an understanding of meanings 'for all practical purposes' (Goffman 1981: 10), but it is by no means restricted to these meanings.

> Culture is not a relatively harmonious and stable pool of significations, but a confrontation between groups occupying different, sometimes opposing positions in the map of social relations, and the process of making meanings (which is, after all, the process of culture) is a social struggle, as different groups struggle to establish meanings that serve their interests.
> (Fiske 1989b: 58)

By using the target society's store of knowledge, but capitalizing on its diversity, speakers make their voice predictable enough to be generally comprehended, but unique enough to be listened to and understood across lines that differ from the ones traditionally encountered in that society. Of course, in this sense native and non-native speakers encounter similar difficulties. However, foreign language learners, who have not grown up in the community that speaks the language, have much greater difficulty identifying the range of potential meanings available in that speech community and selecting the ones appropriate for a given context. Two examples will suffice to illustrate this paradox.

**Example 1:** *Kommst du heute abend zum Essen?* (Are you coming to dinner tonight?) asks my German friend. In my cultural world, such an utterance is a reminder of a previously extended invitation. In the German-speaking world, it expresses a first-time invitation. My instinctive reaction is to feel guilty of possibly having forgotten that I was invited. Remembering the illocutionary meaning of such an utterance in German eliminates my guilt feeling; it does not, however, eliminate my dilemma. For, as a non-native speaker, I need to be accepted by the target cultural speech community and save my positive face by accepting the invitation. At the same time, however, I need to be respected in my own cultural identity and save my negative face by questioning the way the invitation has been formulated. So I can either accept the social meaning of the question on its own terms and answer: *Ja, gerne* (I'd be glad to come), or reject it by imposing my own French cultural meaning on the question *Wieso? ich wußte nicht, daß ich eingeladen war* (I didn't know I was invited), or else point to the cultural paradox itself: *Ja, gerne, aber zuerst dachte ich, daß du mich an etwas erinnern wolltest; wir nämlich in Französisch . . .* (I'd be glad to come, but first I thought you were reminding me of something; in French we . . .). My ability as a non-native speaker to choose a response that satisfies both my negative and my positive face depends on my critical reading of the context of situation, including my self-perception vis-à-vis my own and my friend's social group.

**Example 2:** Judy, a young American student returning from a stay with a German family complained that she never found out how to say 'I'm sorry' in German. For instance, she would enter the living room where the father was sitting, and he would ask her to close the door. As she would go to close the door, she would feel like saying 'Oh, I'm sorry', as she was used to doing from home, to show her sensitive attention to other family members' needs. However, *Entschuldigung* seemed inappropriate, *Verzeihung* seemed too pompous, *Es tut mir leid* seemed excessive. So what should she say?

The student felt obviously awkward replicating the text of prior similar situations in her own family. She intuitively sensed that the German situation did not call for sensitive attention to another person's needs. There was neither the fear of draft nor of noise from the outside and the father did not seem personally inconvenienced by the open door. Rather, closing the door behind you when you enter a room seemed to be the socially appropriate thing to do in Germany. The German father was probably teaching the young foreigner a cultural lesson by asking her to close the door; he was probably not expressing a personal need. Thus a personal expression of excuse could indeed have been viewed as inappropriate and the father would have interpreted it as a puzzling expression of guilt on the part of a foreigner. But Judy wanted to be polite and considerate, so she muttered *Entschuldigung*.[4]

Now one could argue that, by inserting a text from a different context of culture into the new situation, Judy was making a breach into a view of German culture perceived and presented by the father as a monolithic consensual social affair. By personally excusing herself for having left the door open, however awkward the formulation in German, the student was making a statement about the relative distribution of personal vs. societal behaviors in German speech communities and, thereby, for a fleeting moment, she was changing the cultural equation. It could thus be argued that it was legitimate for her to behave as an American in this German situation.

Such paradoxes can only be talked about and reflected upon. It is through the opportunities for dialogue and reflection upon dialogic experiences that cross-cultural exchanges have their value. Rather than tell their students how they should behave in such paradoxical situations, a teachers' responsibility is to give learners a 'space' to make their own meanings and help them interpret those meanings. As the Soviet scholar Mikhail Bakhtin would say, they have to help learners 'be present in their own utterances, . . . appropriate for themselves a language they have not made in contexts they have not chosen' (cited in

Morson 1986: 17). For this, teacher and learners have to develop consciously what Bakhtin (1986: 108) calls a 'double-voiced discourse' by contrast with the single-voiced discourse of traditional education.

## Double-voiced discourse

Bakhtin is interested in the way learners manage to acquire their own communicative competence in a language despite the various voices that coexist in their utterances and that are, as the example of Amy shows, by nature in conflict with one another. 'Language is not a neutral medium that passes freely and easily into the private property of the speaker's intentions; it is populated—overpopulated—with the intentions of others. Expropriating it, forcing it to submit to one's own intentions and accents, is a difficult and complicated process' (Bakhtin, cited in Cazden 1989: 122). Rather than being monolithic speakers of our native language, 'we are the voices that inhabit us' (Morson 1986: 8). So how can learners become the authors of their own words beyond just mouthing the sentences from the textbook, imitating the utterances of their teacher, appropriating for themselves the phrases of other speakers?

It requires first recognizing the extent to which we echo our social environment, then finding new ways of expressing our thoughts in such a way that they are both understandable and original. This process is a dialogic process that Bakhtin scholar Gary Morson describes as follows: 'It includes the listener's identification of the speaker's apparent and concealed motives and of the responses that the speaker invites and hopes to forestall' (ibid.: 6). In other words, it is through dialogue with others, native and non-native speakers, that learners discover which ways of talking and thinking they share with others and which are unique to them.

But, the reader could ask, has not language learning always been based on dialogue? According to Bakhtin, language education has been predicated up to now on the ideal native speaker, speaking with one voice in all situations, through a universal linguistic code. It has been a single-voiced discourse. 'The dictionary, and systematic linguistics, are deaf to the play of voices and insensitive to the cacophony of values' (ibid.: 4). In single-voiced discourse, the sole orientation of the speaker is to the self and to the progress that he or she is making in learning the language.

By contrast, in double-voiced discourse, as Sheldon describes it, 'the primary orientation is to the self, to one's agenda. The other orientation is to the members of the group. The orientation to others does not mean that the speaker necessarily acts in an altruistic, accommodating, or even self-sacrificing manner. It means, rather, that the speaker pays attention to the companion's point of view, even while pursuing her own agenda. As a result, the voice of the self is enmeshed with and regulated by the voice of the other' (Sheldon 1992: 99). In that type of orientation, teacher and learners are interested not only in talking and listening to others talk, but in genuinely exploring the intentions, frames of reference, and reactions of the other participants in the classroom dialogue. By identifying and discussing the dialogic context itself, the participants in the dialogue are given validity and importance as speakers and hearers in that dialogue; their contributions are given breadth and depth.

By attending both to their own agenda and to that of their interlocutors, language learners can start using the foreign language not merely as imperfect native speakers, but as speakers in their own right. It is in this development of the foreign language learner as both a social and an individual speaker that we have to see the emergence of culture in the language classroom. Morson even suggests that Bakhtin's 'double-voiced word', the dialogic utterance, 'could be the new minimal unit of social analysis . . . and could form the basis for the general science of culture' (Morson 1986: 8).

## Dialogic breakthrough

In their reflection on the nature of anthropological fieldwork, Attinasi and Friedrich (forthcoming) describe the dialogues that take place between ethnographers who attempt to describe and interpret the culture of a people's speech community and the people from that community. These dialogues are of two sorts. On the one hand, there are the 'relatively repetitious, formulaic, routine, even banal and vacuous sorts of dialogues that make up the great majority of conversations . . . These ordinary dialogues serve mainly to maintain a status quo in friendships, families, and neighborhoods.'

On the other hand, there are memorable dialogues that Attinasi and Friedrich call 'catalysts of change between dialoguing imaginations'; these dialogues elicit a 'fundamental realignment and reevaluation of psychological values in the minds of the interlocutors. They cannot be pre-programmed or prefabricated. Their meaning is hardly or rarely realized at the time but emerges dynamically as they are ruminated on, reduced, expanded, reactualized, and rerepresented, often with reversal or slowing down of tempo, and otherwise transformed through subsequent imaginings.' Attinasi and Friedrich call such dialogues 'life-changing dialogues'.

I would like to argue that in the foreign language classroom teacher and learners are both participants and observers of a cross-cultural dialogue that takes place in the foreign language across grammatical exercises, communicative activities, and the discussion of texts. The language classroom should therefore be viewed as the privileged site of cross-cultural fieldwork, in which the participants are both informants and ethnographers. In the course of this fieldwork, two kinds of dialogue are likely to occur: the first is an instructional conversation in which forms are practiced and the status quo of the school's educational culture is confirmed and validated; the second is an exchange of ideas and emotions through language, which has the potential of putting in question the status quo. With Attinasi and Friedrich we can distinguish five features of that second kind of dialogue:

1  It involves both language and the use of language—that is, it includes not only words and sentences, but all the aspects of speech and verbal behavior that give language its materiality (e.g. pitch, tempo, interactional dynamics, but also discourse style and the logic of conversations).
2  It is motivated by ambivalent feelings of both empathy and antipathy. Like all human relations, any dialogue is always, potentially, headed toward harmony or order, or toward disorder or chaos. It draws its intensity from the delicate balance it maintains between the two.
3  It is empowering. Since two interlocutors are never completely equal and since they are often politically non-equal, such a dialogue involves a fundamental change in power—as the child gradually grows up to acquire the power of his or her parents.
4  It can happen unexpectedly in the most unlikely places, during a grammar drill, a vocabulary exercise, or the recitation of a poem.

5 It is a 'liminal' experience that creates a special space and time at the boundaries between two views of the world. It involves a sudden grasp of difference and an instantaneous understanding of the relationship between self and other.

I would like to add to this list the profound pleasure that comes from understanding and being understood, from discovering multiple layers of meaning and having the ability and power to manipulate these meanings. As we shall see throughout this book, this pleasure is an aesthetic experience that both engages one totally and leaves one totally free in the dialogic experience.

The foreignness of the foreign language is more likely to foster that kind of experience than teachers usually expect, and, as the example of Amy suggests, they would do well to be on the look-out for the potential occurrence of dialogic experiences amidst the flow of routine pedagogical and non-pedagogical conversations. Culture, conceived here as 'linguaculture', emerges dynamically from actual, concrete exchanges between individuals in the classroom. As we shall see in the next chapter, it is worth exploring such dialogues 'in all their corporeal, emotional, catalytic, political, situational, and bridging aspects' (Attinasi and Friedrich, forthcoming), for they provide the key to the teaching of language and culture at the various levels of language instruction.

At the elementary levels of language learning, learners might discover how much licence the foreign language gives them to play power games with the teacher and with one another, to shape the context of learning by manipulating interactional frames, grammatical forms, sounds and shapes of words to fit their particular meanings. Rather than measure those experimentations only against the socially accepted norms of a given society, the teacher would do well to encourage them also as attempts to test the boundaries of possible referential and metaphorical meanings that culture is made of. Indeed, this is where writing and literature have their uses even at the early stages. At more advanced levels, learners might be made aware of how the choice of one form over another, of one way of speaking over another, has interactional and social consequences that can be looked at critically. They can learn to recognize the social and political implications of linguistic choices and the way cultural reality is constructed through language.

A dialogic pedagogy is unlike traditional pedagogy. Not

only can it not be pre-programmed, but it is likely to question the traditional social and political tenets of foreign language education. Furthermore, it sets new goals for language teachers—poetic, psychological, political goals that are not measurable on proficiency tests and do not constitute any easy-to-follow method. For all these reasons, such a pedagogy should better be described, not as a blueprint for how to *teach* foreign languages, but as another way of *being* a language teacher.

By integrating language and culture in this dialogic framework, it provides for the satisfaction of truly educational (rather than merely instructional) objectives, so long neglected in language teaching.[5]

The next two chapters will explore the implications of a dialogic pedagogy for the teaching of the spoken language.

## Notes

1 'If we don't want to see pedagogy get bogged down in conformism, it must at all times teach the refusal to conform. Constructive pedagogy is always untamed; true pedagogy scoffs at pedagogy.'
2 Both ideologies are shared by the dominant culture of the two countries as it is reflected in the public educational system. They are not necessarily shared by every social group. In order to understand the American concept and its German counterpart, one would have to check its variable meanings across social, racial, gendered, and generational contexts of use. There are in the United States many social groups that do not have the luxury of believing that 'life is a challenge', and there is in present-day Germany a resistance to the German concept of *Bürgerpflicht* (civic duty) especially among young people. There is even in Americanized parts of Germany a certain young entrepreneurial spirit that gives now the word *Herausforderung* the American meaning of challenge, as in the following recent example from the press: 'Solange die deutschen Politiker nicht erkennen, daß ihr inzüchtiges Denken zu eng ist für all die Herausforderungen, die vor uns liegen, ist auf Abhilfe nicht zu hoffen.' (Robert Leicht, 'Zäher Niedergang', *Die Zeit* 18, 3.Mai 1991 p.1). (As long as German politicians do not realize that their ingrained thinking is too narrow for

all the challenges that lay ahead of us, we cannot count on any help from the outside). Even the French seem to have adopted the American meaning of the word. The American press quoted the newly-appointed French Prime Minister, Edith Cresson, as saying: 'I like challenges' (*New York Times* 17 May, 1991 p.1). And indeed, the fact that she was the first woman in French history ever to serve in such a high political post challenged her to take action in hitherto uncommon ways. The French press, however, spoke of her nomination and the challenges she faced as so many *paris*, or bets on an uncertain future ('Edith Cresson: Un Pari' *Le Point* no. 974, 20–26 mai 1991, p.13). The French term *pari* belongs, like the American term 'challenge', to the semantic field of games and sports, but it places the emphasis on chance and the vagaries of fate rather than on individual performance.

3  This entrepreneurial view is often situated within a rhetorically orthodox discourse. I use the phrase 'rhetorically orthodox' here to refer to the unsettling way in which political or educational issues of whatever leanings, such as ecological concerns, equal opportunity, or individual freedom become trapped into their own discourse like the slogans in the first verse of the Domin poem. Depending on how they want to present themselves and exercise power for themselves, speakers use this discourse as a rhetorical weapon against anybody wanting to raise larger questions or point to the complexity of an issue.

For example, in the political arena, the 1989 catastrophic oil spills in Alaska were talked about by some Exxon representatives as so many 'environmental challenges'. That year, nearly 11 million gallons of oil were spilled when the Exxon Valdez tanker ran aground, fouling Prince William Sound and the Gulf of Alaska and killing tens of thousands of sea birds and hundreds of otters, inflicting enormous damages to the fishing industry, the environment, and residents in the area. By calling this worst oil spill in United States history an environmental challenge, the Exxon representatives consciously inserted their discourse into a rhetorically orthodox American ideology and tried to minimize their responsibility for creating this human-made disaster. Similarly, the bureaucratic designation for physically disabled persons in United States officialese is now 'the physically challenged'; this euphemism inscribes itself into a reductionist discourse that in effect avoids any discussion of larger topics such as the consequences of wars, handguns, and drunken driving on citizens' health. By purposely focusing on the positive side of things, such language contributes to conceal human and ecological tragedies.

4　A study by Borkin and Reinhart (1978) show that the English expression 'I'm sorry', by contrast with 'Excuse me' is not necessarily used to convey an apology, but, rather, expresses dismay or regret about a situation perceived as unfortunate.

> 'Excuse me' is more appropriate in remedial exchanges when the speaker's main concern is about a rule violation on his or her part, while 'I'm sorry' is used in remedial interchanges when the speaker's main concern is about a violation of another person's rights or damage to another person's feeling; in other words, the basic concern behind 'excuse me' is 'I have broken or am in danger of breaking a social rule', and the basic concern behind 'I'm sorry' is 'You are or you may be hurt'.
> (cited in Wolfson 1983: 69)

The American student in this case sensed but could not explain that the dictionary equivalent of 'I'm sorry' may indeed be *Es tut mir leid* in German, but that the German expression has quite a different sociopragmatic value in most situations, namely that of an outright apology.

5　At this point, the reader might be discouraged and think: 'I can't see any culture emerging in *my* class of thirteen year olds, or at least not very often!'. It is true, that, as educators, we rarely see the seeds bloom that we sow day after day in the classroom. But this is precisely what distinguishes education from instruction. The Amy anecdote is not recounted here to serve as a model of classroom behavior, but merely to illustrate what may lie beneath the surface of banal classroom routine. If we did not believe such a routine can potentially bring about change, we would have long since given up being language teachers.

# 2 Contexts of speech and social interaction

> The key to understanding language in context is to start not with language, but with context.
> (Hymes 1972: xix)

The previous chapter gave us a glimpse of the complexity of teaching a foreign language if the goal is not only to exchange words with people who speak that language but actually to understand what they mean. Our choice of words is constrained by the context in which we use the language. Our personal thoughts are shaped by those of others. In this chapter, we will explore the notion of context in language teaching.

Foreign language pedagogy has been increasingly aware of the need to teach language in context—for example, by contextualizing grammatical exercises and situating them in socially appropriate verbal exchanges. Yet as the professional rhetoric focuses on context, it is not always clear what teachers mean when they purport to teach language 'in its social context'. So we may ask: what is really at stake when we relate language and context?

## What's in a context?

Consider the following classroom exchange, which will no doubt sound familiar. It has been reconstructed here in English from field notes taken in German. Two beginning students of German are preparing a fictitious role play based on Grimm's fairy tale 'Hänsel and Gretel'. One student turns to the teacher for help.

S: How do you say 'leave'?
T: It depends; it could be 'weggehen' or 'lassen'. What's the context?
S: 'Leave the children'.
T: Well . . . 'lassen', but it depends on the rest of the sentence.

S: 'Leave the children in the woods'.
T: Ah, then it might be 'verlassen'. Who says that to whom?
S: I'm the mother and I say to the father: 'You should leave the children in the woods'.
T: So, you would use the second personal singular, familiar form.
S: And 'should'? 'du mußt' or 'du sollst?'
T: Ah well . . . that depends . . .

Constructing a speech event means not only having a choice of grammatical and lexical features, but deciding which to choose from, depending on one's assessment of the whole situation of communication, and on the expectations raised in the speaker and the listener by that situation. In order to solve a seemingly simple problem of vocabulary, the student in the example above would really have to assess, among other things, the degree of situational urgency that prompted the mother to make such a statement, the intentions of the mother and the effect she wanted her statement to have on the father. And, having made the decision to choose, for example, the moral imperative (*du sollst*) instead of a simple imperative (*laß sie allein*) or a milder form of command (*du solltest* or *warum läßt du sie nicht . . .*), the student would set the scene for the response by the father and thus create a context for the rest of the dialogue.

The fact that beginning students rarely consider all these factors when they prepare role-plays in the foreign language, but just use whatever forms they know best, does not relieve the teacher from the responsibility, whenever possible and appropriate, to make them realize what meanings they convey by choosing one form over the other. In fact, this is exactly what a functional approach to language teaching should do.

This small example shows that there are different ways of looking at a situation of communication. Each of them highlights a different dimension of the communicative event. The first dimension is linguistic. The choice of one linguistic form over another is determined by the co-text—that is, those linguistic elements that precede or follow and that ensure the text's cohesion. Thus, if the sentence contains a direct object, German cannot use the verb *weggehen*, which is intransitive; if the first sentence of the narrative is in the past tense, the other verbs can be expected to follow suit; if a speaker starts an argument with 'on the one hand', the logic of the spoken text—that is, its cohesive structure—leads the listener to expect 'on the other hand' to turn up somewhat later on. Cohesion is established by a host of textual features such as pronouns, substitutions, deictics (see Chapter 4).

The choice of a linguistic form is also determined by the internal context of utterance, constituted by 'all the factors which, by virtue of their influence upon the participants in a language event, systematically determine the form, the appropriacy and the meaning of utterances' (Lyons 1977: 572). Context here refers to the intentions, assumptions, and presuppositions of speakers and hearers, which ensure that their discourse is perceived as coherent and therefore makes sense for the participants. For example, the fact that Grimm's fairy tale reveals later on that the mother had the intention of 'getting rid' of the children, could retroactively justify the student's choice of the verb *verlassen* (abandon) over *lassen* (leave). Intended meanings depend on the speech acts that preceded as well as on those that will follow them. The coherence of a text relies on the illocutionary force of its component parts and their perlocutionary effect on the hearer/reader.

Meanings also depend on the external context of communication, or *situational context* of the speech event. The most well-known definitions of the situational context are those by Roman Jakobson (1960) and Dell Hymes (1974). Among the six factors that Jakobson sees as constituting the speech event (addresser, addressee, context, message, contact, code), context is that which the message refers to, 'seizable by the addressee, and either verbal or capable of being verbalized'; it is, in other words, the topic or propositional content of utterance (Jakobson 1960: 353). The language function associated with context is the referential function. In the example above, it is the topic of conversation between the mother and the father. As can be expected, what the topic is about might be a matter of disagreement between the two of them. Although they might both agree that the general topic is 'finding a solution to the problem of hunger', the father might view the real topic to be a power play, which he is not willing to engage in, between him and his wife; the mother might consider the topic to be 'looking for a way of giving the children a chance of survival'. As Jakobson points out, verbal messages do not fulfill only one function; even though the words refer to 'leaving children in the woods', the meaning of that reference cannot be disambiguated without taking other factors into account.

The refinement of our way of viewing context has been well described recently by sociolinguists (see, for example, Wardaugh 1986, Preston 1989, Berns 1990). Firth, inspired by the work of the anthropologist Malinowski, was the first to include in the context 'not only spoken words, but facial expression, gestures, bodily activities, the whole group of people present during an exchange of utterances, and the part of the environment in which these people are engaged', and to call the totality of these factors 'context of situation' (Berns 1990: 10). Hymes (1974), picking up on Malinowski and Firth, and expanding Jakobson's notion of context, devised his own set of factors to describe the situational context of the speech event. He lists these under the acronym SPEAKING, which I will explain below with reference to the language classroom. According to Hymes,

**Setting** refers to the time and place—that is, the physical set-up of the class. Place includes: the space occupied by teacher and students; the movements of participants within that space; the seating arrangement; the temperature, background noise, place, size, and quality of the blackboard, etc. Time includes: the time devoted to each activity, its timing within the whole lesson, its relative length, its pace, the presence or absence of concurrent activities.

**Participants** include combinations of speakers and listeners in various roles, that are either given to them or taken on during the lesson.

**Ends** refers to the purposes of the activities and what participants seek to accomplish. These can be short-term learning goals such as the linguistic, cognitive, or affective outcomes of a particular activity, or they can be long-term goals such as motivations or attitudes or specific professional outcomes.

**Act sequence** refers both to the form and the content of utterances, both to what is said and what is meant by the way it is said.

**Key** refers to the tone, manner, or spirit in which a particular message is conveyed: serious or ironical, matter-of-fact or playful. The key can be conveyed verbally and non-verbally and the two may sometimes contradict one another.

**Instrumentalities** refers to the choice of channel (for example, oral or written), and of code (mother tongue, foreign language, or a mix of codes or code-switching).

**Norms of interaction and interpretation** refers to the way participants in the lesson interact and interpret what is said or what they are reading.

**Genre** refers to the type of oral or written activity students and teacher are engaged in: casual conversation, drill, lecture, discussion, role-play; grammatical exercise, written summary, report, essay, written dialogue.

The work of Goffman enables us to detail Hymes' characterization further by diversifying the notion of setting and participants. In particular, we can distinguish between various orientations or 'footings' that speakers and hearers take toward each other and toward various audiences in the classroom. Goffman (1981: 128) defines footing as 'the alignment we take up to ourselves and the others present as expressed in the way we manage the production or reception of an utterance'. It represents the way we frame events and the stance we take toward these events and the participants in the social encounter. Consider the following example, taken from an English class in Germany. The class is doing an exercise on the negatives in English, Jenny and Peter are characters in the textbook.

> **Bernd:** Peter don't like jazz music.
> **Atnam:** (*raises his hand*)
> **Teacher:** Atnam.
> **Atnam:** That was wrong.
> **Teacher:** Why? Can you say it in the right way?
> **Atnam:** Peter, Peter don't likes, likes . . .
> **Teacher:** (*writes on chalkboard: Jenny likes jazz music. Peter does not like jazz music*). Hatte zunächst die Namen vertauscht. Jetzt haben wir's umgekehrt, ist genau falsch rum. [I had first mixed up the names. Now we have the exact opposite, it should be exactly the other way around.]
> **Manfred:** Is doch egal. [It's all the same.]
> (Butzkamm 1983: 80)

Within three turns at talk the teacher switches footing four times, as she changes codes, tone of voice, and instrumentality. In her first turn, the teacher responds to Atnam's bid for the floor and orients her attention to him as her sole addressee. By granting him the floor, she asserts her position as a teacher in control of speaking rights, or, using Goffman's term, as 'principal' (in the legalistic sense) — that is, 'someone whose position is established by the words that are spoken' (Goffman 1981: 144). In her second turn, she addresses the same pupil but it is for the didactic benefit of the other pupils in the class, whom she hopes to engage in the correction of Bernd's sentence. The other pupils become thereby the ratified bystanders of her exchange with Atnam. In her third turn, realizing that Atnam was trying to correct not Bernd's grammar, but the truth value of Bernd's statement, she first repeats the textbook sentence, writing it down on the board and reciting, that is, 'animating', the textbook's words as a paradigm of correct language use. She then spontaneously makes a side comment in German, almost talking to herself in the presence of pupils who are 'eavesdropping' on her remark. Manfred, as one of the eavesdroppers, reacts to her side comment on *her* footing, establishing thereby a kind of intimacy in their common mother tongue. At the same time, what Manfred says only reaffirms the teacher's traditional role as an interlocutor only interested in the form, not in the truth of utterances.

In the course of these changes in footing, the teacher puts on different hats: she first gives Atnam the floor with the authority of a foreign language teacher, she then quotes the sentence from the book with the correctness of a native speaker, and finally speaks as a private German citizen in her mother tongue. In Goffman's terms, within a few seconds she has switched from being the principal, to the animator, to the author of the words she utters.

We can see from this example how much the simple notions of 'speaker' and 'hearer' need to be differentiated. We can distinguish in the social context of the classroom three different types of speakers:

**principals:** participants addressing each other according to their position in the social structure. In the language learning event, teachers and learners view each other as the representatives of an institution, of a given culture, a given generation, race, or gender, and address each other accordingly.

**animators:** participants reciting or reading aloud a prepared text or isolated sentences; for example, teacher or students modelling or displaying utterances in the foreign language without any particular addressee.

**authors:** participants speaking their own words, either as part of the dominant communication of the classroom or as part of 'sideplays' such as the side comments made by the teacher in the above example, or the hushed words exchanged entirely among bystanders in the classroom.

Hearers too must be differentiated into ratified and unratified participants. They are of three kinds:

**addressee:** the student to whom the teacher is asking a question.

**bystanders:** the rest of the class while the teacher is asking a question of that student. The presence of bystanders is the rule in most of our daily conversations, but there, bystanders are supposed to politely disavail themselves of the opportunity to listen in. In classrooms, by contrast, bystanders are expected to attend, as if they had been addressed.

**eavesdroppers:** the teacher eavesdropping on what students say during group work or a student from one group over-hearing what is being discussed in another group, or a visitor observing the classroom.

The behavior of a teacher thus aligns itself in myriad impercept-ible and often unconscious ways to the microaspects of the social context of the classroom. That is why every recording of the event (audio or videotape, field notes) can reveal only partial truths. It cannot provide the ultimate understanding of what has gone on during the lesson.

To this microlevel of various forms of talk, Ellis and Roberts have added the notion of prototypical contexts or 'domains', by which they mean 'a grouping together of recurring situation types' such as the family, the church, the classroom (1987: 8). People enter churches or classrooms with expectations based on their 'scripts' of such environments, and tend to first behave according to these expectations. However, these scripts are by no means uni-form nor is there any reliable homogeneity among these situation types. Even the classroom context can hardly be considered a unit-ary domain, given all the variations that occur from classroom to classroom. In addition, the fact that, for instance, what anyone says in a classroom can be overheard by others or used by the teacher for the benefit of others can potentially turn any type of classroom discourse, even the most natural, into an interview situ-ation, a theater production or a court proceeding.

The notion of domain can therefore be useful as a general frame, but it is difficult to define and to use when teaching foreign language behavior. However, by drawing attention to the perceptions and expectations of participants in the speech event, Ellis and Roberts have expanded our understanding of context to include its interactional dimension, to which I will now turn.

The third dimension of context is that which is created by the interaction itself, through the beliefs and presuppositions that the interlocutors bring to the encounter. Ellis and Roberts (1987: 20) define this interactional context as follows:

> Context is created in interaction partly on the basis of particular and individual choices by speakers at a local level and partly by those speakers being able to make inferences about each other on the basis of shared knowledge and assumptions about the world and about how to accomplish things interactionally.

Goodwin (1981), studying the social organization of conversation, shows how the perception by the speaker of the extent to which the information conveyed is shared or not by the other participants can affect the 'recipient design' of the speaker's utterance. Topics are introduced not only because of participants' intentions, but also because of perceived local interactional needs and the constraints imposed by multiple audiences. For example, as in Allwright's famous Igor case (1980), a student may ask a question, not because he is seeking information, but because he wants to show the rest of the class that he knows something the others do not know, such as the features of tax-icabs in Moscow, or because his interaction with the teacher develops its own dynamic of which both become prisoners without having intended it (Edmondson 1983: 115).

In the last ten years, research on interaction in language classrooms has made great strides (see, for example, Day 1986, Long 1983, 1989, Pica 1987a, among others). It has shown how non-native speakers of a language negotiate with other non-native speakers (their peers in the classroom) or with native or near-native speakers (e.g. the teacher) to clarify the meaning of each other's utterances in the performance of classroom tasks. Beyond the mechanics of turn-taking, the requests for clarification or confirmation, and repair strategies, this research has investigated the effect of such factors as task type (Doughty and

Pica 1986; Long 1989; Tarone and Yule 1989; Pica, Kanagy, and Falodun forthcoming) and expertise knowledge (Woken and Swales 1989) on the quantity and quality of participation in classroom interactions.

For example, Pica, Kanagy, and Falodun (forthcoming) found that the tasks that fostered the most negotiation of meaning, and thus, interaction, were the jigsaw and information-gap tasks, in which participants had to share information in order for the group to solve a problem or arrive at one decision. The open-ended opinion-exchange tasks offered the least interactional 'pull'. Yule and Macdonald (1991) found that pairing a low-proficiency learner and a high-proficiency learner in an informa-tion-gap task, but giving the low-proficiency learner the greater information to share—that is, putting him or her in a position of expertise—increased the amount of participation of the low-proficiency learner. Researchers are beginning to look into the effect of gender on classroom interaction (Gass and Varonis 1986, Pica *et al.* 1991), but it is difficult to isolate the gender factor from other factors such as class and ethnicity, and the results are as yet inconclusive.

We have seen how individual choices in the shaping of the context are constrained by the intratextual linguistic demands of cohesion and coherence, the situational demands of, e.g., the physical setting and the participants, and the interactional demands of exchanging utterances both for display and for com-munication. According to Halliday, individual choices in the creation of texts are constrained by yet two other larger kinds of context.

One is the *context of culture*, a term originally coined by Malinowski to describe the institutional and ideological back-ground knowledge shared by participants in speech events. This context, called by Fowler (1986: 19) 'the community's store of established knowledge', consists of 'structures of expectation' that allow people to make sense of the world around them. (Tannen 1979: 144) describes these structures as follows:

> People approach the world not as naive, blank-slate recept-acles who take in stimuli as they exist in some independent and objective way, but rather as experienced and sophisticated veterans of perception who have stored their prior experiences as 'an organized mass', and who see events and objects in the world in relation to each other and in relation to their prior

experience. This prior experience . . . then takes the form of expectations about the world, and in the vast majority of cases, the world, being a systematic place, confirms these expectations.

Native speakers of a language speak not only with their own individual voices, but through them speak also the established knowledge of their native community and society, the stock of metaphors this community lives by, and the categories they use to represent their experience (Lakoff and Johnson 1980, Lakoff 1987). This makes native speakers' ways of speaking predictable enough to be understood by other native speakers, but it is also what makes it so difficult for non-native speakers to communicate with native speakers, because they do not share the native-speaking community's memory and knowledge. And all the more so if they are fully socialized adults who carry with them twenty or thirty years of their own speech community's ways of talking. Even if they have mastered the forms of the new language, they might still have difficulty in meeting the social expectations of speakers from the new speech community (Saville-Troike 1991, Becker 1992).

One might argue that in a foreign language classroom, unlike second language contexts, the risks of misunderstanding are minimized. After all, do not the students share a common native culture, and does not the teacher by definition understand everything a student says? This seemingly unproblematic communication is precisely the problem in teaching a foreign culture. For, beyond the structures of the language they use, teachers and learners are often not aware of the cultural nature of their discourse. Furthermore, as we will see in the next chapter, the increasingly multicultural nature of foreign language classrooms and the hesitations of many teachers to recognize deeper misunderstandings due to social and cultural factors, are making the foreign language class as complex as the traditional ESL class. For example, in the United States, foreign language learners try to replicate in French or German such untransferrable Anglo-American concepts as: 'to be in control', 'to be committed to', 'setting one's priorities', 'creating opportunities—'without even realizing how ideologically laden such phrases are. Is it enough for the teacher to point to the lexical inappropriateness of such terms in the foreign language? Does he or she not have to examine those terms critically for their ideological content and make the students aware of that ideology?[1]

By teaching a foreign language we should objectivize the learner's native discourse patterns and help them adopt those of the new language. The question is, however, to what extent can and should we teach foreign forms of discourse and insist on their production by foreign language learners? The sociolinguist Saville-Troike gives the example of the Japanese learner of English who bows a lot to her professors.

> One of her professors told her that she shouldn't bow in English or to American professors, because that wasn't considered appropriate. This professor was trying to teach her a sociolinguistic rule in English. She was crushed. 'I know Americans don't bow', she said, 'but that's my culture, and if I don't do that, I'm not being respectful and I won't be a good person.'
> (Kramsch and McConnell-Ginet 1992b: 280)

Saville-Troike concludes from this event that 'the sociolinguistic rules can be talked about, but it should be left to the learners' own decision to adopt them or not for productive use' (ibid.).

The foreign language educator Jorden agrees with Saville-Troike, but points to the dilemma:

> Without forcing the person to change her ways, I think it's extremely important to explain to her how the average American reads that particular signal. The person can then make her own decision. In one ESL class, for example, Japanese students were asked to introduce themselves by their first name. So they said: 'My name is Taro' and so on, but then suddenly one man, the oldest in the class, said: 'I will be called Mr. Tanaka'. The teacher was very upset and asked me what to do about it. And I told her, of course it's all right for him to be called Mr. Tanaka, but he must know how Americans are going to react to someone in this culture who says: 'Don't call me by my first name, call me only Mr. Tanaka.
> (ibid.)

This teacher probably felt it was her responsibility to socialize the student into American society so that he could function appropriately outside the classroom. Would she be abdicating her responsibility if she left him free to flout the conventions of that society? Or was she overestimating the amount of consensus about the use of first names in American society? This is a very difficult question, and one that is ultimately a matter of judgment on the part of the teacher.

The two examples above point to the ambivalence of social roles and to the teacher's pedagogical responsibility to make that ambivalence explicit. But, given the traditionally normative nature of everything that is taught in classrooms, it is difficult for teachers to present a type of knowledge that does not automatically translate into normative behavior. The teacher in the example above was building on a series of prior texts in the educational culture she was trained in: conversations, textbooks, interviews, model lessons, and so on. These texts were part of a teacher-training pattern that views the teacher as the expert knower, who represents a native-speaking host speech community, and whose role is to impart a certain body of knowledge to non-native speaking non-knowers in order to facilitate their integration into the speech community. Prior texts constitute an intertextual context that I shall examine below.

Beyond the context of culture, of which we have seen the complexity, Halliday (1989: 49) introduces yet another kind of context, that arises from the friction between the texts that people generate and the contexts that are thereby shaped by them: the *intertextual context,* that is, the relation of a text with other texts, assumptions, and expectations. Halliday writes:

> Every lesson is built on the assumption of earlier lessons in which topics have been explored, concepts agreed upon and defined . . . At a deeper level, the entire school learning experience is linked by a pervading 'intertextuality' that embodies the theory and practice of education as institutionalized in our culture.
> (ibid.: 47)

The American ESL teacher may believe that by teaching Mr. Tanaka the proper American uses of the English language she is helping him get the 'equal opportunity' promised to any immigrant to the United States. She is therefore not only echoing mainstream ways of speaking (i.e. use of the first name in informal situations), she is also echoing texts from well-established American educational philosophy. Her distress at the student's lack of compliance has much deeper roots than the local fear of losing authority or of having her student use improper American English. Its causes are to be found to a large extent in the many other educational texts she is implicitly citing.

The reverse example is equally illustrative of the complexity of intertextual context. Like many native English speakers teaching ESL, native speakers of Japanese who teach Japanese in American schools often use pedagogical methods typical of their native culture: teacher-centered classes, emphasis on the written language, discipline, academic hierarchy. However, as Jorden (1992) points out, in addition to replicating, sometimes unconsciously, the context of their own educational culture, they also replicate the views of many Japanese educators who believe that it is impossible for foreigners to learn perfect Japanese, so what they should teach is a watered-down form of Japanese for foreigners. Thus the context that is slowly built-up from one text to the next across the syllabus reflects the larger cultural assumptions about the role of foreigners in Japanese society.

In our exploration of the notion of context we have seen that contexts are alignments of reality along five different axes: linguistic, situational, interactional, cultural, and intertextual. Context is shaped by persons in dialogue with one another, saying things about the world and thus making statements about themselves and their relationship to one another. Through this dialogue, they exchange and negotiate meanings that belong to a community's stock of common knowledge and that draw on a variety of past and present 'texts'. Context is the matrix created by language as discourse and as a form of social practice.

Context should therefore be viewed not as a natural given, but as a social construct, the product of linguistic choices made by two or more individuals interacting through language. These choices in turn hold together, control, manipulate, and maintain the social order, that is, the social organization of classrooms, homes, and workplaces. Ellis and Roberts (1987: 22) note that:

> It is [usually] taken for granted that the control exercised by the teacher in the classroom through her choice of language is the only way that education can be done, or that the language of the housing officer or of the job interview . . . simply reflect, uncritically, the commonsense way of doing things . . . [In fact] in their discourse, they actively create their institutionalized role.

Ellis and Roberts (ibid.) quote Fairclough, who writes: 'Discourse makes people, as well as people making discourse'.

## Discourse and culture

In the foreign language class, culture is created and enacted through the dialogue between students and between teacher and students. Through this dialogue, participants not only replicate a given context of culture, but, because it takes place in a foreign language, it also has the potential of shaping a new culture.[2]

The French linguist Charaudeau (1983) gives an interesting analysis of this emergence of culture at the discourse level. He shows how every speech act, rather than being the production of a message by one sender to one receptor (the way most language learners imagine communication to be), is in fact a dialectic encounter between four participants: an addresser, an addressee, a communicator, an interpreter. Let us assume here that the addresser is a man, the addressee a woman. The addressee is not merely a recipient of a message issued by the addresser, but also an interpreter of that message according to how she perceives the situation and the intentions of the addresser. In return, the addresser, finding himself interpreted by the addressee, discovers another self, which is the product of the interpretation by the addressee.[3] Thus a speech act is at the confluence of two processes:

—a production process, by which an *I* addresses a *YOU* whom he or she believes (and wants) to match his or her communicative purpose;

—an interpretation process, by which an addressee *YOU* builds an image of *I*'s intentions and purposes, and possibly sends back to *I* a different image from that which *I* wanted to project. *I*, upon discovering that the interpreting *YOU* is not the same as the one imagined (and wanted), discovers in himself or herself another *I* (*I'*), which is the *I* perceived and constructed by the interpreting *YOU*.[4] Of course, this process does not end there, but continues back and forth, across turns-at-talk, generating each time new levels of interpretation, new dimensions of self-and other-understanding—the essence of hermeneutic dialogue.[5]

Charaudeau thus makes the distinction in every speech event between four minimal units: an Enunciating Addresser (I), a Communicating Addresser (I'), a Receiving Addressee (YOU), an Interpreting Addressee (YOU'). In foreign language learning, where communication is made difficult by the dearth of linguistic resources, social roles which are normally welded together are for the first time experienced as dissociated. In the example given in the previous chapter, Judy was confronted by native speakers in Germany with an image of herself as a communicator that jarred with the one she wanted to project. This 'culture shock' was directly linked to the language she used. It did not at first put in question her personal identity as a polite, sensitive young woman; it did, however, give her an alternative role as participant in social interactions across cultures. It made clear to her, in a flash, how what she had seen up to now as one, namely her personal and her social self, could in fact, be seen as two different parts of her way of being in the world: one was her right to behave in a person-to-person manner, the way she had been taught from home, the other was the obligation to take into account the way she was interpreted by others, namely as a foreigner in need of a cultural lesson on open and closed doors.

Participants in the foreign language classroom create their own cultural context by shaping the conditions of enunciation/communication and the conditions of reception/interpretation of classroom discourse. With every turn-at-talk, teachers either perpetuate or subvert the traditional social culture of the classroom. On the one hand, together with the students, as we saw in the example above, they enact the traditional culture of the instructional setting in which they were trained; they echo the native culture of the society in which they were socialized; they act out the behavior of speakers from the target society, which they have studied; their discourse and that of their students are full of invisible quotes, borrowed consciously or unconsciously from those who taught them—parents, teachers, mentors—and from those who have helped build the discourse of their discipline. In fact, language teachers are so much teachers of culture that culture has often become invisible to them.

On the other hand, it would be wrong to view speakers only as mouthpieces of a monolithic social environment. The dominant culture of the classroom is constantly contested, avoided, put in question, confronted with linguistically deviant 'minority' cultures. Many learners resist the self-evident and invisible culture teachers try to impose. As observers have abundantly documented and as we shall see below, learners find the most ingenious ways of playing with schismatic meanings, pretending they do not understand, double-guessing the grammatical exercise, beating the system, sneaking in the forbidden native tongue, creating a counter-culture with foreign sounds and shapes.

As foreign language classrooms are composed of students from an increasingly diverse background, language teachers can no longer count on a stock of common knowledge against which to teach the foreign language and culture; they cannot build on common schooling habits, common conversational styles; they cannot even count on shared levels of knowledge of a common native tongue. The notion of a generic native speaker has become so diversified that it has lost its meaning. Attention to this diversity forces teachers to take into consideration differences in class, gender, race, and ethnicity in the design of classroom activities. For example, cultural differences in the distribution of silences may force them to rethink their communicative language teaching practices (e.g. Philips 1972); and gender differences in conversational style may prompt them to diversify the discussion format in their classrooms (Treichler and Kramarae 1983).

Thus teachers themselves become instrumental in creating alternative contexts of culture. The consensus they used to take for granted, the fixed point from which to view the foreign culture has become an illusion that demands to be looked at with the same critical distance as the foreign culture itself. In the classroom, teachers can learn to 'read' their students' attempts to define and make sense of its various contexts.

As we shall see in the following section, much of the beginners' pleasure in speaking a foreign language can come from the power and the license it gives them to play with various footings, to manipulate frames, to experience what Goffman (1981: 173) calls 'the partition between the inside and the outside of words' despite their limited linguistic resources. Later, the pleasure can come from experiencing and critically examining the struggle for control between the individual and the social voices present in the popular culture of the classroom.

## Contextual shaping

In the classroom, the success of any communicative activity is heavily determined by the way the participants perceive the context of situation and shape it accordingly through their verbal and non-verbal behavior. In the following examples, I will look at how learners and teachers shape the context of learning through the way they define each of Hymes' eight aspects of the speech situation: the speech genre the participants think they are engaged in; the norms of interaction and interpretation they think are called for; the code and register they view as appropriate; the key they believe they share; the type and level of act sequence they believe they should attend to; the ends or purpose they attribute to the exchange; the role they think they should play as participants; and, finally, the meaning they attribute to the whole setting or scene.

In each example, several of these factors can contribute to the success or failure, the pleasure or frustration, of the intended communication. I will use each here to illustrate one factor in particular, well aware, however, that each example can illustrate also other factors and that each factor is correlated with many others within one given speech encounter.

## Genre

One of the favorite strategies of beginning language learners is to play at changing the genre of the verbal exchange taking place between them and the teacher. For example, they might try and transform a formal exercise into a sample of naturally-occurring communication. Consider, for example, the exchange below from an English secondary school class in Switzerland, where the teacher is trying to elicit from the students the phrase 'to suffer from a heart condition':

> **T:** he has difficult with his heart . . . of course everybody'll understand but
> **Marianne:** he've got a difficult heart
> **T:** a difficult heart (*everybody laughs*) yes ok good yes
> **Hansueli:** troubles
> **T:** ja
> **Hansueli:** with his heart
> **T:** trou trouble with his heart . . . yes we know what you mean and therefore people with a weak heart what do they sometimes suffer from what's the problem with a with a weak
> **Hansueli:** they must sit down and drink drinking a beer
> (*everybody laughs*)

**T:** drink a beer is it good for a heart patient do you know
**Hansueli:** I don't know but he must drink something
**T:** aha
**Hansueli:** a glass of water
**T:** glass of water good yes ok anyway you must give some-
one with a heart condition with a weak heart if he has a
fit you must give him what . . .
(Spycher 1988)

It is clear that the genre the teacher is trying to impose, namely lexical search, is consistently refused by Hansueli who tries to impose another genre, namely 'life story'. The student success-fully forces the teacher to provide the lexical item himself and imposes a message-oriented type of natural communication where comprehension is the goal. However, the reverse can also occur. In the previous example (p.38), we saw that it was the teacher who was struggling to uphold the genre 'natural com-munication' and the student who defined it as a mere formal exercise.

Differing views between persons in authority and persons in subordinate roles, such as teachers and learners, concerning the genre of talk they are engaged in can lead to disappointments on both sides. VanLier (1989), for example, has observed such divergences between tester and testee in an oral proficiency situ-ation. Oral proficiency interviews are meant to test the ability of speakers to behave in naturally-occurring conversations. VanLier observed how the learner's definition of the exchange as an interview rather than as a casual conversation determined his decision to respond to the tester's questions by simply pro-viding information. By doing so, however, he helped confirm the definition of the situation as an interview. Had he challenged that definition, he would have sometimes questioned the form or even the validity of the tester's questions, thus adopting a behavior more typical of an informal conversation. These find-ings are supported by other studies (e.g. Bacon 1990, Wildner-Bassett 1990) and by the studies done by Gumperz, Jupp, and Roberts (1979) in cross-cultural encounters.

## Norms of interaction and interpretation

Because at the beginning stages of language learning the mean-ings of words are still quite fluid, students are unusually attuned to both indexical and symbolic meanings (Widdowson 1991: 14). They are, of course, attentive to the way words *refer to* the world through their dictionary definition (indexical meaning), but they are also highly sensitive to the various ways in which words can *represent* a certain state of the world through shapes, sounds, and metaphors, and to the way these words interact with the context in which they are used (symbolic meaning). Taking advantage of the multiple levels of meaning is one way for them to counteract the fundamental powerlessness brought about by what Harder (1980) has called the 'reduced personality' of the language learner and gain control over the norms of interaction and interpretation established by the teacher. For example, Nold (1983: 310) reports on German students doing an exercise on English gerunds:

S1: We stopped reading this book last year in July
T: Last year in July
S2: Stimmt ja net! [It's not true!]
T: And today it is not raining, but yesterday it was raining and there is no rain today—so—
S2: You can go out
T: It has stopped raining

Clearly, not all participants in the class accept the 'dutiful student' image of themselves that the teacher imposes on them. The difference in obedience between addressee S1 and bystander S2 is a case in point. The teacher in turn refuses the image 'friendly conversational partner' attributed to him by S2. The negotiation of the norms of interpretation is marked by the notable switch to the native language common to both students and teacher. By changing the footing, this switch poses an implicit challenge to the norms of interaction between teacher and students: are they going to interact as compatriots only pretending to be native speakers of another culture, or is the teacher going to be the full native speaker, pretending that he does not know any other culture than the target one? By switching to German, the student makes apparent the many different norms of interaction available to participants in language classrooms. The teacher can interact with the students as an instructor of textbook English or as conversational partner of vernacular English, the students can interact with the teacher as learners, or as conversational partners, teacher and students can follow the norms of interaction expected of fellow native speakers of German or of make-believe native speakers of English. As Gremmo *et al.* (1985) have shown, each of these roles demands a specific form of interaction and calls for a different way of interpreting what is meant. The side comment *Stimmt ja net!* not only denies the genre imposed by the teacher (gerund exercise), it also tries to impose other norms of interaction.

In situations where the norms of interaction are less clearly defined than those between teacher and students, the ability to impose one's own norms depends a great deal on the participants' perception of speaking rights and power, and, as a corollary, on their tolerance to loss of face. In a study of six female American learners of Japanese in conversation with six female native speakers of Japanese at an American university, Jackson (1990) found that the usual NS–NNS power differential took on other aspects than those observed when the NS was the English speaker and the setting was the United States. The genre chosen for the study was casual conversation with no pre-determined topic. Thus, the only pressure on the interlocutors was to continue carrying on the conversation, rather than accomplishing a given task. Contrary to Long's (1983) findings, that the NS usually has the control over topic selections, Jackson found that the Japanese NSs tried to stay on one topic longer and hesitated to change the subject too often, whereas the American NNSs did not hesitate to switch topics when things became linguistically too difficult. In one of the pairs, the NNS switched topics seven times while the NS only changed topic twice. Two examples of such switches and their respective interpretations by the speakers are given below in their English translation. In the first, it is the Japanese native speaker who switches topic. The Japanese NS and the American NNS have just found out that they have a mutual acquaintance.

> NS:  Oh, ah, Kozue? . . . Oh, I know her. (hee) (*expression of surprise*)
> NNS: Ahh . . . (*long pause*) ahh, time is long. ah, xxx I have telephone number, but . . . I, time xx xx ah, don't have, so . . . Telephone does not connect.
> NS:  Uuun, huun, ah, yes . . . Have you been to Japan? (Jackson 1990)

Upon listening to the tape, the Japanese native speaker was surprised that she had changed the topic so abruptly, but she explained to the investigator that she had probably detected some problem between the American NNS and their common acquaintance and that's why she avoided talking about it any further. However, the investigator, herself native Japanese, comments: 'What the NS said toward the end of the conversation convinced me that at this point she actually did not understand what the NNS was trying to explain. I believe that the NNS's failure to show greater coherence between her utterance and that of the NS caused the NS to perceive that the NNS's utterance was somewhat irrelevant and, hence, embarrassing.' It is interesting to note, if Jackson's intuition is correct, that the NS retrospectively rephrased a linguistic embarrassment into a referential embarrassment, which provided her with an explanation as to why she had switched topics, but did not cause her to lose face by admitting that maybe she had not understood what the NNS was trying to say. In the next example, it is the American non-native speaker who switches topic:

NNS: Mrs. X, ah, when you came to Ithaca, . . . you came to Ithaca, how long ago?
NS:  I came in August last year. It has not yet been one year.
NNS: (*nod*) Is the Cornell law school program three years?
NS:  Well it is one-year program. ⌈Ah,
NNS:                                ⌊Really?
NS:  Yes, I don't know if it is one year or two years, but it is the course called LLM. Ah, my husband looks like xxxx finishing LLM in one year.
NNS: Ahh, (*nod*) Do you suppose going home?
NS:  Yes. He is dispatched by the company, and the company has set the time limit to two years for his stay, so we must go home exactly in two years.
NNS: (*nod; pointing at window*) This weather is not like Ithaca's spring, but . . .
NS:  That's right. Summer seemed to come suddenly from winter.
     (ibid.)

In a subsequent interview, the American NNS admitted that she did not have the slightest clue as to what the Japanese NS was saying between lines 11 and 13. Asked why she had so abruptly changed the topic, she too said she was surprised that she had initiated this sudden change. However, since, to her knowledge, she does not usually switch topics in such an abrupt manner, she firmly believes that she must have heard the NS mention something about the weather, or that the NS must have indicated non-verbally her desire to talk about the weather.

Both examples show that the loss of face entailed in admitting that one has not understood one's interlocutor can be immense. As Goffman (1981: 26) writes, 'To ask for a rerun can be to admit that one has not been considerate enough to listen or that one is insufficiently knowledgeable to understand the speaker's utterance or that the speaker himself may not know how to express himself clearly': hence, for example, the other-directed motives given by the American NNS for switching topics. However, switching topic might cause an equally threatening loss of face, especially if it has to be done abruptly with simple markers like *ano* (well . . .), because the NNS does not know more subtle topic-switching devices, e.g. *hanasi wa kawarimasu kedo* (to change the subject) or *hanasi wa chotto chigaimasu kedo* (this is a slightly different subject). Requesting clarification and switching topic both require conversational courage and the willingness to keep the dialogue going. When learners engage in conversation with peers, their propensity to abandon topics or switch to new ones rather than negotiate in the face of misunderstandings is well-known (Long 1983: 131; Pica 1992: 203). The price in the loss of face for admitting non-understanding might be too high.

## Instrumentalities / code

As we have seen, the favorite way for learners to shape the learning context of the classroom is to switch footing. The subtle ways in which learners use code-switching or turn novice teachers into ambulant dictionaries by incessantly asking for the L2 equivalent of L1 words illustrate the struggle for control that goes on in classrooms. The teacher's insistence on the exclusive use of the foreign code is one of the most powerful countermeasures the teacher can take to impose his or her definition of the context of situation and, thereby, his or her authority, as the following example shows. This English teacher at a German school has been drilling the difference between *this* and *that* in English, getting confused himself in the process:

T:   This is a cat. Jürgen, what is it?
S1:  It is a cat.
     (*Ss in the background*: Nein nein es heißt anders) [No no you don't say it like that.]

> **T:**  This is a cat. Jürgen?
> **S2:**  Es muß ja heißen [You should say]: That is a cat.
> **T:**  We speak English, not German. That is a cat. Good. That is a cat.
> (Goethe Institut 1969)

Before Jürgen has had time to respond, S1 and S2 contest the authority of the teacher by questioning the linguistic accuracy of his statement. By castigating them for their use of the mother tongue, the teacher both regains control of the code and reinstates his authority.

## Key

With their limited resources, even beginning learners can try and affect the key of exchanges. Consider the following example, taken from a very tightly teacher-centered class. The teacher has been pulling various stuffed animals from his briefcase to build the students' vocabulary. One student raises his hand:

> **S1:**  (*with a smile*) Have you a mouse?
> **T:**  (*with surprise and feigned regret*) Oh no! I haven't got a mouse. (*didactic tone*) I haven't got a mouse. Who can draw a mouse on the blackboard? on the blackboard? (*A student is sent to the board. He draws a mouse.*)
> **T:**  What is this? Bernhard?
> **S2:**  This is a mouse.
> **T:**  Yes, yes. Is it a big mouse or a small mouse? Jürgen?
> **S3:**  This mouse is big. (*a student raises his hand*) Christoph?
> **S1:**  (*with a cunning smile*) That is a louse!
> **T:**  Is it a louse? No, I think it is a mouse (*didactic tone*) a mouse a mouse. (*Turning to his briefcase to fish out yet another stuffed animal*) What have I in my bag?
> (Goethe Institut 1969)

The pleasure at having gained however fleeting control over the boring ritual of the formal vocabulary drill through this remarkable pun is far from trivial. It is all the greater as it is done for the benefit of multiple audiences (including the cameraman!) that appreciate the challenge to the teacher's authority while enjoying that authority.

## Act sequence

At a more advanced level, there can be disagreement about the level of the act sequence at which the misunderstanding is taking place. In their study of different styles of negotiation of meaning in task-based situations, Ehrlich, Avery, and Yorio (1989) show how a different understanding of the level of communication breakdown can lead speakers to use different negotiating styles (skeletonizing or embroidering), which in turn help or impede relevant information transfer. The following excerpt from their data (ibid.: 409) will serve as illustration.

In an interaction between a female NS of English and a female Japanese learner of English at the University of Toronto, a breakdown occurs while the speaker is describing the positioning of the stem of a tulip on a picture that the listener has to replicate on her piece of paper.

> NS: it goes/has a round bottom/the stem is fairly thick/could you draw it/it's right in the middle/now the stem doesn't start on the line/it starts about an eighth of an inch above the line/a little bit above the line and it's fairly thick
> NNS: eighth?
> NS: eighth of an inch above the line/the bottom/it doesn't touch the bottom line

The NS goes on to describe the leaves, their precise location on the stem, and the tulip's shape. After a few turns, it becomes apparent that the Japanese NNS had not understood the word 'stem':

> NNS: what is top of the stem?
> NS: the stem is the line you drew going up the middle
> NNS: middle?
> NS: yeah/you know the line you drew that ends/it's what a flower stands on/it's like the trunk of a treee or the stem of a flower/well the very top of it/where the stem is the highest/the beginning of the stem
> NNS: stem?
> NS: you don't know what the stem is?
> NNS: no.

The authors comment:

> It is likely that the NNS on hearing the word stem for the first time did not attend to this item because it was not deemed important. Thus, the overt indication of non-understanding (the word *eighth*) does not lead to a felicitous repair. Because the NNS's overt indication of non-understanding (*eighth?*) occurred with an item deeply embedded within the discourse, both interlocutors were unable to locate the more important source of difficulty ... and, consequently, the speaker was unable to repair the utterance successfully.
> (ibid.)

Ultimately, they found, it is one's willingness to abandon one's context of reference at deeply embedded points of misunderstanding and instead redefine the context itself, rather than continue to embroider on the same one, that leads to satisfactory communication.

## Ends

At all levels of proficiency, perceptions vary also among participants in the classroom concerning the purpose of tasks and activities and the concomitant expectations by the teacher. In a 1988 study by Soulé-Susbielles, two NNS of English in pair work in an ESL class were assigned to tell each other their life story. Each of them interpreted the purpose of the task and their role differently. David, an Iranian male student, took the assignment to be a one-way telling task; Haeran, a Korean female student, took it as an opportunity to get acquainted with another student in the class. Haeran and David's differing interpretation of the purpose of the activity accounted for differences in the quality and quantity of input they provided for each other and in the type of control each exercised over the topic. Samples of their conversation are given below:

### D's story

**D:** my name is D I'm Persian and I
**H:** Persian?
**D:** Persian yes I came from Iran
**H:** you mean you came from?
**D:** Iran yes

H: but it's tell Persia?
D: Persia is the old name you know of my country
H: ah yes yes Persia
D: and hm I've been here for two years . . .
H: you came here
D: ya
H: for study?
D: ya

## *H's story*

H: my parents very old and I have been here almost three years and I have been working and and studying and my major was German literature in our country
D: ya
H: but I I want to change it
D: hm hm
H: now I didn't decide yet and I want to help poor child poor ch poor children
D: ya
H: in education
D: education for children
H: ya early childhood education
D: ya

The differences in purpose definition resulted in a sense of frustration as the participants misinterpreted each other's intentions and did not have their expectations fulfilled. In a subsequent conversation with the investigator, David complained that Haeran was always interfering in his story and not letting him talk, Haeran complained about David's lack of interest in her story. The interlocutors' perception of the purpose of the task imposed on each other differing images of interlocution, possibly based on cultural and gender differences, themselves the product of social perceptions (Tannen 1990).

## Participants' roles

Differences in task definition can be due to differences in the way speakers view their role as language learners in general, as can be seen from the following exchange between two low-intermediate-level students A and B following a conversation B had with another student:

**A:** was spricht sprich
**B:** sprech
**A:** sprecht bahh (*laughs impatiently*)
**B:** wir haben über Deutsch gespricht (A: ah) gesprochen
gesprochen
**A:** gesprochen ja
**B:** wir haben wir haben über Deutsch gesprochen weil eh ich
weil ich nach Deutschland will gehen fahren will fahren
fahren will eh vielleicht in ein oder zwei Jahr

[A: what does he talk you (*2nd PSg*) talk B: talk (*2nd PPl*)
A: talk (*2nd PPl*) bahh (*laughs impatiently*) B: we talk about
German (A: ah) talked talked A: talked yes B: we talked
talked about German because er I because I to Germany want
to go to fly want to fly to Germany er maybe in one or two
years]

A sees himself mainly as a communicator, B mainly as a language learner. The overmonitored behavior of B makes A impa-
tient, but he does not dare interrupt such laudable attempts at
getting the grammar straight, although he has got the message
a long time ago. These differences in role perception account for
B's lack of cooperation when A later appeals to him for help as
illustrated below:

**A:** wenn man von M.I.T ist und eh eh wie dich eh hat ein
ein graduate degree (B: ja) es ist nicht eh eh how do you
say 'difficile'? (*French pronunciation*)
**B:** (*chuckles*)
**A:** es ist nicht eh es ist sehr 'possible' (*French pronunciation*)
**B:** sehr
**A:** sehr möglich einen Job zu finden?
**B:** ah ja es ist leicht   einen Job zu finden
**A:**                          ja leicht (*laughs*), ja es ist leicht einen
Job zu finden
**B:** für mich

[A: when one is from M.I.T and er er like you er has a a
graduate degree (B: yes) it is not er er how do you say (*Fr.*)
'difficile'? B: (*chuckles*) A: it is not er it is very (*Fr.*) 'possible'
B: very A: very possible to find a job? B: ah yes it is easy to
find a job A: yes easy (*laughs*), yes it is easy to find a job B:
for me]

After three consecutive attempts by A to get at the word he was looking for (*leicht* [easy]) without any help forthcoming from his interlocutor, B at last produces the word and A is bailed out. B might have been waiting for the context to clear up, but, considering his preference for self-monitored learning, he certainly did nothing to speed up the process, as contrasted with the help A provided him a little later on:

B: Waren war deine Eltern deine Großeltern in Deutschland (*4 seconds*)
A: ge ⌈boren?
B:       ⌊geboren
A: ja meine Großmutter war in Deutschland geboren.

[B: were your parents your grandparents in Germany (*4 seconds*) A: born? B: born A: yes my grandmother was born in Germany]

In other cases, students can view their role as quite the opposite. Depending on how the task has been defined, some students can view it as their responsibility to take over the role of the teacher and duplicate in peer work the kind of instructional discourse usually found in teacher-fronted classes (Kinginger 1989).

As we have seen, learners are not mere victims of other people's definition of their role, but rather, they can take an unconsciously active part in realigning their participation to fit their needs and to gain control over the situation. For example, Frawley and Lantolf (1985) describe an experiment where ESL learners and native speakers were to tell a story based on a series of six drawings. Drawings 1 through 6 represented the following events:

1 A boy walks along a road.
2 He sees an ice cream vendor.
3 He buys a 50 cent ice-cream cone.
4 He gives the cone to a small boy.
5 A man approaches the small boy.
6 The man takes the cone from the small boy; the small boy cries.

Advanced ESL learners and native speakers saw the task as a test of their ability to relate information, and they dispatched the task quite well, as can be seen from their opening utterances below:

1 Well, there's a young boy . . .
2 guy standing in the road . . .
3 a little boy on the sidewalk . . .
4 a little boy is walking down the street . . .
5 a little boy standing in the street.
6 there is a young boy in shorts . . .
   (ibid.: 24)

By contrast, intermediate ESL learners, who were still grappling with linguistic difficulties, unable to consider the task as 'relating information', redefined it as the familiar dialogic social situation of the classroom:

1 This is Tom
2 this road—what's this? Let me just call John. John is standing on the road.
3 this picture—do you want to tell me, I tell you where he is or . . .?
4 you want me to say what they are doing?
5 he's a boy!
6 so, we saw a rather young guy on the lane
7 I see a boy who stay on the way
8 I see a boy that the boy have the hand in your pants
9 I see a boy on the road
   (ibid.: 26)

In the absence of a real addressee, caused by the testing situation, intermediate ESL learners broke the frame imposed by the teacher and recreated an imaginary addressee to help them control the task. Students were attending to context, but to the interactional, as well as to the linguistic context.[6]

This example is interesting on many counts. First, we see how text shapes context. The learner's level of proficiency changes the social relationship between participants in a speech event. The role that a so-called low-proficiency learner constructs for the teacher (or tester) is different from the role in which more proficient learners cast him or her. In other words, the learner makes the teacher as much as the teacher makes the learner.

On the other hand, context shapes text. Emmanuel Schegloff, introducing the concept of conversational presence, shows that from the official absence of an answer, conversational partners infer the physical and interactional absence of the prospective answerer (Schegloff 1972: 77). In contexts in which one conversational partner does not do his or her share of the conversational tasks, such as in a test situation, the 'absence' of a prospective answerer has repercussions on the structure of the speaker's discourse itself. In this study, the student transformed an artificial display of information transfer into a natural dialogic situation.

A third observation we can make from the Frawley and Lantolf experiment has to do with what Goodwin calls the 'knowing vs. unknowing recipient' differential (1981: 156). Goodwin shows the lengths to which conversationalists will go to incorporate something new in their utterances, when they are put in the difficult position of having to convey some information or tell a story which one of the participants knows already. The queries and exclamations of the second ESL learner in the example above reinstate a natural information gap in an exercise that has none since the tester knows the pictures already. This is a situation familiar to learners in a classroom, who have to answer display questions to show that they know what they know. Depending upon the amount of natural communication the learners perceive is going on in the class, there will be more or less reluctance on their part to provide mere display responses. For example, their silence in response to a teacher's comprehension check, that requires them to lift the answer from the printed page, might be a sign of social embarrassment, not of poor linguistic ability.

## Setting

Finally, differing perceptions of the general physical and psychological circumstances of the verbal exchange can foster or inhibit conversational cooperation. These perceptions have to do with the various contexts of culture that coexist in the language classroom. In the following excerpt, taken from a German classroom in Cameroun (Ngatcha 1991: 126), teacher and students have to define their place among the many discourse contexts available. Observe the remarkable amount of frame-work that takes place.

The teacher is trying to engage his 50 students in a dialogue on the theme of the lesson in the textbook: 'Tourism—The Mueller family spend their vacation in Africa'.

T: Der Text spricht über Tourismus. Was ist Tourismus?
S: (*silence*)

**T:**   (*puts his hand under his chin*) Was ist Tourismus?

[T: The text talks about tourism. What is tourism?]

The setting, as defined by this first engagement by the teacher, is the institutional school setting represented by the topic in the textbook. It is an abstract setting, as evidenced by the decontextualized question of the teacher, which requests a decontextualized answer. The question is too broad and too far removed from the students' experience to be answerable. They remain silent. The teacher then tries another path.

**T:**   Ihr kennt bestimmt das Wort Tourismus. Was bedeutet Tourismus?

**Ss:**   (*silence*)

[T: You (*2nd PPl familiar*) surely know the word tourism. What does tourism mean?]

The teacher redefines the participants as a group of students he knows well (hence the use of the familiar form of the second person pronoun) and with whom he has some common classroom history to which he can refer (hence the use of the word 'surely'). However, even this new definition fails to engage the students, so he tries yet another contextual approach.

**T:**   Wir sagen, wir machen Tourismus. Was bedeutet das?

**S:**   Tourismus bedeutet eine Reis auf ein andere Land, wenn man macht eine Reise in andere Land (*plays with his fingers*).

[T: We say, we do tourism. What does that mean? S: Tourism means a trip to another country, when one makes a trip to another country.]

This time the teacher has narrowed the distance between himself and the students by using the cooperative pronoun 'we'. This 'we' refers to the community of learners and users of the German language; the first 'we' refers to the instructional context of the lesson; the second 'we' is a grammatical paradigm with no other reference than itself. This definition of the task as a collaborative endeavor entails quite a different act sequence. Whereas in excerpt 1, the teacher required a dictionary definition, in excerpt 2, a translation, in excerpt 3 he appeals to an experience he shares with the students. In excerpt 4, a student not only responds to the teacher, but she builds on the collaborative 'we' he had offered previously to formulate her answer.

T: Wenn ich nach Yaounde fahre, ist das kein Tourismus?...
S: Wir kann sagen
T: Wir können sagen
S: Wir können sagen, Tourismus ist eine Reise über ein neuer Ort.

[T: When I go to Yaounde, isn't that tourism? S: We can (*1st PSg*) say T: We can (*1st PPl*) say S: We can (*1st PPl*) say, tourism is a trip over a new place.]

Beyond the institutional and the instructional setting, there is, however, also another level of context to which the class must pay attention, namely the physical and psychological setting of the German characters in the text, namely, the Müllers and their German mindset.

T: Was macht Frau Müller? Sie geht in ein Reisebüro und sie bekommt solche Papier (*shows the travel brochure*). Sie liest das sehr sorgfältig durch. Was ist hier? Das ist Kamerun. Was kann man in Kamerun finden? Aha! schöne Landschaft, Folkloregruppe, Museen, Wasserfälle . . . Das ist interessant! . . . Hier haben wir einige Hotels: Yaounde, Mont-Febe, das ist sehr teuer. Wir haben nicht sehr viel Geld.

[T: what does Mrs. Müller do? She goes to a travel agency and she gets a paper like that one (*shows travel brochure*). She reads it very carefully. What is here? This is Cameroun. What can one find in Cameroun? Aha! beautiful landscape, folkloric groups, museums, waterfalls. That is interesting! Here we have a few hotels: Yaounde, Mont-Febe, that is very expensive. We don't have very much money.]

The 'we' in line 6 simulates the foreign cultural setting by taking on the role of a German speaker planning a vacation in Cameroun. By reading this passage of the textbook aloud, the teacher tries to include his students in this foreign perspective on their own country. However, as the following segment shows, this foreign perspective on Kamerun is based on a view of Germany that does not seem to fit the students' expectations.

T: Hier kann man segeln, fischen, schwimmen, und es steht: 'Das Wasser ist warm und sauber'. Warum ist das Adjektiv 'sauber' für die Deutschen sehr wichtig?
Ss: (*silence*)

T:    Wie ist das Wasser in Deutschland? Wer hat eine Idee?
S:    (*timidly*) Es gibt keine Krankheiten.
T:    Keine Krankheiten? Es gibt vielleicht zu viele Krankheiten
      im Wasser (*silence*). Sie haben letzte Woche einige Filme
      über Deutschland gesehen. Wie sah das Wasser aus. War
      das sauber?
Ss:   (*chorus*) Nein.
T:    Das Wasser war ganz schmutzig wegen der Industrie.

[T: Here one can sail, fish, swim, and it says: 'The water is
warm and clean'. Why is the adjective 'clean' so important
for Germans? Ss: (*silence*). T: How is the water in Germany?
Who has an idea? S: (*timidly*) There are no diseases. T: No
diseases? There are maybe too many diseases in the water
(*silence*). You have seen last week a few films about Germany.
How did the water look like? Was it clean? Ss: (*chorus*) No.
T: the water was quite dirty because of the industry.]

The students' interest in air and water pollution in Germany is
only moderate, since they generally view Germany as a desirable
industrialized country to visit or live in. Their responses show
accordingly little enthusiasm.

T:    [In Deutschland] ist das Wasser sehr schmutzig und sie
      haben Angst vor Krankheiten. In Afrika ist das Wasser
      sauber und warm. Und dort wie ist das Wetter?
Ss:   (*no answer, some students have fallen asleep*)
T:    Was haben wir jeden Tag in Afrika?
Ss:   (*some mumble the word*) Sonne.
T:    Wir haben fast jeden Tag die Sonne, sehr interessant für
      die Europäer, sie können braun werden.

[T: In Germany the water is very dirty and they are afraid of
diseases. In Africa the water is clean and warm. And there,
how is the weather? Ss: (*no answer*) T: What do we have
every day in Africa? Ss: (*some mumble the word*) Sun. T:
Every day we have sun, very interesting for Europeans, they
can get a tan.]

This last shaping of the setting as the common native culture of
the learners fails to establish the intimacy necessary for active
dialogue. This is due in part to the fact that the textbook imposes
a foreigner's view on the students' culture that is of little relevance to these learners' lives.

## Conclusion

We have adopted in this chapter Halliday's definition of context as 'the total environment in which a text unfolds' (1978: 5). This definition is part of a view of language as social semiotic, in which context always includes and is in a dialectic relationship with a text. As Halliday pointed out recently, 'Language is at the same time a part of reality, a shaper of reality, and a metaphor for reality' (1990). This definition puts into question purely structuralist views of language and context (see Becker 1984).

In sum, the notion of context is a relational one. In each of its five dimensions: linguistic, situational, interactional, as well as cultural and intertextual, it is shaped by people in dialogue with one another in a variety of roles and statuses. Because language is at the intersection of the individual and the social, of text and discourse, it both reflects and construes the social reality called 'context'.

Because of the multiplicity of meanings inherent in any stretch of speech, contexts are not stable; they are constantly changed and recreated by individual speakers and hearers, writers and readers. The dominance of any established 'culture' is alternately adopted and contested, adapted and ironicized, by the emergence of new meanings. In the creation of spoken and written texts, individuals manipulate and shape imposed contexts to fit their own individual needs and bring to the fore their own meanings.

Teaching a language is teaching how to shape the context of the 'lesson' as an individual learning event and as a social encounter with regard to its setting, its participant roles, the purpose of its activities, its topics of conversation, its tone, modalities, norms of interaction, and the genre of its tasks. The way context is shaped through the foreign language determines the types of meanings the students will be allowed to explore, discover, and exchange. The more potential meanings they are encouraged to discover, the richer the opportunities for learning. In the next chapter, we will look at a few case studies of contextual shaping by foreign language teachers and learners in actual classrooms.

## Notes

1 For example, in a fifth semester German language class in the United States, American students who were reading Kant's essay 'Was ist Aufklärung?' were asked by their teacher 'Nun, was ist Aufklärung?' [Well, what is enlightenment?]. For a while, there was silence in the classroom, either because no one had done the reading, or because the answer could easily be lifted off the page. The teacher, a native speaker of German, having repeated her question, a timid finger was raised, and the student muttered a response that had to do with 'Freiheit' [freedom] and the ability to have 'Kontrolle' over one's life. The teacher exclaimed: 'Was? Kontrolle? Nein! Was hat Kontrolle mit Aufklärung zu tun?' [What? Control? No! What does control have to do with enlightenment?] One student then looked at the text and read: 'Es ist der Mut, sich seines Verstandes zu bedienen' [It is the courage to use one's reason]. 'Gut', said the teacher, 'es ist die Fähigkeit, sich seines Verstandes zu bedienen. Nächste Frage . . .' [It is the ability to use one's reason. Next question . . .] The German teacher never did realize what the American student was referring to by appealing to such American concepts as 'control' and 'freedom' that belong to a different tradition. The student's misperception of what enlightenment meant for Germans in 1783 would have been worth a critical comparison between commonly held American views about freedom of action and individual control, and eighteenth century German views about freedom of the mind and social control.

2 Of course, the potential of shaping a new culture exists even if one is not communicating in a foreign language, if we take, as I do here, the term 'culture' to encompass more than the speech communities of nation states.

3 This linguistic analysis does not claim to depict or predict psychological reality. The fact that one is interpreted by another does not necessarily mean that one is ready, willing, or able to reinterpret oneself.

4 This way of viewing the self in social interaction echoes the view of social psychologist George Herbert Mead (1863–1931), who described the two aspects of the self in relation to the other as *I* and *Me*. The ego or I is the response of the organism to the attitude of others; the censor or Me is the organized set of the attitudes of others which one assumes

oneself. The attitudes of others constitute the organized Me toward whom one reacts as an I. Charaudeau's perspective differs, however, from that of Mead, in that Mead's description of the dialogic situation is a purely behaviorist one, whereas Charaudeau operates within a discourse analytic, social semiotic framework that is closer to language teachers' concerns, because it captures the dialogic nature of all linguistic utterances.

5 The fear of the hermeneutic dialogue turning into a hermeneutic circle should not be minimized. Learners of a foreign language may reach a stage of acculturation and empathy for the foreign language and culture, in which perceptions and counterperceptions seem to reflect each other ad infinitum, and where every interpretation seems so relative to any other that there is a real fear of losing oneself in the process. In Chapter 8, I will suggest ways to break the cycle of relativity and to 'find a home' both in one's native and in the foreign language.

6 My interpretation of the data differs slightly here from that of Frawley and Lantolf, who see in the inner speech displayed by the weak ESL students merely evidence of their attempts to gain control over the task at hand. I do not think that the authors' Vygotskian perspective is incompatible with Bakhtin's notion of double-voiced discourse in the construction and production of texts (see Chapter 1).

# 3   Teaching the spoken language

Nicht weil Unterricht unbekannt, sondern weil er zu gut
bekannt ist, läßt sich so schwer über ihn reden[1]
(Hans Hunfeld 1990: 9)

The number of imaginative and creative activities and techniques
designed over the last fifteen years to help classroom learners
develop communicative competence is remarkable. These pedagogical practices have revolutionized the teaching of oral skills
and rekindled the belief that in order to understand other people
you first have to be able to converse with them. This truth,
however, is so difficult to put into practice precisely because it
is so obvious. As Hunfeld writes (see above), the difficulty in
talking about language teaching is not that people do not know
what it is about, but that most people believe they already know
what it is all about.

This chapter will not discuss what can now be assumed to
be good communicative language teaching. Instead, with a few
selected case studies, I will take a critical look at how these
activities are in fact carried out in actual classrooms and examine how language and context interact to produce meaning. I
will then make suggestions for a communicative approach that
focuses not only on talking and listening, but on multiple levels
of contextual understanding through dialogue.

## Five case studies

The following five case studies are based on genuine observations of actual classes conducted at various colleges in the
United States. My purpose is not to evaluate the pedagogical
qualities of the teachers depicted, but rather, to examine the
way in which, through their choice of verbal and non-verbal
behavior, teachers and students set up contexts of social interaction that in turn affect the way students use the language
they are learning. I will look especially at the cultural implications of these choices, and at the opportunities they provide
for thematizing the link between the language and the cultural
values it encodes.

## Case 1

Having heard much good about the benefits of group work, this teacher decides to try group work for the first time in an intermediate-level French class. The students have just finished the chapter in their textbook which features the following: functions of expressing and reacting to feelings, opinions, and facts; and the grammar points of verbs taking the subjunctive, and reflexive verbs. The teacher has prepared the following 50-minute lesson plan for the day:

> 5': presentation of the exercise
> 30': group work
> 15': presentation of group work.

As the teacher enters the room, the twelve students are sitting in a circle along the classroom walls. She sits down behind the table, her back to the blackboard and announces in French the activity for the day: now that they have finished lesson 6 in the textbook, they are going to do group work to practice expressing feelings and voice reactions using the subjunctive. They will have 25–30 minutes to prepare their role in writing. Then they will present it to the rest of the class. As they listen to the presentation of others, they should write down vocabulary they have not understood or errors of grammar they might have picked up. They should, in the end, write a one-sentence evaluation of the other groups' presentations. The teacher then breaks up the class into groups of 3, 4, and 5 and distributes a task (in French) to each group:

1   (Group of 3) Starting next January, every student has to take a 20 hours a week course entitled 'Survival course for the year 2000' in order to graduate. This course will teach the art of verbal negotiation and elements of first aid. The following persons express their feelings about this curricular initiative: one student enthusiastically in favor; one student against; one representative of the administration.

2   (Group of 4) You have just come out of an audition that will determine whether or not you are admitted in a drama/dance/music group at your school and you are awaiting the result. With you are two friends, one optimistic, the other pessimistic, and one of your teachers. All

four of you express your impressions and reactions to the audition, you express your hopes and fears.

3   (Group of 5) The administration of your school has just forbidden shorts and bare feet on campus during the week. The following persons give their reactions to the news: a male student; a female student; a chemistry professor; a librarian; a representative of the administration.

During the 30 minutes of group work, students work partly individually and silently, partly they ask each other for translations (e.g. '*J'ai peur que* . . . does that take the subjunctive?', 'How do you say "topic" in French?'). The teacher moves from group to group, helping students with their roles. She shows interest only in the form of students' utterances, not their content:

**S1:**  (*to teacher*) Qu'est-ce que je dois écrire ici?
**T:**   Utilisez seulement les structures que nous avons apprises au chapitre 6: subjonctif, indicatif . . .

[S1: What should I write here? T: Use only the structures we have learned in chapter 6: subjunctive, indicative . . .]

**S2:**  (*to teacher*) Mais ce n'est pas vrai.
**T:**   Ça ne fait rien; c'est seulement un exercice.

[S2: But it is not true. T: It doesn't matter, it is only an exercise.]

**S3:**  (*to teacher*) J'aime les topiques que vous choisissez.
**T:**   Attention temps du verbe.
**S3:**  que vous avez choisi.
**S2:**  subjonctif.
**T:**   subjonctif après 'aimer': oui? non?

[S3: I like the topics (*anglicism*) you choose. T: Watch out verb tense. S3: that you have chosen. S2: subjunctive. T: subjunctive after 'to like': yes? no?]

Most groups, as soon as the teacher has her back turned, start speaking English with one another. They ask each other in English what they should say and then write the sentence down in French on their hand-out. When the thirty minutes have elapsed, the teacher asks each group to make its presentation. Students read their written statements, with great care for structural accuracy. They address exclusively the teacher who, sitting behind the table, listens attentively and notes down errors of grammar and vocabulary. When the group is finished, the teacher turns to each student and draws his or her attention to one or two errors she has made. Groups 1 and 2 perform their task with care but with little of the expressiveness one could expect of such expressions as *Je suis heureuse que ...* [I am happy that] or *Je crains que ...* [I fear that].

Students in group 3 start, like the others before them, by reading their statements in subdued and monotone voices, when all of a sudden one member of the group turns to another member of the group and challenges his opinion directly: *Ah non alors, je ne suis pas d'accord!* [No, I don't agree!]. Within a split second, the reading of statements to the teacher turns into a fiery debate within the group for and against the wearing of shorts on campus. Students turn around to face each other, they take sides, opinions and reactions fly with or without subjunctives, grammatical accuracy becomes much more random, some forms are correct, many are not, but the students keep talking and vie for the floor with enthusiasm. The teacher interrupts the debate after five minutes.

The teacher then asks the students to write down one sentence evaluating each group's activity (hoping to elicit once again a discussion of verbs of feelings and opinion); however, what the students turn in is not the expected report of other students' choice of forms, but a *summary* of how each group discussed the topic. At the end of the class, the teacher asks the students how they liked the group work. The reaction is positive: they say they enjoyed learning from one another, not only from the teacher; they found the discussion topics amusing, and they liked most of all the debate of group 3.

In a follow-up conversation with the observer, the teacher admits she is not quite satisfied with the lesson. Her goal was to have students interact with one another so that they would have more opportunity to use the language for communication. She feels she has given the students too much to do, that they would have needed more time, and that they have not interacted as much as she had hoped within the groups. She is pleased that group 3 has been more active, but she does not quite know how that came about. Considering that students seem to like group work, she is prepared to try it again, but she thinks that next time she might give them the task to prepare at home before coming to class.

## Discussion

Within the very first two minutes of the lesson, the teacher has already defined the ends, the norms of interaction and the instrumentalities of this day's class. By seating herself behind the desk, by announcing that they are going to do group work 'in order to practice the subjunctive after verbs of feeling', and by asking the small groups to write down their feelings and reactions and then their evaluations of other students' statements, she has defined the following parameters of the context of learning:

—The purpose of this activity is to practice formal structures of speech.
—The students should interact mainly as learners, and only incidentally as communicators.
—Speaking is not a spontaneous affair, but a matter of getting one's grammar straight. Writing serves to slow down the production process and ensure greater accuracy.
—Learning a language is a matter of applying formal rules of grammar and vocabulary.

However, at the same time, by relinquishing her authority to the groups and letting them negotiate among one another both the content and the form of their utterances, also by choosing provocative and imaginative topics for discussion, she is giving the situation the following structures of expectation:

—Learning a language is having the choice of deciding what one wants to say and how one will say it.
—What one says need not reflect one's 'true' opinions; imagination is in fact encouraged.
—Students can learn from one another; i.e. learners can take on the role of teachers.
—Interaction in groups helps prepare for a display performance at a later date for the benefit of the teacher.

By accepting the ends, the norms of interaction, and the instrumentalities set by the teacher, the students implicitly collaborate in shaping the context of the lesson the way she presented it. It is therefore not surprising that the interaction in the groups is not as lively as the teacher had hoped, for this is not the expectation she has set up. Despite the wording of the hand-outs, the activity is perceived as a tutoring activity, not as a communicative event. The pragmatic functions are not acted out, they are only realized grammatically.

The context as set up by the teacher is not unambiguous: on the one hand, students are to be imaginative, creative in their verbal participation; on the other hand, what counts is only the grammaticality of their utterances, not their creativity. They are to learn from one another as learners, but for that they have to adopt the role and even the discourse of a teacher for one another; they are to react to an event and to other participants' feelings in a discussion about that event, and yet they have to *read* their reactions to someone who has not participated in the discussion, namely the teacher. So the situation in itself invites subversion, and that is exactly what happens.

The turning point in the lesson is indeed the arbitrary and unexpected redefinition by group 3 of the whole context of situation. How did that come about? First the students redefined the instrumentalities. They abandoned the prepared scripts and addressed their peers directly. Then, they opened up the debate to other norms of interaction and interpretation; they changed the nature of the audience from the teacher to their interlocutors in the group, thereby instinctively introducing an element of unpredictability or information gap that provided its own rhetorical momentum. Finally, they changed their text from a formal display act to a negotiation of divergent meanings.

Note that they did not resort to English in the fire of the debate, but maintained the use of French throughout. Contrary to Prabhu's (1987) suggestion—namely that learners in monolingual classrooms tend to use their mother tongue during small group work, and that therefore group work should be discouraged in foreign language classes—the amount of native language spoken in foreign language classes seems to vary with the parameters of the context: time constraints, perceived purpose of the activity, interactional pull, size of the group, and so on. The stricter the time limit, the more precisely defined the purpose of the activity, the greater the negotiative nature of the task, the easier it is for the students to immerse themselves in the target language for the duration of the communicative activity.

However, in this particular class, as the students' use of French became more fluent and more spontaneous, their grammar became also much less controlled and the subjunctives were even ignored under the communicative load and the pressure to argue fast and persuasively. Teachers do well, as this teacher did, to make a note of the main errors and correct them *after* the activity. But an exclusive correction of low-level grammar is likely to encourage the assumption that linguistic forms bear no relationship to the expression of meanings in context. While one could argue that some linguistic forms have no direct communicative value (e.g. some of the French subjunctives), the teacher would be well-advised to pick up also on those linguistic errors that account for erroneous meanings (e.g. wrong verb tenses, agreements, etc.), and to deal with them not as errors in morphology, but as ambiguities in communicative intent.

How does this class fulfill the goals the teacher has set for herself? As we have seen, by attending only to the grammatical forms of the language, she has constrained the context to its linguistic dimensions. However, the students changed the context, thus potentially provoking sociocultural inquiry. For example, the topic summaries offered by the students at the end of the class would have been an opportunity to broaden the context of communication to include its referential aspects. The divergent behavior of group 3 could have a provided insights into different ways of debating a topic. As we shall see in the other case studies below, the language classroom offers a range of contextual possibilities — linguistic, situational, interactional, cultural — that can all be made available to the language user.

## Case 2

In this beginning German class based on a natural approach textbook, *Kontakte. A Communicative Approach* (Terrell *et al.* 1988; published by Random House), students are learning the forms of the past tense. To help the students practice these forms, rather than have them produce them on meaningless drills, the teacher has distributed slips of paper containing several interrogative sentences in the past tense. The teacher has made sure that these sentences are relevant to American students' lives, e.g. *Als du ein Kind warst, hast du gern Spinat gegessen? hast du mit Barbie Puppen gespielt? hast du Sesamstraße geschaut?* [When you were a child, did you like to eat spinach? did you play with Barbie dolls? did you watch Sesame Street?]. Students are to move around the class, read each other the questions and note down the yes/no answers. Of the seventeen students in the class, three are Japanese, two are Korean, three are from India, and the rest are Anglo-Americans. While there is much laughter among the Anglos as they ask each other the questions and enjoy both the cultural innuendos and the interactional spin-offs of the activity, the Asian students seem to be in trouble, not because of the linguistic difficulty of the questions, but because of their referential opacity. Why should they have not liked eating spinach? what is a Barbie Doll? and what is Sesame Street? and, most of all, why are the other students laughing? By the time they have tried to find answers to these questions, the activity is up and they never did get to practice their past tenses. The three Indian students seemed to be Americanized enough to know what the topics were about.

In the follow-up conversation the teacher said he had noticed the difficulty, and was concerned about the cultural problem presented by the Asian students. His goal had been to engage students in natural communication, using specific grammatical forms, but the different learning styles and different life experiences of learners in beginning language classes made it difficult to reach this goal. Unlike ESL classes, he said, that operate on the principle of sociocultural immersion, the natural approach in foreign language teaching encourages the students to talk about their own familiar lives and concerns, assuming that this shared reality will compensate for the learners' meager linguistic resources, and make communication possible. However, he added, if there is no such shared reality, how can communication come about?

## Discussion

By conducting this activity as described, the teacher defined the context of learning in the following manner:

—The purpose of the activity is to learn grammatical forms. This is done by hearing the forms and producing them over and over again in interaction with different interlocutors.
—The situational context proposed by the teacher is the here-and-now of students' lives.
—Scene, participant roles, key, and norms of interaction are as close as possible to those of the social context outside the classroom. This should increase the students' motivation to talk and thereby fulfill the purpose of the activity.
—The instrumentality 'talk' is presented as an exchange of personal meanings, and students try to give 'true' answers to the questions posed to them.

How does this definition of context match the teacher's stated goals? Using social interaction as a means to acquire grammatical forms certainly provides a better incentive to talk than pattern drills, but at the same time, it can constrain students' discourse options if speakers are made to feel that the purpose of the activity is to practice grammatical forms, not really to get to know each other. Thus, defining the instrumentalities as an exchange of true personal meanings seems to contradict the real purpose of the activity.

Most American students tolerate this contradiction as part of the language learning game; they are satisfied with what they perceive to be a cocktail-party type of social interaction, and the teacher feels gratified at having a lively class. However, some students, like the Asian students in this class, are caught between their view of themselves as learners and the teacher's view of them as cocktail-party communicators. How can they ask or answer a grammatically correct question if they do not understand the cultural context of that question? In their view, natural communication would require a negotiation of meaning that goes far beyond the meaning of the mere past tense. Moreover, this type of small talk does not fit their expectations of what classroom learning should be like.

Under the surface of a simple grammatical exercise, we are faced here with the paradox of the multicultural classroom. The teacher tries to avoid the strangeness of foreign topics by choosing a setting that is transparent to mainstream Anglo-American students yet provocative enough to generate surprise and desire to talk. That setting, however, is opaque to many minority students in the class. In addition, as has been shown by Kachru (1986), besides imposing an interactional pedagogy that might be strange to non-mainstream students, such a definition of context asks students to engage in interaction types (e.g. conversational chit-chat, the use of straightforward questions requiring straightforward answers) that might go against the way they have been socialized into behaving, especially with teachers and other learners in classrooms. This is not to say, as has been pointed out in Chapter 1, that foreign language teachers should not try and shape the instructional context in more natural ways. Rather, it points to the necessity of teaching context itself explicitly, and not assuming that it is transparent and agreed upon by everyone in the class.

This second case study offers insights that are not usually

available in monocultural classrooms. By problematizing usual pedagogical practice, it opens up the possibility, as in natural settings, of jointly deciding on the context of language use. For example, by brainstorming and discussing with the students some of the things they did 'when they were young', and basing the list of past tense utterances on student input rather than on the teacher's assumptions of students' interests, the teacher can begin to make explicit the very tenets of his or her pedagogy. By enabling the students to articulate their varied cultural/historical contexts, the foreign language classroom thus promotes cross-cultural interaction and opens new possibilities of understanding.

In sum, this case study has illustrated yet another way of identifying and understanding the cultural implications of language instruction. It not only suggests making the purposes of tasks and the rationale for the choice of interactional format as clear and explicit as possible, but it suggests reflecting on that choice as well.

## Case 3

The topic of this low-intermediate German lesson is the function 'Giving and receiving advice'. This function in German can be realized by such phrases as *Was rätst du mir? Was soll ich tun?* [What do you advise me? What should I do?] and its rejoinders *An deiner Stelle würde ich . . ., du solltest . . .* [If I were you I would . . ., You should . . .] requiring the use of the subjunctive of politeness and an infinitive construction. Eighteen students are sitting in two long rows of nine. The teacher, sitting in front of the class, engages the students in a fifteen-minute conversation in German on the topic: 'How did you feel the first time you came to this school? What did you expect? What did you find?'. Many students enjoy the chatty atmosphere, and participate; many look like they are waiting for the real lesson to begin. The teacher then breaks up the class into groups of three or four: one student is to play the role of a new student at the school, who asks for advice on where to live, what courses to take etc., the others give relevant advice. For the next 15 minutes, the teacher goes from group to group, mostly listening, sometimes reviving a sluggish conversation, occasionally providing an item of vocabulary. The students talk readily, using as opener exclusively the modal phrase *Was soll ich ... / Du sollst ...* [What should I ...? You should ...]. As they want to say things related to their immediate cultural environment, they have to ask the teacher for many typically American vocabulary items like 'fraternity', 'admissions', 'campus', 'registration', which he is not always able to provide, or they have to resort to code-switching, which seems the preferred way out for most students. The rest of the lesson is spent again with the whole class, the teacher conducting an informal conversation about what has been discussed in the small groups, what one should and should not do as a first-time student at the school.

The teacher was satisfied with the lesson. His main purpose, he said, had been to create an atmosphere that was non-threatening to the students, so that they would be motivated to talk and participate without interference from the teacher. He was somewhat worried about the incorrectness of their speech, but he felt that their grammar and pronunciation would improve with time and with conversational practice.

## Discussion

How did the teacher set up the context of this lesson? By seating himself next to the desk (not behind it) and remaining on the same physical level as his students; further, by adopting an easy-going, conversational tone, by not focusing on how things are said, but only on what is said, the teacher is defining the genre, the tone, the code, the norms of interaction, and the purpose of the lesson. Students can expect the following:

—Learning a language is best done through conversation on familiar topics in which the learners talk as much as possible.
—The tone of this conversation is casual.
—The purpose of the activity is both to practice the language and to 'socialize', i.e. to get acquainted with other students in the class, not to learn about Germany or about how German speakers socialize.
—The code is exclusively German, but any variety of German interlanguage is acceptable if it brings one's message across. What is important is what you say, not how you say it.
—The norms of interaction have been implicitly established by default, so to speak. By not demonstrating nor insisting on

German ways of speaking, the teacher has led the students to assume that norms of interaction in German are the same as in American settings outside the classroom.

How did this teacher's set-up help him meet his goals? The focus here is mainly on the interactional and situational aspects of the context, not on its linguistic or cultural/intertextual dimensions. This, in fact, has the effect of making the students more, not less, dependent on the teacher. Since no linguistic restrictions are imposed on the context and the students are encouraged to say whatever they wish, their need for vocabulary is insatiable and the teacher has to perform encyclopaedic feats of translation on demand. In addition, since comprehensibility is predicated on a shared knowledge of the situational context, it does not seem necessary to negotiate meaning because of possibly ambiguous syntax, incomprehensible pronunciation, or even cultural misunderstandings. Students are confident that the teacher will understand everything they say, and if the teacher or their fellow students do not understand them, topics are just dropped and switched. In short, the students are engaged in shaping a context of communication where what one says is not really of any consequence. Thus it seems that the very lack of structure runs counter to what the teacher wanted to achieve, namely, autonomous speakers in control of their conversational topic.

Interestingly, by exercising as little control as possible, the teacher has constrained the discourse choices of the students rather than broadening them. Whenever a topic was dropped for lack of vocabulary, whenever the same opening gambit was used for lack of an alternative, or a superficial answer was given for lack of reflection, there was an opportunity to enable students to go beyond their current knowledge and stretch their cultural and linguistic resources. Several suggestions have been made to create such enabling conditions. For example, by tightening up the group task through a shorter time limit, and by setting clear objectives that make negotiation necessary—such as jigsaw, information-gap, or decision-making tasks—students are encouraged to clarify their utterances and make demands on their listeners; by observing how native speakers realize speech functions with their culturally appropriate linguistic markers, students are given a range of sociolinguistic choices according to the situation.

Drawing the students' attention to the interactional context of communication could have led the students beyond communicative fluency and made them aware of the cultural meanings encoded in the foreign discourse.

## Case 4

The topic of this other low-intermediate German class is 'expressing/reacting to opinions'. The class, composed of fifteen students, has been given the lesson to read and the tape to listen to at home. Without preamble, the teacher starts the lesson by distributing to the students slips of paper that contain the following four items:

> Wie findest du . . . Madonna/Kevin Costner?
> Was hältst du von . . . San Franzisko/New York?
> Was meinst du zu . . . Rockmusik/klassiche Musik?
> Bist du der Meinung, daß George Bush/Dan Quayle . . .?
>
> [How do you find Madonna/Kevin Costner? How do you like San Francisco/New York? What do you think of rock/classical music? Do you feel that George Bush/Dan Quayle . . .?]

Students are to mill around the room and ask each other questions based on the elements given. After five minutes, the teacher asks the same questions of the class at large, generating quite a bit of laughter and some humorous responses. The teacher then distributes a prefabricated dialogue which he has prepared and asks students in groups of four to read it silently, then aloud, each one taking a part (excerpts of the hand-out are given below):

> 1: Also, wie habt ihr den Film gefunden?
> 2: Eigentlich fand ich ihn ganz schlecht. Die Charaktere waren total eindimensional.
> 3: Ja, du hast vollkommen recht!
> 4: O nee! ich sehe die Sache ganz anders. Habt ihr denn wirklich kein Mitleid mit dem Mann gehabt? . . .
> 4: Tscha, leider kann ich eure Meinung ganz und gar nicht teilen. Ich fand die Situation mit der Stiefmutter völlig glaubwürdig.
> 2: Na ja, ist egal. Wir brauchen auch nicht alle der gleichen Meinung zu sein
> 1: Ja, das stimmt. Hauptsache, es hat uns Spaß gemacht.

3: Genau!
2: Richtig!  } *(alle zusammen)*
4: Klar!

[1: Well, how did you find the film? 2: Actually I thought it was really bad. The characters were totally one-dimensional. 3: Yes, you are absolutely right! 4: Oh no! I am of a totally different opinion. Don't you feel pity for the man? ... 4: Well, unfortunately I disagree with you. I found the situation with the mother-in-law absolutely convincing. 2: Oh well, it doesn't matter. We don't need to be all of the same opinion. 1: Yes, that's true. The main thing, it was fun. *(together)*: 3: Exactly! 2: Right! 4: Sure!]

The students are to use the functional phrases underlined in the written dialogue to debate in their groups the following topic: 'Sollten Sportler solche hohen Gagen bekommen? Pro und Kontra' [Should athletes be paid as much as they are? For and Against]. The small groups are slow at getting a discussion going, the topic proves to have little pull, and no one uses any of the phrases on the hand-out. So after two or three minutes, the teacher proposes another topic to be discussed with the whole class: 'Sex education in schools. For or against?' The sudden thickness of the silence in the class reveals that this topic is of relevance to everybody. Students speak up. The first to speak, with great conviction, is a female Chinese-American student. She feels very strongly (*ich bin fest davon überzeugt* [I firmly believe]) that sex education should be a private matter, up to the parents, not the school. The teacher acknowledges her opinion and asks for others. During the next five minutes, six or seven other students speak up, both men and women, all in favor of having schools, not the parents, deliver sex education. They generally start their statement with the culturally appropriate openers *ich finde* [I feel] or *meiner Meinung nach* [in my view]. The teacher listens and gives the floor to whoever raises a hand, but refrains from giving any opinion of his own, or from probing deeper into the reasons for the arguments on both sides. When the students have finished, the teacher admits that he himself was given sex education at school, but he does not enter the argument one way or the other. He then closes the activity by saying: *Na ja. Jeder hat seine Meinung. Wir brauchen auch nicht alle der gleichen Meinung zu sein* [OK, everyone has an opinion, we don't need to be all of the same opinion].

The teacher was pleased with the liveliness of the class. He did not quite understand why the debate topic had not generated more conversation, but he felt that the goals of the lesson had been fully reached in the second half of the class when students, using the German language throughout, participated freely in the general discussion over sex education in schools, and even used many of the German floor-taking gambits introduced in the lesson.

## Discussion

Unlike the teacher in the previous case study, this teacher foregrounded right away the linguistically appropriate form for the speech function of the day and set up a context of social interaction that valued both form and content. As can be inferred from the last statement in the written dialogue on the hand-out and from his last remarks in the lesson, this teacher clearly sees 'expressing one's opinion' as the essence of a pluralistic society in which, as the saying goes, 'everyone is entitled to his or her opinion'. From the way the teacher set up the activities, we can reconstruct his definition of the context as follows:

—Learning a language is learning how to perform certain speech functions in dialogue with other people.
—Learning how to express an opinion in German is a matter of identifying the appropriate opener, learning it and plugging it into the appropriate situation, as one has learned to do with other linguistic structures.
—Expressing one's opinions is everybody's right in a pluralistic society; no one should impose his or her opinion on anybody else. Germans are believed to hold in this respect the same view as Americans.
—Since different people hold different opinions, it is not worthwhile finding out why they are of a different opinion.

How well did this definition of the context help the teacher achieve the goals of the lesson? Inasmuch as the goal was the free exchange of opinions and the use of German gambits, this class had been successful indeed. It did, however, offer interesting opportunities for cross-cultural inquiry that could have served to enrich further the context of the lesson. The fact that the Chinese-American student's voice got drowned in the discussion, and that the discourse style adopted by the class was quite different from what one would expect among German native speakers, were two culturally salient aspects of the discourse of this lesson.

The students were exposed to various opinion markers in German, but, because these idiomatic phrases were not accompanied by a philosophy of conversational behavior, the linguistic forms became dissociated from their German discourse context and were put in the service of an American way of expressing opinions. American students, even in an academic context, are generally much less seriously committed to defending their opinion than German students would be in a German academic context, where opinions are more likely to be *Stellungnahmen* (personal stands) that are worth justifying and defending. In American classrooms, foreign language teachers generally shy away from too conflictual a clash of opinions, especially if they pertain to sex education, religion, or politics, which is probably why the students did not pick up on the Chinese-American student's contribution. In Germany, by contrast, such issues are eminently debatable, especially in educational contexts.

This is certainly not to say that learning to use a foreign language *necessitates* conforming to the cultural norms of its speakers, but teaching context does mean making the students aware of cultural differences in discourse styles. Such an awareness can be fostered either through role-play (e.g. by temporarily adopting a German discussion style), or through explicit metatalk on the discourse style employed by the students. In both cases, the teacher has to be an intercessor of the textbook; he or she has to help the students interpret the linguistic forms presented in the text and embed them in the appropriate cultural context.

Broadening the contextual options in this manner is no easy task. The reasons offered for not dealing explicitly with the social and cultural differences in students' opinions and discourse styles usually include ideological motives ('you can't talk about these things in democratic classrooms'), or the limited scope of one's legitimate expertise ('I am only a language teacher'), or time constraints ('I still had this or that item on my lesson plan for the day'). However, these reasons are often excuses for inexperience or for conservative political attitudes. If routine maintenance dialogues are to lead to cross-cultural breakthroughs, moments such as the one observed in this class must be remembered, played back, examined in retrospect, and possibly evaluated as a missed cultural opportunity in the very name of conversational practice.

## Case 5

At the end of a beginning German course, four different instructors devise communicative activities to teach a short story by Helga Novak, entitled 'Schlittenfahren' (1968). This is the first literary selection in their first-year textbook (see Appendix I).

The story tells of two children, 'one who cannot talk yet', and another 'older one' playing in the garden and fighting over the sled. It is winter; the sun is big and red. Every time the little one screams, a man comes out of the house, shouts *Wer brüllt, kommt rein!* [He who screams comes in!] and slams the door. This happens five times until the older child screams *Daaaddy, daddydaddydaaaaaaddy! Now Andreas has fallen into the brook!* The door opens just a crack wide; a man's voice shouts *How often do I have to say it: He who screams, comes in!*

The way the story is told is intriguing. First, the title is ambiguous. The German expression *mit jemandem Schlitten fahren* has, beyond the literal meaning 'going sledding with someone', also the metaphorical meaning of 'giving someone a hard time'. Then, the initial sentence of the story is unusual. The phrase *Das Eigenheim steht in einem Garten* [The private home stands in a garden] gives prominence to the fact that the man is the owner of the house. This seems to be superfluous information since all the action takes place in the garden and the man only appears on the scene to monitor the children and to repeat the same impersonal injunction *Wer brüllt, kommt rein!*. The little one cannot talk yet, but the narrator gives his screams a variety of flavors: he cries, he screams, he sobs, he squeals, he howls, he whines. The man is always referred to as 'the man', the children as 'the smaller child', 'the bigger child'. The impersonal distance kept by the narrator vis-à-vis the characters and their actions enhances the brutality and emptiness of the phrase *Wer brüllt, kommt rein!* as counterpoint to the seemingly innocuous title 'Sledding'. Andreas, who ends up falling in the ice-cold stream, not only cannot talk, but he is given a name only indirectly through the voices of others. The children are being socialized into an impersonal social behavior that has no other meaning but itself and does not fit the changing events happening in the garden. The story, written by a (then) West-German woman, is a moving indictment of a man's world, hostile to children and other voiceless creatures—of a world frozen in its fossilized stereotypes and routinized talk.

The story is followed by the usual 'Comprehension Questions'. The young instructors find these questions too teacher-centered, so they design activities that would make the students talk and generate a lively discussion. They give the reading as a homework assignment for the next day.

### TEACHER A

After the usual comprehension questions to ensure that everyone has understood the plot, teacher A breaks the class into groups of four; each group is given five minutes to prepare orally a rendition of the story as seen from the perspective of one of the protagonists. Each student is responsible for telling two events. The students seem to have difficulty at first telling each other a story that they know already and to take on the voice of one the characters, but after a while they do that quite well. The teacher then has each group stand up in front of the class, announce the narrator's perspective and recount the events of the story, keeping close to that perspective. After class, the teacher is pleased with the linguistic exercise, but expresses a personal dissatisfaction: she is not sure that the students understood the story any better by doing this and she has not been able to draw any conclusions from it.

### TEACHER B

Rather than ask the usual comprehension questions, teacher B decides to summarize the story himself for the students, but to intermingle errors of fact that the students have to identify and correct. Every time they detect an error they are to raise their hand and say *Quatsch!* [rubbish]. The teacher reports having had great fun preparing the exercise; the students in turn were kept on their toes, they loved correcting the teacher, and it made for a very enjoyable and lively activity. When asked whether he had discussed with his students why the erroneous elements were not likely to be part of the story, he answered that the main thing at that elementary level was not to have the students interpret the text, but to give them practice in listening comprehension and in taking the floor.

### TEACHER C

Teacher C has the students reconstitute the story by asking each of them to write a word on the board that they consider to be important in the story, (e.g. *der Vater* [the father], *schreien* [to scream], *Schlittenfahren* [sledding], *der Bach* [the brook]). The class then makes statements connected with those words. She then has the students write on the blackboard alternative titles for the story ('Find a title that better captures how *you* understand what the story is about'). One writes *Der böse Vater* [the bad father], another *Wer brüllt, kommt rein* [he who screams comes in], and yet another *Andreas*. After class, the teacher says she is satisfied with the lesson but she does not find that the titles produced by the students were very imaginative.

### TEACHER D

Teacher D draws up the following scenario. Let us assume the child died as a result of the accident. Let us put the man on trial. Three groups have to build their case representing, respectively, the defense lawyer, the district attorney, the key witness (older sibling). The groups are given ten minutes to prepare their arguments and to decide how they are going to present their case before a panel of two or three judges, who may ask additional questions and have to decide on a verdict. The teacher writes on the board some useful words such as *Fahrlässigkeit* [negligence], *Gleichgültigkeit* [indifference], *Opfer* [victim], and so on. Students have a great time; the teacher goes from group to group, spurring on the conversation, giving some vocabulary, at no point correcting the grammar explicitly, but only rephrasing correctly a student utterance. In their presentations to the jury, the imagination of the students knows no bounds: the father defends himself by stating that the mother was sick inside the house and the screams of the children were disturbing her; he did not suspect that the child could drown, he thought the ice was too thick; no, he could not go to the rescue because he had lost a leg in the war and he could not find his wooden leg. The students roar with laughter. The father is declared not guilty of the charges. The teacher evaluates this class as a most successful class, the students have been very active, the ratio of student-talk to teacher-talk has been very high.

## Discussion

In the course of each of these lessons, the four teachers have
defined the context of learning as an interactive one, in which
learners are given the freedom to manipulate the setting and the
scene of the story, the roles and the perspectives of the participants; in addition, teacher C has given them leeway to use whatever norms of interpretation they wish, teacher D has varied the
genre from interaction with a written text to a face-to-face court
trial of the argumentative type. The linguistic aspect of the context has been subordinated to its situational and interactional
aspects.

In all four classes, the teacher set up a context for students'
expectations as follows:

— Discussing a text is talking about what happened in the story.
— A good story provides an incentive to talk. Creating and
   expressing personal meanings in a foreign language can be
   fun.
— In a language class, talking and responding to what others say
   (in speech or in writing) are the two most important activities.

Let us look at each class in turn to see how well this contextual
set-up facilitated the achievement of each teacher's goals. In
teacher A's class, assigning different students to different renditions of events was a good starting point for eliciting divergent
perspectives on the text and provided a good incentive for students to talk. It appears, however, that such an activity did not
automatically bring about an understanding of perspective and
point of view. The differences in perspective in the various
retellings were left unexamined, they were performed as routine
lexical and grammatical exercises and as exercises in information retrieval. Had the class subsequently engaged in comparing
the nature and the form of the information provided by each
of the protagonists, maybe by writing some of the students'
productions on the blackboard, different patterns of voice and
power might have emerged that could have been compared with
the original text. The students' texts could have then led to a
richer interpretation of the story.

Teacher B used a well-known communicative activity ('Catch
the liar') to practice listening comprehension. Such an activity
encourages attention to detail and to a text's linguistic and situational context. However, it is not clear how the exercise as it

was conducted contributed to an understanding of the text that was better than the traditional comprehension questions the teacher had rejected. It was dealt with as a referential, not as an interpretive exercise. Moreover, although it engaged the students' attention, it could hardly be called student-centered, since the students were not asked for their personal reactions or responses to the text.

Teacher C's alternative-title exercise was potentially an excellent way of bringing to the fore students' understanding of the story. It required on their part an analysis of its theme, an interpretation of its meaning, and a personal recasting of the story into a title. However, teacher C used this activity purely as an exercise in imagination and creativity. As such it was valuable enough, but it did not in itself yield a deeper understanding of students' responses. That understanding can only come through dialogue and negotiated interpretation. For example, the teacher would have had to ask herself and discuss with the class: What did the title *Der böse Vater* say about the way the student understood the story? Did the student believe the father was a bad father or an angry father (the adjective can have both meanings in German)? Was the adjective *böse* meant in a moral or in a psychological sense?

Teacher D's class had the potential of having students understand the story by performing it. Holding a press conference with a character in a story or putting a character on trial are some of the more imaginative communicative activities recommended for dealing with narrative or dramatic texts in the language classroom (see Chapter 5). Here, the student performance could have been further explored for its deeper cross-cultural meaning by discussing, as I show below, the role in which the students had cast the father.

One of the most difficult things for American students to understand is the pressure exerted on the individual in an older, traditional, rule-governed society like the one encountered in many parts of Germany. The phrase *Wer brüllt kommt rein*—like other similar impersonal phrases displayed in public places, *Rasen nicht betreten* (keep off the grass), *Hunde sind an der Leine zu führen* (dogs should be kept on a leash), *Spielen verboten* (no playing), *Rauchen verboten* (no smoking)—does not need any local legitimation. It derives from the generic injunction *Ordnung muß sein* (there must be law and order), and is sanctioned by tradition and the social order. As a typically single-voiced phrase, it has taken on a life of its own, which is precisely the point of the story.

In its cultural and social value, this phrase has no American equivalent. For, in most parts of American society, there is no consensus as to what children should or should not do irrespective of the situation. Children should keep quiet *for a reason*, and teacher D's students invented all kinds of reasons why the father of the story wanted his children to keep quiet. But by doing so, they created a cultural context which was radically opposed to that of the story. It would have been enlightening to make this cultural clash explicit by reflecting on the text performed by the students.

The way the context of learning was set up in all four classes encouraged the students to use the text as a springboard for their own creativity in interaction with their peers. By having them do this, the teachers were tapping a rich source of cross-cultural material. However, this material is too valuable to remain unexplored. To increase their linguistic options and their chances at cross-cultural understanding, students' input should be given the importance it deserves as a unique window on the dialogic emergence of culture in the classroom.

## Problems and paradoxes

In each of the five case studies above, the teacher's main goal was to have the students talk and interact, in the hope that through interaction and minimal interference from the teacher the students would practice the linguistic forms they had learned and enter into meaningful dialogue with one another. However, we have seen the important role that context played in the construction of meaning. By failing to take advantage of the full range of contextual possibilities, the teachers often unwittingly constrained classroom discourse to superficial, linguistic exchanges, thus only partly achieving the goal they had set for themselves. Doing justice to the full context of the foreign language classroom raises interesting issues that require a new type of pedagogy:

1 *Multicultural classrooms.* As Königs pointed out recently: 'Internationalization will force us to develop a concept of multilingualism that goes beyond the mere accumulation of foreign language skills and is much more closely linked to

the societal context [in which they are used]' (1991: 80 my translation). Cases 2 and 4 show how complex such a link can be when teaching foreign languages to multicultural classes. The problem of teaching students from multiple mother tongues is nothing new to ESL teachers. However, in English-speaking countries, ESL teachers can at least rely on a common language being spoken outside the classroom. In foreign language education, the language taught is not spoken in the environment, and the link between the foreign language and any specific speech community is an arbitrary one. Hence the paradox: we have to make culture more explicit, and link more closely together language and culture, yet we must constantly stress the arbitrariness of that link and examine it critically (Saville-Troike 1992). How should we deal with this paradox?

2　*Cognition and communication.* We have to teach contrastively and cognitively, yet we do not want to loose the momentum of the communicative approach. Case 3 raises the question 'To what extent have the expectations raised by "natural" approaches made it difficult to introduce a more reflective, cognitive type of learning, that has no quick rewards and puts greater demands on the students' affective and cognitive understanding?'

3　*Pedagogy of sociocultural competence.* Teaching how to shape contexts of interaction cannot be done directly by a well-dosed administration of facts. Cases 1 and 4 show that it is not by learning a list of useful phrases like so many items of vocabulary that students will know how to use them to become fluent conversationalists. Pragmatic knowledge, as Valdman (1992) suggests can only be acquired through observation and analysis and a feel for the whole social context. It is not an 'if-then' affair. It requires, therefore, a totally different pedagogic approach. Are teachers capable of switching gears? Can they meet an educational challenge that requires action, but mainly as food for reflection?

4　*Teacher on the line.* As we encourage teachers to make the context of culture and the intertextual aspects of the discourse of their students more explicit, they have to be aware themselves of the extent to which their own discourse shapes and is shaped by their environment. Teacher personality has been up to now 'a largely tabu research topic' (Königs 1991: 81). Cases 4 and 5 raise the question

'Are teachers ready to examine their own cultural premises, reveal their opinions and their own interpretations of texts, and engage in double-voiced discourse with their students?

5 *Cultural stereotypes*. If the learners' different voices are to be taken seriously, we have to systematically bring these differences to the fore. Even if learners share a common native language, the fact that they partake of a multiplicity of 'cultures' (e.g. socioeconomic status, gender, sexual orientation, visible and invisible disabilities) is rarely acknowledged. However, as case study 5 illustrates, there is great resistance to exploring social and physical differences for fear of generating stereotypes. Can we debunk stereotypes without perpetuating them?

The analyses of the classroom lessons described above show how complex and at times paradoxical the task of teachers and learners can be. In fact, many teachers would prefer not to know too much about the contextual factors that affect their teaching and that make them in turn shape the learning environment the way they do. They feel already all too powerless in the face of the incredible constraints imposed on the language learning enterprise by the institutional setting, the educational traditions, the societal attitudes and expectations vis-à-vis foreign language learning and language teachers in particular. Moreover, as we will see in Chapter 5, there are severe cultural limits on the amount of cross-cultural discussions they feel they can entertain in their classes. Trying to apply the insights of psycholinguistic or educational research to the day-to-day achievement of lessons in overcrowded classes, within a conservative educational culture, for little academic or financial recognition, seems utopian indeed (see, for example, one such reflection on the United States' educational context in Freed and Bernhardt 1992).

And yet, the classroom is not the totally socially controlled context it seems to be. As we have seen, it is constantly challenged by the learners themselves, in ways that are as varied as its potential meanings. What often constrains teachers is their fear of the imagination, of unexplainable and uncontrollable meanings, of paradox and ambiguity. If they listen to and explore further what their students are saying through their ill-formed utterances, their silences, their non-verbal language, they will discover where the forces of change are and where teachers can, as the saying goes, 'make a difference'.

For this, however, they have to embrace the full context of learning in all its facets. And that is more than just adopting an eclectic methodology (see Introduction). It means 'pulling out all the stops'. That expression refers to the way in which experienced teachers play on the keyboard of the classroom as on an organ, using all the registers, keys, group configurations, tempo, and voices to make the richest music possible.

## Teaching language as (con)text

The pedagogy I would like to suggest strives to exploit the rich meaning potential of all the activities we conduct in the classroom. As has been pointed out several times in this chapter, teachers seem to pull the brake at precisely those points in the give-and-take of the lesson that could allow for a discovery and discussion of individual and social meanings. In the following, I will describe ways of expanding and deepening the contextual parameters of classroom dialogue.

### Expanding the context

If communicative activities are not only to meet the needs of social *maintenance*, but potentially to bring about educational and social *change*, then we have to search for ways of explicitly varying all parameters of the interactional context. These variations are not just to introduce diversity in an otherwise monotonous lesson; they are to provide food for thought.

I will take as an example a typical interactional activity, in which student A has to narrate a story to student B. Each variation in the context can bring to the fore potential variations of meaning in the text. After each activity, the class should consciously reflect on these different meanings, give them a name and relate them to others.

### *Setting*

By keeping interlocutor and text constant, but varying the spatial and temporal setting, student A can focus on changing her style of delivery, and her choice of words. For instance, A can tell her story to B as they sit face-to-face or back-to-back, in the presence of one or several observers, at a simulated cocktail party or in a fictitious job interview. The same exercise can be done either face-to-face in the classroom, or as homework over the phone, or on tape. The speakers can be asked to talk, shout, or whisper; they should either talk and listen with no overlap, or they should try and interrupt each other, or even overshout each other, in an attempt to impose their story on one another. The presence or absence of a visible interlocutor can change the equation of silence and talk, the amount of redundancy, the order in which information is transmitted.

Time, too, is an important feature of context that can be varied. If A tells the same story to B, C, and D, A can be given three minutes to tell her story to B, then 2 minutes to tell it to C, and only 1 minute to tell it to D. The topic remains constant, but A's fluency increases and so can the students' sensitivity to subtle shades of meaning.

## Participants

Sensitizing learners to the notion of audience is an important step towards making them aware of the dialogic nature of communication. One way of doing this is to vary the recipient while keeping all the other parameters constant. For example, B, C, and D are asked to be, each in turn, responsive listeners to student A's story. They are shown how to react, ask for clarification, show interest by asking questions, and so on. Every time A changes interlocutor, the text remains constant, but the questions and requests for clarification vary. A gets better and better at telling her story, and can add various details in response to local interactional needs. Further variations can be introduced in the sequence of interlocutors: for example, A tells the story to B, B tells A's story to C, C tells A's story to D, and so forth.

## Ends

Irrespective of the topic chosen, teachers can vary the purposes of the activities. There are a variety of task types available to the teacher who wants to vary the interactional parameters of pair and group work: tasks based on information gap, jigsaw, problem-solving, decision-making, opinion-exchange, surveys, role-play, simulation—all impose varying degrees of cooperation, negotiation of meaning, and consensus seeking among interlocutors. For instance, in the first case study described earlier in this chapter, the task type chosen for all three groups was opinion-exchange—a task with low interactional pull and low pressure to exchange information and negotiate meaning. We saw how the group members, while keeping the topic imposed by the teacher, changed the nature of the task from an opinion-exchange to a decision-making contest.

## Act sequence

Language can be used to express a variety of functions within one activity: for example, interlocutors can ask for clarification, give and request information, complain, apologize, agree, disagree, ask for advice/help, and express and react to opinions. In the first case study, the teacher had designed the task so that only one function, namely, describing and displaying information, was asked for. As we noticed, one group automatically enriched the context by enlisting additional speech functions that introduced intentional ambivalence and a sense of empowerment typical of more meaningful dialogues.

## Key

In an exercise in story-telling, A, B, C, and D can be given different instructions as to which tone they should adopt. Retelling, for instance, a story originally told by the teacher, A can be asked to adopt an emotional, B a sensationalist, C an ironic, D a matter-of-fact, tone of voice and to add whatever asides, exclamations, and body language they deem necessary for their rendition of the text.

## Instrumentalities

Spoken and written language can be contrasted with each other as a means of illustrating the relationship of form and meaning. For instance, once students have written paragraphs or full-length essays, they can be asked to tell (not read) their story to one or several other students as shown above. Once A has told her story to B and the same story has been told by B to C, then by C to D, each of the four interlocutors is asked to write a two or three sentence summary of the story on the blackboard. The four versions can then be compared for subtle differences in meaning caused by slight changes in the syntax. As an example, this activity yielded the following results in an advanced German class:

**A:** Als Katharina letzten Sommer in Paris war, ging sie auf den Eiffel Turm. Als sie herunterkam, wollte sie nach Hause, aber die U-bahn geht nicht nach Mitternacht. Gott sei Dank war ein Amerikaner in der Nähe, der sie nach Hause fuhr.

[When Katharina was in Paris last summer, she went on to the Eiffel Tower. When she came down, she wanted to go home, but the subway does not run after midnight. Thank God there was an American nearby who drove her home.]

**B:** Letzten Sommer war Katharina in Paris. Als sie vom Eiffel Turm herunterkam, wollte sie mit der U-bahn nach Hause, aber sie hatte vergessen, daß nach Mitternacht die U-bahn nicht mehr fährt.

[Last summer Katharina was in Paris. When she came down from the Eiffel Tower, she wanted to go home with the subway, but she had forgotten that the subway does not run any more after midnight.]

**C:** Das ist die typische Geschichte einer amerikanischen Touristin in Paris. Als Katharina nach Mitternacht vom Eiffel Turm herunterkam, merkte sie, daß die U-bahn nicht mehr fuhr.

[This is the typical story of an American tourist in Paris. When Katharina came down from the Eiffel Tower after midnight, she noticed that the subway didn't run any more.]

**D:** Als Katharina letzten Sommer nach einem schönen Tag in Paris vom Eiffel Turm herunterstieg, versuchte sie, mit der U-bahn nach Hause zu fahren, aber sie wußte nicht, daß die U-bahn nach Mitternacht nicht mehr fährt.

[Last summer, when Katharina came down the Eiffel Tower after a nice day spent in Paris, she tried to go home with the subway, but she didn't know that the subway doesn't run any more after midnight.]

It was easy to see and discuss with students how the use of tenses, choice of verbs, and ordering of information by the various narrators all try and elicit a greater or lesser empathy in the reader for Katharina's plight.

## Norms of interaction

These vary automatically with the choice of setting, and with the status and role given to the participants. For example, if B is to assume the role of a child, A will tell the story differently than if B is an older person who is hard of hearing. A and B will use culturally different norms of interaction if they simulate native-speaker roles than if they are allowed to interact as they would in their native tongue.

## Genre

The same topic can be dealt with either as a monologue, whose delivery is only punctuated by the listener's feedback, or as an interview shaped in response to the interviewer's questions, or as a homily, a publicity pitch, a lecture, or a debate. Each of these genres has of course its own key, norms of interaction, participants' roles, and appropriate speech functions.

By varying the parameters of the context, students are given the opportunity to experience and express a variety of meanings and to be made aware of these variations. Metatalk need not be in the form of a theoretical lecture. Contextual variables can simply be given a name, or pointed out. They can also become identified quite naturally in the course of such activities as 'reader's theater', which I describe below.

## Exploring the various layers of the context

As an example of exploration in deeper layers of dialogue, or, to use Goffman's terms, of experimentation with different groundings or footings, I will describe an intermediate-level German class in which the teacher had decided to use a reader's theater approach for teaching the same Novak's story as that discussed in case 5 above: 'Schlittenfahren'. This approach is based on the belief that the construction of meaning is a social process that takes place both within and between individuals as they try to make sense of language in discourse. Reader's theater involves scripting a text for a future reading performance in front of an audience (Coger and White 1973, Kramsch 1984: 146), or for teasing out and interpreting the various 'voices of the mind' that give the text depth and meaning (Cazden 1992). The ultimate goal is a group reading of the text that highlights its different voices while maintaining absolute fidelity to its wording.

The teacher first selected three other students to demonstrate the activity in front of the class, choosing a simple fable by Kafka that the students had read the week before.

## Kleine Fabel

'Ach', sagte die Maus, 'die Welt wird enger mit jedem Tag. Zuerst war sie so breit, daß ich Angst hatte, ich lief weiter und war glücklich, daß ich endlich rechts und links in der Ferne Mauern sah, aber diese langen Mauern eilen so schnell aufeinander zu, daß ich schon im letzten Zimmer bin, und dort im Winkel steht die Falle, in die ich laufe.'—'Du mußt nur die Laufrichtung ändern', sagte die Katze und fraß sie.

[Little fable. 'Oh,' said the mouse, 'the world is becoming narrower everyday. At first it was so large, that I got scared, I ran and ran and was happy to see at last in the distance some walls right and left, but these long walls are closing in so rapidly that I am already in the last room and there in the corner stands the trap into which I am running.'—'You only need to change direction', said the cat and ate it up.]

The teacher had scripted the text according to the following voice distribution: A (the mouse) and B (the cat) sitting facing the audience, A' (mouse narrator) and B' (cat narrator) standing behind them.

A:      (*helpless*) Ach
A':     sagte die Maus
A:      (*with annoyance*) die Welt wird enger mit jedem Tag.
A':     Zuerst war sie sooooo breit (*movements of arms and hands*)
A:      (*with anxiety*) daß ich Angst hatte
A':     ich lief weiter
A:      (*sigh of relief*) und war glücklich
A':     daß ich endlich rechts und links in der Ferne Mauern sah, aber diese langen Mauern eilen so schnell aufeinander zu
A:      (*in panic*) daß ich schon im letzten Zimmer bin
A':     (*breathless*) und dort im Winkel steht die Falle
A/A':   (*together in the pitch of despair*) in die ich laufe!
A/A':   (*together*) ahhhh!
B:      (*which had its back to the audience, turns around suddenly and says in a calm but firm voice*) Du brauchst nur die Laufrichtung ändern
B':     sagte die Katze

B':   (*simulating holding up a mouse by the tail and lowering it into its mouth*) und fraß sie.

B:   (*rubbing its stomach and wiping its mouth with a napkin*) mmmmm! (*burp*)

After the demonstration, the fourteen students in the class were divided into two groups of seven. Each group was given the task of performing a similar activity with the Novak story. The students were first to decide who was going to be which of the three characters and which of the three characters' narrators, and what role the seventh group member would play. They then had to negotiate who was going to read which sentence or portion of sentence, with which intonation, using which accompanying gestures, exclamations, sounds, and props. Only after several rehearsals and much discussion, were students given highlighters to mark their part.

During the groups' discussions, some interesting points of interpretation were negotiated. It was obvious that the small child should not speak at all, but only whine, cry, howl, and squeal and that anything that pertained to him should be read by his narrator. However, opinions were divided as to whether the seventh group member should be the door of the house, the whole house, or the house and the garden, and whether sentences such as 'The man opens the door' should be read by the narrator of the man or by someone representing the door. In group 1, it was finally decided that the door was an important enough feature of the story to justify having its own reader. Students felt it was the dividing line between the home and the garden, the man and his children, between the static world of private homes and the changing world of sleds and nature.

Much discussion went into deciding how the first paragraph should be read. At first, the students were pretty skeptical about the whole exercise. It seemed so uncontroversial: since the group did not include an 'ominiscient' narrator, the father's narrator should read the whole paragraph! The teacher helped consider other options. Who should take responsibility for the first sentence 'The private home stands in a garden': only the father's narrator, or all the characters in chorus? After all, the house and the garden involved all three characters. Or perhaps the student representing the door, since it was a part of the house, but stood at the interface of the house and the garden. The students started to see the possibilities.

The teacher continued. And who should read the second sentence? Should a statement like 'The garden is big' be uttered by the narrator of the small child, or by that of the older child, or by both together? And what should the tone of voice be: matter-of-fact, mysterious, threatening? Given the larger context of the story, should the sentence be read as a mere statement about the physical dimensions of the garden or as an intimation of potential pleasures, or as an ominous warning of things to come ? As they started deciding how the different voices were going to interact and how they were going to block the stage, the students became more and more intrigued at the host of potential meanings. The mere discussion of the second sentence gave mythic proportions to the word 'big'—one student even suggested 'the garden' might be seen as the garden of Eden before the fall. How can it be the garden of Eden, said another, with a house in the middle?

Group 1 finally decided to script the first paragraph in the following manner:

**Father's narrator** (*falling intonation*): The private home stands
**The two children's narrators**: in a garden.
**Small child narrator**: The garden is big!
**Older child narrator**: Through the garden there flows a brook.
**Both children's narrators**: In the garden are two children.
**Small child narrator**: One of the children cannot talk yet.
**Older child narrator**: The other child is bigger.
**Both children's narrators**: They sit on a sled.
**Small child narrator**: The smaller child cries.
**Small child**: (*cries*)
**Older child narrator**: The bigger one says
**Older child**: Give me the sled.
**Small child narrator**: The smaller one cries.
**Small child**: (*cries*)
**Small child narrator**: He screams.
**Small child**: (*screams*)

The students from group 1 chose the following configuration to perform the story:

| A′ | B | C′ | D′ |
|----|----|----|----|
| A | ↓ | C | D |

A   =   father
A′  =   father's narrator
B   =   door and environment
C   =   older child
C′  =   older child's narrator
D   =   small child
D′  =   small child's narrator

Every time the door opened and closed, student B stepped forward and opened a book, then stepped back and slammed the book shut. The man stood with his back to the audience, and turned around to utter the senseless phrase without moving from his designated place. The ritualistic character of his interventions became clear as the 'door' stepped forward and backward, and the interaction between the characters became more and more predictable. The students decided to give the door the last word and to slam the book shut after the man's last statement.

After both groups' performances, the class discussed how the various characters had provided various interpretations of the text. Two different readings of the older child's utterance *Vaaati, jetzt ist Andreas in den Bach gefallen* [. . . Daaaddy, now Andreas has fallen into the brook] revealed unexpected layers of meaning for this simple sentence. One group decided to have it read by the child, the other group decided that the 'now' was a rhetorical marker, a signal that the voice was that of the narrator reflecting on the sequence of events within the narrative. In other words, the sentence should be glossed as saying to the reader: 'Now, after all that, Andreas fell into the brook'. Since the text omits quotation marks throughout and since the present perfect in German can express both recent events within the story and the narrator's stance outside the story, the group insisted that their interpretation was justified and that the sentence should be read by the child's narrator. This interpretation sounded all but implausible to the native reader. However, it did make the class stop and think about the meaning of 'now' in the sentence 'Now Andreas has fallen into the brook'. Upon reflection, this sentence seemed pretty complacent as a cry for help. One would have expected from a child in that situation a simple *(der) Andreas ist in den Bach gefallen!*. Could it be that the older child had already internalized some of the self-righteousness of the adults and that his cry was less a cry for help than an accusation of the father? The class would never even have discussed the matter had it not been for the somewhat unusual interpretation of the second group of readers.

The students playing the father in each of the groups admitted that they had had a hard time identifying with the role given to them in the story; they did not feel comfortable having to say *Wer brüllt kommt rein* over and over again; they just could not imagine their fathers acting like that. American fathers just did not talk like that, they said. One student admitted that that was the reason why he chose to be the father's narrator, and not the father. Some women students felt one of the 'fathers' had spoken with too kind a voice for a man and that this was a feminist story. However, some men in the class interpreted the father's voice not as kind but as indifferent and numb. They were convinced that the man had only become so insensitive because of his many responsibilities and the pressures of society. The man, they said, was in fact a victim of a consumer's society that gives priority to privately owned homes over children. The sad thing was that he was raising his children into that kind of materialistic society. A cultural issue? A gender issue? Or both? The tone was set for a discussion of the substantive issues raised by the story.

## Discussion

As Shweder wrote recently: 'Every human being has her or his subjectivity and mental life altered through the processes of seizing meanings and resources from some socio-cultural environment and using them' (1990: 2, cited in Cazden 1991). By having students externalize their interpreting processes and confronting them with others in the group, and by having them commit themselves to one interpretation among the many considered, reader's theater is emblematic of what Hymes has called 'the ethnography of communication'—that is, the way dialogue can be used to both enact and reflect upon the construction of meaning as social practice.

The dialogue generated by this activity, both in the discussion and in the performance phase, enlisted the participants in all five aspects of context:

*Linguistic.* During the negotiation of roles and parts, students had to weigh each word of the text as to its information and symbolic value in the global context of the story; they had to decide how to segment the text into those units of meaning and choose those prosodic features of speech that are appropriate for their interpretation of the text.

*Situational/interactional.* Besides having to activate the speech functions necessary to take part in group decisions, students had to decide how their different voices were going to interact, for which effect on the audience and for the representation of which situation.

*Intertextual/cultural.* Students had to base their decisions on their global apprehension of the context: the genre, the real and symbolic setting, the reference to prior texts they might have experienced first hand (e.g. utterances by their own fathers) or vicariously (e.g. the father in Kafka's *Metamorphosis*). They had to construct their meaning of that context through verbal and non-verbal paratextual accoutrements.

As we shall see in the next two chapters, this activity also served to demonstrate that the meaning of a text is not in the text itself but in the interaction between the text and a reader who actualizes its meaning potential. It further illustrated the indissociable nature of form and content and helped students find meaning not only in what a text said, but in the way it was structured.

Finally, the type of dialogue generated around this activity created a climate of intimacy and deep cooperativeness among the members of the group. This intimacy, stressed by many educators as being essential for cognitive and emotional growth (Ochs and Taylor 1992) can lead to cultural change precisely because students discover the range of their power to assign new values to a seemingly stable and predetermined universe of existing meanings.

With reader's theater, we are at the boundary between the pedagogy of spoken and written language, between speech acts and reading acts, between the voices of a speech community and those of individual readers and writers. In the next chapter, we shall expand the notion of context to include the contexts of meaning that writers and their distant readers create through written texts.

### Note

1 'The reason why teaching is so difficult to talk about is not because it is so unfamiliar, but because it is too familiar.'

# 4 Stories and discourses

Ecrire, c'est déjà organiser le monde, c'est déjà penser . . .
Il est donc inutile de demander à l'autre de se réécrire,
s'il n'est pas décidé à se repenser.[1]
(Roland Barthes 1966: 33)

Because most of our ways of speaking remain unconscious to us and others—a kind of invisible grid on which human interactions are built—conventional pedagogic practice tends to view context as a given, pre-existing reality that serves to disambiguate the meaning of language forms (see Chapter 2). Both teachers and learners tend to ignore the degree to which their use of language constructs the very context in which they are learning it. As we have seen in the previous chapter, this illusion is particularly tenacious in the use of the spoken language, but it is also prevalent in the way learners are taught the written forms of the language.

Language learners often believe that language is only a manifestation of pre-existing thoughts. Writing is just 'writing thoughts down'—writing in a foreign language is just giving L1 thoughts a L2 form. Learners do not realize at first that the foreign language structures are also making thoughts available to them that they had not had quite in this form before—a phenomenon which Britton et al. describe as 'shaping at the point of utterance' and which E. M. Forster noted when he quipped 'How do I know what I think till I see what I say?' (both cited in Nystrand 1986: 28).

Conversely, when faced with written texts, they often have the feeling of being confronted with a ready-made world of meanings upon which they have no control. Not only are many of the words unknown to them, but even if they know the words, their use is often out of the ordinary, with socio-historical connotations that are unknown to the non-native reader. Literary texts, that require an additional familiarity with a particular author, genre, period, or style, may be intimidating. Not only is all language, as Ortega says, 'both deficient and exuberant', meaning both less and more than it says (Ortega y Gasset 1959: 2), but literary language adds a dimension of particularity that seems like an added difficulty.

Literary texts may present a dilemma for communication-oriented language teachers. On the one hand, teachers have to socialize their students to the universally shared meanings of everyday language, on the other hand they have to show them the potentialities of the ordinary by exposing them to particular texts that break with the ordinary. Thus, many teachers view the two activities as unrelated: here, oral communicative activities, there, the reading of literary texts.

In order to avoid returning to earlier practices of teacher-centered exegesis and translation, it has been suggested that teachers use the story-line of narratives as springboard for oral or written communicative activities (Collie and Slater 1987, di Pietro 1987), that they exploit the cultural information found in popular literature (Swaffar 1992) or use information-processing strategies to discover literary techniques (Isenberg 1990). In so doing, however, particular voices risk being recycled into the voices of the community, potential meanings are liable to be subordinated to existing, ordinary meanings. By failing to examine the particular meanings expressed by the writer, teachers deprive themselves of a unique opportunity to lead learners beyond the looking-glass and to help them distinguish between what Frank Smith calls the 'shunting of information' and the 'creation of worlds' (Smith 1985: 195).

If using language in communication means shaping contexts of discourse, then we need to look more closely at how writers use language to create particular meanings.

## Dimensions of particularity

At a seminar attended by colleague teachers and researchers at the 1985 LSA/TESOL Institute, the linguist A. L. Becker did a short experiment designed precisely to demonstrate the ways in which writers shape the context of communication to produce meaning (Becker 1985). He asked the participants to write a sentence which could be as long as they liked—as many clauses, compoundings, and embeddings as they felt inclined to use—in which they described the simple action he was about to do. The only constraint was that it be a single sentence. He then slowly walked up the steps to the podium and laid a book on the desk. After asking the participants to read their sentences aloud, he wrote down a few on the board:

1 He walked up the steps across the stage to the podium, and slapped the book down on it as he arrived there.
2 You stepped onto the stage holding a book, walked to the podium, and put the book on the podium.
3 He walked slowly toward the podium, placed the book he was carrying on it, and looked at us.
4 He was walking up the steps to the podium being careful not to trip.
5 The man with the small paperback book in his hand who was standing at the edge of the stage began to walk up the steps onto the stage and then crossed the small semicircular platform to the podium where he put the book down onto the surface of the podium.
6 The linguist, though he had removed his spectacles, walked up the stairs without tripping.
(Becker 1985: 21)

The first striking thing was that not one of the sentences was the same, despite the seemingly obvious nature of the simple event observed. These differences would not have been so marked had he not asked the participants to write them down, but just to speak them out from aural memory. After about five or six, people would have started saying: 'Well I said just what he said'. Becker notes: 'The inventiveness of new versions, of new "takes" on this situation seems to dry up under the pressure of the oral situation' (ibid.: 23). It appears that the very act of writing, the medium itself, is part of what shaped these sentences.

Another major difference is the particular relationship chosen by each writer to the person described: 'he', 'the man', 'the linguist', 'you', all specify a dimension of variation, and a different position adopted by the narrator vis-à-vis the 'story'. Likewise, the use of grammar: main and dependent clauses, tenses, punctuation, choice and place of pronouns, definite articles, all establish a hierarchy of part-whole relations, of new-old information, that is tailored to the reader's assumed state of knowledge: indeed, it seems that, through its syntactic choices, each sentence is shaping a different reader for itself. For example, the definite articles in sentence 1 indicate that the reader of that sentence is assumed to know who the person depicted is, which podium is being referred to, and which book the man puts down on the podium. The two-clause rhythm of the sentence, combined with the verb 'slapped', depicts a goal-directed action and conveys a strong feeling of closure, that is perhaps supposed to express determination. By contrast, sentence 2, which has a more personal relationship with the reader since it addresses the reader himself, and which embeds his action in a three-part syntactic structure with rhapsodic repetition ('to the podium', 'on the podium'), seems to highlight the way rather than the goal. It might be significant that sentence 1 was written by a man, sentence 2 by a woman.

Each of these sentences both reshapes the past and creates the present. As Becker points out, some of the sentences sound like the beginning of letters, or poems, or novels, or short aphorisms, or metacomments, or newspaper stories, or police reports. Each of the authors was reaching back in memory to prior texts and made his or her text a variant of those prior texts. But at the same time, by expressing the event in that manner, each writer created it and obligated his or her reader to see that event in the same manner. Referential truth thus becomes subordinated to language. Such questions as 'What really happened?' or 'Which one of these sentences is most correct?' are impossible to answer independently of the language used to report the event. 'Describing the event,' writes Becker, 'creates it' (ibid.: 24).

Finally, one last dimension of difference among the sentences is what people chose not to write in order to write other things. These silences vary from writer to writer, but also from language to language. Becker uses a quote from Ortega to illustrate the point:

> Each language represents a different equation between manifestations and silences. Each people leaves some things unsaid in order to be able to say others ... Hence the immense difficulty of translation: translation is a matter of saying in a language precisely what that language tends to pass over in silence.
> (ibid.: 25)

In sum, through an ongoing process that Becker calls 'languaging', prior texts are constantly being reshaped to present needs along six aspects of context, or dimensions of particularity:

1  medial—by shaping the medium
2  structural—by making grammatical sentences
3  interpersonal—by negotiating interpersonal relationships
4  referential—by looking through language to a believed world
5  generic—by evoking prior language
6  silential—by leaving many things unsaid, some of them unsayable.

Understanding and creating written texts-in-context is an exercise in particularity. Most of the oral communicative activities in the language classroom are based on the premise that language, as a referential system, is universal, and that what needs to be negotiated is this reference to a common reality. Written texts, by contrast, stress the particular. It is precisely that understanding of particularity that reading can bring to the language class.

## Understanding particularity

As we have seen, there are six aspects of the shaping of context through text that learners need to be made aware of as they engage in reading a foreign language text. Like the contextual factors examined in Chapter 2, these aspects are difficult to discuss separately from one another, for they are heavily interrelated. They will be presented here one after the other for reasons of exposition.

### Shaping the medium

The best way to gain an understanding of what written language does and does not do is to have the students experience writing themselves. Several intermediate-level readers, such as Schofer and Rice (1987) for French, suggest creative writing as a pre-reading activity in intermediate-level French classes. For example, before reading Prévert's poem 'Le Message', students are asked to compose a story, a poem, or an essay according to the Prévert model:

La porte que quelqu'un a ouverte
La porte que quelqu'un a refermée
La chaise où quelqu'un s'est assis
Le chat que quelqu'un a caressé ...

| Un objet | Que ou où | Une personne | Un verbe (au passé composé) |
|----------|-----------|--------------|------------------------------|
| 1 | | | |
| 2 | | | |
| 3 | | | |
| 4 | | | |

(ibid.: 18)

These exercises are meant to explore the lexical or grammatical treatment of the theme and to create a parallel student text. However, they fail to realize their full potential as pre-reading activities, as they are not followed by any reflection on the languaging process the students have just experienced. Students are not asked why they chose this word, tense, or structure rather than that one, what kind of reaction they hoped to elicit from their reader, which things they chose to leave unsaid, nor are they asked to compare their texts with the Prévert text along any of the dimensions of context discussed above. Comprehension questions ('Questions sur le texte') do offer a pathway into a deeper understanding of Prévert's poem, but it is not a trail that students have first blazed for themselves. We have seen in the previous chapter (p.96) how having students write a text they have spoken can make them aware of the way the written language shapes particular meanings. The following experiment, conducted at a seminar for language teachers, will serve here to analyze more specific differences between spoken and written language. Replicating similar experiments done by Chafe (1985), or Hildyard and Hidi (1985), I asked three or four language teachers each to recount in English a happy or frightening experience to a small group of listeners. I then asked both the teller and the listeners to write up the story for the next day. What follows is the oral and the written rendition of 'One of my happiest experiences' by the storyteller herself.

## Tammy tells her story

Transcription key

| .. | short pause (<0.5 second or short breath intake) |
| ... | 0.5-second pause |
| .... | 1-second pause |
| | etc. |
| *p* | piano (spoken softly) |

*pp* pianissimo (spoken very softly)
*acc* spoken quickly
: lengthened vowel sound (extra colons indicate greater lengthening)
underline emphatic stress
CAPITALS very emphatic stress

I'd like to tell you the story of the .. one of the happiest days of my life .. which was Mother's Day a few years ago. Normally I don't .. believe in Mother's Day, I think _acc_ it's you know a kind of a silly holiday, but my children .. _acc_ um .. really made it special for me that year (*coughs*) especially .. in this case my son .. .. So I have to give you a _acc_ little bit of a background my son is not a very good student he doesn't like school and we were having trouble getting him to do his homework, so .. um .. on .. .. Satur= day morning just before Mother's Day I had told him that he could not play with his friend until he had finished his homework .. He didn't like that too much bu:::t he .. decided to sit down and do his homework and .. about twenty minutes later he said that all of his homework was done .. I was sort of suspicious but .. he showed it to me and it looked like it was all done so I said he could play with his friend ....... (*deep breath intake*) which he did .. _acc_ That evening we were watching television a movie on TV at .. home .. and when the movie was all finished I turned to my son and I said: Gee isn't it nice to have all your homework done! .. You don't have to worry about it! .. He didn't say anything and I knew immediately that he had NOT done his homework like he said so I said: Did you REALLY do your homework? and he .. didn't say anything and I got REALLY mad at him and I said: 'You didn't do your homework and not only did you NOT do your homework, but you lied to me didn't you?' I was really angry at him and so for the first time that I can remember I put him to bed without a cuddly ..

—a cuddly is a tradition that we have .. just a hug and a <sub>acc</sub> kiss before going to bed .. And ... he however did not ... go <sub>acc</sub> to bed right away which I found out later .. The next day <sub>acc</sub> was Mother's Day and when I got up .. I went in .. and my kids had prepared some special things for me for breakfast .. and then I found out that my son when I put him to bed angry last night .. had .. set his alarm clock for one o'clock in the morning .. gotten up .. finished his homework .. cleaned up the living room .. and made me a lovely Mother's Day card that said how much he loved me and how much he <sub>acc</sub> <sub>acc</sub> appreciated (*chuckle*) all of the work I put in on him. (*Deep <sub>acc</sub> breath intake*). So ... (*breathing out*) that's what I found when I got up the next day. I .. my daughter had also given me a very special present .. She had for the f .. she is only ten .. <sub>acc</sub> she had gone out shopping all by herself without anybody knowing about it and had bought me a ceramic heart with her own money. And my husband gave me a big bunch of flowers. So that was a very special ... Mother's Day present and I still have those .. things from Mother's Day ...... I forgot <sub>p</sub> <sub>pp</sub> to mention that my son was twelve years old at the time.

## *Tammy writes her story*

Editing key

(  )    indicates deletions

NARRATOR A (female English native speaker)
My most memorable experience happened during Mothers' Day four months ago. We had gone through (sev) a little crisis a couple of days (before that) earlier when we found out that our (el) 12 year-old son—we have two children; my daughter is 9—wasn't doing his homework for school. So that Saturday before Mothers' Day I told him that he wasn't going to be allowed to play with his friends until he finished his homework. After some time he came downstairs and told me that his homework was done. He showed me what he was supposed to do and that he had finished all the work.

But I was suspicious. After he came back later that night from playing I asked him again whether that had been all the homework he was supposed to do. Since my son is a poor liar he admitted that he had not finished his homework yet. (Boy was) I was very mad. I didn't talk to him all night, and he had to go to bed without the hug he usually gets from me.

When I woke up (on) the (next) morning of Mothers' Day I found a big surprise. Feeling guilty because of his lies and realizing that he had done something wrong, my son had set his alarm clock for 1:30 a.m. Then, (after) he (had) finished his homework (,) and (he had) cleaned the living room. That was a very happy moment in my life.

The two renditions have some striking differences. The spoken narrative requires on-line processing, so to speak, and a recipient design that is sensitive to the immediate reactions of the interlocutors. The speaker uses pitch, stress, and speed to distinguish between important and less important information ('Did you REALLY do your homework?'), she addresses her interlocutors directly ('I'd like to tell you ...'), gives them additional information when she realizes they might not understand a word (e.g. 'a cuddly'), adds an afterthought to add coherence ('... which he did' *acc.*) or to make sure her interlocutors appreciate the meaning of her story ('I forgot to mention ...'). The written narrative, by contrast, leads the eye linearly across the page, allowing the readers to go back and retrieve some information they might have missed along the way. Rather than speed and pitch, the writer used syntax and paragraph structure to differentiate the important from the less important. By doing that, she conveyed a greater sense of detachment as a narrator vis-à-vis the event narrated.

However, if we look at the self-corrections that Tammy made while she was writing, and if we compare Tammy's written narrative with the written accounts of the same story by three of her listeners (see below), we realize that the differences might not really be due to the fact that the one is spoken whereas the others are written. For example, as we shall see, Tammy's spoken story contains so few false starts and repetitions that it sounds almost as if she were telling a written story. By contrast, her written story has a distinct oral flavor to it. When the other narrators read her story, one of them even exclaimed: 'This is almost verbatim what she told us yesterday!'.

Rather than making a distinction between the spoken and the written medium, it might be more useful to view the differences in speech as two different modes of language, one more 'orate', the other more 'literate', on an orate–literate continuum (Widdowson 1992b). For example, a personal letter might be at the orate end, an academic essay at the literate end of the continuum. The three other written versions of Tammy's story below display various combinations of orate and literate features.

NARRATOR B (female English native speaker)
This is a story that reflects the juxtaposition of the trials and rewards—the ups and the downs occurring back to back—of motherhood. Tammy has two children: a boy of 12 and a girl of 9. There is an ongoing struggle in their home between (her) mother and (her) son over the 'h' word—homework. One Mother's Day eve was no exception. Having lied to his mom saying he had finished his assignments, the 12-year-old found himself in big trouble when he finally admitted he still had work to do. (Tammy was hurt) Mother was hurt over the lie and son went tearfully to bed.

Mother's day arrived and Tammy (is) was showered with a big bouquet of flowers from her husband and a ceramic heart from her daughter ((a) the first gift her 9 year-old ever bought with her own money). But it was her son's gift that touched her heart the most. For he had set his alarm for 1.00 a.m., (he) got up, did all his homework, (made) cleaned the living room and made a beautiful card for his precious mama stating how much he loved her. Tammy, moved to tears, celebrated her best Mother's Day ever.

NARRATOR C (female Japanese native speaker)
We are born with an empty pot and with it we begin our journey of life collecting stars called happiness.

Happiness—such an easy word to use but hard word to define. Happiness is infinitely abundant and yet sometimes so hard to recognize.

We are sometimes so busy seeking for it that we forget to appreciate those already in the pot. And sometimes we find a dull colored stone in the pot which we thought was a shining star.

Now I want to tell you a story about Tammy who recently found a genuine star of happiness.

Tammy is a mother of a 9-year-old girl and 12-year-old boy. A girl seemed to be a sweet thing every mother wishes to have, but a boy was a bit of a problem for the family. He just didn't like school work especially his homework.

It was a day before mother's day of the year. Tammy asked her boy if he did his homework and to her surprise he said 'yes'. But Tammy found out later that it was a lie. 'Oh, no! He never lied to me before!' disappointed mother said to herself.

Next morning, however, as she came down to neatly cleaned living room, she found a hand-made card on the coffee table situated in the middle of the room. As she was reading the card, her boy entered the room and told her proudly that he set alarm clock at 1:00 in the morning, and finished his homework and made mother's day card. Not only that, he woke up early and cleaned the living room for her. She thought that her boy looked taller today.

Is this happiness? Indeed.

Tammy without any doubt will keep collecting star of happiness, but she knows that the star she unexpectedly found in her living room on this year's mother's day will continue to shine in her pot.

NARRATOR D (male English native speaker)

The Homework (beginning)

Sam hated homework. He'd much rather be outside skateboarding, throwing water balloons, and playing with his friends than sitting inside and doing homework. Who wouldn't? After all, it was that teacher who wouldn't even let you play paper football in the classroom, even during recess, who assigned the dumb homework. Sam knew homework was <u>not</u> cool, definitely not cool. And what good did it do you anyway? You didn't make any friends by doing homework. You certainly didn't have fun. What a drag!

The thing Sam didn't understand was why his mother made such a fuss about it. 'Did you do your homework, dear?' 'Not yet, Mom.'

'Well, go do your homework. You have to finish it before you go out to play.'

'But Mo...om!'

'You heard me.'

'But ...'
'No buts. Go do your homework.'
Boy, Junior High was going to be so much better. No homework ... Just assignments.

What are some of the characteristics of the orate and literate modes of language used in these texts? Linguists have identified several of them (see in particular: Chafe 1982, 1985; Hildyard and Hidi 1985; Ong 1982, Scollon and Scollon 1981; Tannen 1985; Torrance and Olson 1985). The orate mode (or what Tannen calls the 'involved' mode), based on face-to-face interaction, is a participatory mode that relies heavily on the presence of an interlocutor. It is characterized by:

1 Involvement: ego involvement ('Normally I don't believe in Mother's Day'), involvement with the audience ('I have to give you a little bit of a background'), involvement with the subject matter through exclamations ('Boy was I mad'), direct quotations ('I said: Gee, isn't it nice..'), emphatic particles, ('Did you REALLY do your homework?'), and sometimes the use of the historical present.

2 A rhapsodic style (from the Greek *rhapsodein*: to stitch together), i.e. paratactic constructions and redundancies that make up for the quick pace of delivery: hesitations ('my children .. um .. really made it special for me'), fragmentation in short clauses ('when I got up ... I went in .. and my kids ..'), loose connectives (and, so, but), formulaic phrases that monitor the flow of speech and regulate the attention of the listener ('well .., you know .., I mean ...'), reliance on context ('it was that teacher who wouldn't even let you play ..').

3 Inductive evaluation of the evidence: assessing the reliability of knowledge ('it's a kind of a silly holiday'), use of evaluative metacomments ('normally I don't .. believe in Mother's Day', 'what a drag!', 'who wouldn't?', 'Boy, junior high was going to be so much better'), hedges ('I was sort of suspicious'), reference to sensory evidence ('it looked like it was all done').

By contrast, a more literate mode of speech, that is predicated on the absence of immediate interlocutors, is topic- or message-oriented. It relies on explicitness of reference and a more linear, sequential, analytic rendition of events. It is characterized by:

1 Detachment: a higher proportion of nouns and noun phrases than verbs ('happiness—such an easy word to use but a hard word to define'); a preference for impersonal constructions ('Happiness is hard to recognize').

2 Integration of idea units into more complex sentences: subordinate clauses ('after he came back later that night from playing, I asked him again ...'; 'since my son is a poor liar, ...'), participial clauses ('Feeling guilty because of his lies, ...').

3 Deductive evaluation of the evidence: 'Is this happiness? Indeed.' 'Tammy without any doubt will keep collecting ...'

We have seen how a comparison of the four written renditions of the same story can illustrate the possible variations along the orate–literate continuum in written speech. They highlight also the way the writers use the forms of the language to convey meaning.

## Shaping experience with grammar and vocabulary

As painters express their experience through shapes and colors, so do writers with words. Besides the paraphrasable content of the subject matter, there is a non-paraphrasable message expressed through the textual structure of the written medium. We have to distinguish *what* the narrators said from *how* they said it in order to have what kind of relationship with their readers.

How do narrators establish a shared universe of discourse with their readers? Following the useful analyses provided in, for example, Chatman (1978), Fowler (1986), Rimmon-Kenan (1983), and Traugott and Pratt (1980), we can identify six important ways in which the narrators of Tammy's story have used grammar and vocabulary to express their experience of the events related: these ways are now discussed.

### Point of departure

All narrative beginnings typically orient the reader by going from what he or she is assumed to know to what is new information. They differ in the type and amount of information they assume as given and as new. In a more orate mode, much background information can be assumed to be shared by the storyteller and the readers. Narrator A, by using a personal frame that establishes a first-person narrator ('*my* most memorable experience') and a specific time anchored deictically in the here-and-now of the reader ('Mother's Day four years ago'), establishes a direct, almost intimate contact with her readers. By contrast, in a more literate mode, narrator B uses a general philosophical frame of common wisdom (trials and rewards of motherhood), of which the story will be an illustration. She adopts an omniscient perspective with a point of reference that is outside the narrative ('One Mother's Day eve'). Narrator C establishes a general metaphorical frame ('stars of happiness') and draws the reader into a community of people ('we') sharing in the same human condition. Narrator D's story plunges the reader right *in medias res*, by assuming the identity of the character as known, thus establishing a more orate type of contact with the reader. It conveys, however, less a sense of oral immediacy than the orate flavor of a literary piece of prose.

The narratives differ greatly in the length of text they devote to orienting the reader. The effect on the readers can vary with their cultural background. For instance, American narrator D's extensive orientation creates in American readers a climate of complicity with the character by letting the reader in on his thoughts and feelings. An equally long orientation by Japanese narrator C can give Japanese readers a sense of philosophical intimacy, but it might have a different effect on Western readers.

## Spatial and temporal frames of reference

The perspective of the speaker is anchored in space and time through the use of pronouns and adverbs called 'deictics' (establishing speaker orientation), such as 'we', 'my most memorable experience', 'now', 'I', 'you', 'this story', 'four years ago'. The speaker positions him or herself either outside the narrative (narrators B, C, and D) or inside it (narrator A). As we have seen, the latter positioning of the speaker achieves a closeness with the reader that is more typical of the orate mode.

The first three narrators in Tammy's story place themselves on the Saturday before Mother's Day. While narrator A positions herself at the mother's injunction to her son to do his homework, narrator B places herself at a somewhat later point in time, namely after the discovery of the son's lie. By reducing the lie to a past participle ('Having lied to his mom ...'), and syntactically subordinating it to the son's failure to do his homework, the narrator somewhat weakens the importance of the lie. Narrator D, by contrast, places himself at a much earlier point in time, while Sam is doing his homework.

The use of tenses also serves to position the narrator vis-à-vis the events narrated. Prior events and the state of affairs are narrated either in the pluperfect (narrator A 'we had gone through a little crisis'), or in the present tense (narrator B 'There is an ongoing struggle'), or in the past tense (narrator C 'a boy was a bit of a problem ... he just didn't like school work'). Each of these decisions, in the way they are combined with the other decisions concerning point of departure, point of view, text time, and so on, increase the sense of closeness or distance between narrator and reader, between narrator and events related.

## Text time versus story time

Another important clue to understanding the meaning conveyed by a story is the order in which the events are narrated, their duration and the frequency in which they occur as compared to the amount of text space devoted to them.

For example, narrator A and narrator C start the story when the mother asks her son if he has done his homework. This allows them to give a certain narrative space to the telling of the lie. The reader understands the mother to be doubly hurt, first by the son not doing his homework, then by his lying about it; the joy of the mother the next day is all the more enhanced as the disappointment has been extensively narrated. This focus on the mother is reinforced, of course, in narration A, by the choice of a first-person point of reference, and of a personal point of departure.

Narrator A devotes much more space to her questioning of her son and to the account of his lie than narrator B; through the relative weight given to that part of the story, A's reader is made to empathize with the mother's pain at being deceived, and is led to interpret the subsequent actions of the boy as a sign of penance and remorse. In narration B, by contrast, a large amount of narrative space is devoted to the gifts received by the mother on Mother's Day. Embedded in a progression of increasingly important presents, the son's gifts are endowed with climactic importance as signs of love from a son to his mother. Of course, the reader has been prepared for this theme by the opening frame of the story.

## Characterization

Characters can be described directly, as in 'she had a boy of 12 and a girl of 9', or indirectly through their actions, their speech, their external appearance. Narrator D gives the reader many indirect clues regarding Sam's age, temperament, and relationship to his mother, by the way he is made to talk and by the references he makes to his environment. It is sometimes more difficult for the reader to trust the reliability of a character depicted through indirect means than that of a direct characterization given by an omniscient narrator outside the story. In narrative D, the character being so young and restive, it is difficult to believe him when he says that 'Junior High is going to be so much better'. This lack of reliability is here precisely what the narrator wants to convey. It is reinforced by the impetuous point of departure, and the amount of text space devoted to the boy's thoughts and feelings.

## Point of view

By choosing his or her position within the narrative, the narrator is deciding not only how much distance to have vis-à-vis the character, but through whose eyes the events are going to be seen (a narrative device called 'focalization'). In A's story, the events are seen through the eyes of the first-person narrator; in narratives B and C, the narrator is external to the story; in narrative D, the narrator sees and speaks through the eyes and mouth of the boy. Together with the other features of discourse structure, the choice of point of view appeals to different responses from the reader, for example: trust or distrust, identification or detachment.

## Speech representation

Different choices are available to the narrators when reporting characters' speech. Narrator D inserted a dialogue into his narrative ('Did you do your homework, dear?'), and used free direct discourse—that is, direct discourse without quotation marks, the typical form of first-person interior monologue ('Boy, Junior High was going to be so much better'). Both techniques give his narration a clearly orate flavor. The others used either bare report ('Tammy found out it was a lie'), or indirect discourse ('She asked her boy if he had done his homework'), or direct discourse ('To her surprise he said "yes"'), which are common to both orate and literate modes of speech. Free indirect discourse as used by narrator D is a literate device that simulates the spontaneity of an interior monologue ('Who wouldn't? After all, it was that teacher who wouldn't even let you play paper football in the classroom'). Speech representation is one of the many features that contribute to placing narrative D at the more literate end of the orate–literate continuum. It also identifies it as the literary genre 'children's story', rather than a personal letter (narrative A) or a folktale (narrative C).

Reader response is constrained and directed by all the textual features described above, which establish various types of narrator–reader relationship. By bringing the narration closer to one or the other end of the orate–literate continuum, by adopting familiar genres (personal letter, essay, folktale, children's story), the narrator strives to establish closeness or distance between the text and the reader. The choices he or she makes manipulate the reader into feeling sympathy for one or the other character, empathy for the one or the other point of view. For example, the way in which the information is provided in A's and C's stories leads the reader to identify with the mother and her moment of happiness. In B's story, the information given about the son in the first paragraph and the mother in the second makes the reader identify with the relationship between the son and the mother. In all these ways, the structure of the text invites the reader to respond to it and assign it a meaning.

Each of these choices also evokes prior texts with similar narrative discourse features and raises expectations based on intertextual recognition. Foreign cultural readers might be reminded of prior texts that are different from those of the narrator's intended readers, or not be reminded of prior texts at all. Narrator D's story, for example, starts like American children's stories, familiar to anyone born and raised in the United States' educational culture. Readers from other cultures might not recognize the style, hence might misread the focalization and the title 'The Homework' as being characteristic of a parent's point of view. What might have been intended as an American children's story might be viewed by foreign readers as an adult cautionary tale. If it is the ability to recognize prior texts that makes for fluency in reading, then teaching reading in a foreign language requires a contextual dimension that is lacking in most traditional approaches.

Because the discourse features of texts appeal to the reader and only receive meaning through the reader, they are not culture-free categories that can be taught like so many recipes for the interpretation of texts. They have to be named and interpreted through the continued dialogue between readers and texts and among readers. Thus we turn now to the third dimension of particularity, namely the negotiation of meaning between a reader and a text.

## Negotiating interpersonal relationships

Because texts encourage one to enter the writer's subjective world view, they appeal to the reader's own subjective response. In her discussion of the relationship between reader and text, Louise Rosenblatt distinguishes between a *text*, or 'set or series of signs interpretable as linguistic symbols' and a *poem*, that is, 'an event in time ... a coming-together, a compenetration, of a reader and a text ... the experience shaped by the reader under the guidance of the text' (Rosenblatt 1978: 12). She adds:

> We cannot simply look at the text and predict the poem. For this, a reader or readers with particular attributes must be postulated: for example, the author-as-reader as he is creating the text; the author as he reads it years later; contemporaries of the author with similar backgrounds of education and experience; contemporaries with different backgrounds; other individuals living in specific places, times, and milieus. Thus both text and reader are essential aspects or components ... of that which is manifested in each reading as the poem.
> (ibid.: 15)

There is indeed one text, but there are as many discourses as there are readers of that text.

Rosenblatt distinguishes two kinds of reading. In one type of reading, 'the reader's attention is focused primarily on what will remain as the residue *after* the reading—information to be acquired, logical solution to a problem, actions to be carried out' (ibid.). This is the reading that is fostered at the beginning stages of language learning, where learners are taught to skim a text to retrieve its gist, to scan it to pick out specific information, to predict from the title what the story will be about, to infer from the context the meaning of specific words. This type of reading, in which the primary concern is with what the reader will carry away from the reading, Rosenblatt calls 'efferent reading', from the Latin *effere*, 'to carry away'. It is an essential skill if you need to know how to find your way in a foreign city, how to bake a cake, how to be informed about the daily news ... or how to answer comprehension questions on a reading test.

In the second type of reading, by contrast, the attention of the readers is focused on what happens *during* the actual reading event. Although they must decipher the images, or concepts, or assertions, that the words refer to, readers also have to pay attention to the associations, feelings, attitudes, and ideas that these words and their referents arouse within them. As Rosenblatt writes: 'Listening to himself, (the reader) synthesizes these elements into a meaningful structure. In aesthetic reading, the reader's attention is centered directly on what he is living through during his relationship with that particular text.' (ibid.: 25)

In efferent reading, a knowledge of grammar and vocabulary, as well as a knowledge of the social conventions constraining the use of language in social settings, are enough to ensure reading speed and efficiency in the performance of practical tasks. Rosenblatt gives the example of a mother, whose child has swallowed poisonous liquid and who is frantically reading the label on the bottle to discover the antidote to be administered. Obviously, the more she concentrates on the objects, ideas, and actions designated on that label, the more she ignores the rhythm, sound, or associations of the words, and the more she makes herself impersonal and transparent, the more efficiently she reads.

However, when it is not the practical outcome of the reading that is of paramount importance, but the understanding of someone else's experience, then we need another approach, for this experience cannot be shared directly. It must be mutually recreated and constructed through the joint collaboration of text, author, and audience under the mediation of the written word; this construction is bound to remain as incomplete and selective as language itself. Hence the possibility for the reader to fill in the deficiencies with his or her own experience.

Rosenblatt shares with Roger Fowler (1986: 7) the belief that the classification of texts into literary and non-literary is misleading; the same text may be read either efferently or aesthetically. *Efferent* and *aesthetic* are to be viewed as dimensions of the reader-text dialogue, some texts being more likely to activate aesthetic dialogue than others. Indeed, the frequent disappointment of intermediate language learners may stem from the fact that they are asked to read efferently as stories texts that yield their best when read aesthetically as discourses. Concentrating only on the information contained in the story, they attribute their failure to 'get the point' to yet another lack of information, namely their deficient knowledge of the culture. In fact, what they are missing is not an ever greater amount of information, but an awareness of their own frame of reference and of their dialogue with the text during the reading process.

## Referring to a believed world

To understand texts, readers draw on prior experience and knowledge. Indeed, much research on reading in a second language has shown the crucial effect of background knowledge on the reading ability of foreign language learners (see, in particular, Lee 1986, Carrell *et al.* 1988, Barnett 1989, Bernhardt 1991, Swaffar *et al.* 1991). Called alternately 'frames', 'scripts', or 'schemata', this background knowledge makes it possible to anticipate incoming information, relate it to previous knowledge and thus make global sense of the text as it unfolds. Fillmore (1981) has distinguished three kinds of schemata: *text schemata* that deal with grammatical and cohesion structures; *genre schemata* that pertain to the rhetorical structures of different text genres (fairy tales, letters, newspaper articles, etc.); and *content schemata* that refer to the topic. To this list of linguistic textual characteristics, Canale adds a discourse dimension by including the social and cultural context of production, and the personal and cultural context of reception of the text by the reader. He summarizes readers' processes as follows:

> The reader assigns increasing confidence to these [Fillmore's] various schemata and their integration according to whether each schema is: (a) explicitly justified at the literal word-by-word, sentence-by-sentence level of a text; (b) soundly based on inferences that are clearly provided for and invited at the level

of cohesive groups of sentences; (c) not necessarily provided for nor invited by the text but consistent with it, given common social and cultural knowledge; and (d) not motivated so much by the text as by the reader's personal, idiosyncratic experiences.
(Canale 1984: 350)

Learners who lack any of these four schemata can badly misunderstand the topic, the tone, the genre, or the purpose of the text, or the intentions, goals, and plans of the characters in a fictional text.

The debate among foreign language reading specialists currently revolves around Canale's condition (c): 'How much background information should I give my students and should I give it to them before they read or after?'. Some teachers advocate giving it beforehand, arguing that readers cannot understand what they read unless they can predict meanings based on global schemata. Others feel that they will develop the appropriate schemata precisely through the process of reading. By focusing on quantity of background and timing of delivery, teachers are making themselves prisoners of the 'bottom-up' versus 'top-down' dichotomy that we examined in the Introduction. Rather, we should rephrase the question in qualitative terms. Not 'how much' and 'when', but *what kind* of background knowledge should be given?

In *literature* classes, teachers have traditionally provided text and genre schemata—that is, the rhetorical knowledge necessary to appreciate the craft of the writer: information concerning author, period, genre, tone (ironic, metaphorical, tragic, comic), the internal logic of a narrative, the illocutionary force of utterances. This information constitutes what Fowler calls the linguistic 'context of utterance' (Fowler 1986: 86). In *language* classes, teachers and textbooks usually give content schemata—that is, referential knowledge concerning the author, the theme and its social and cultural value. This information constitutes the situational 'context of reference' (ibid.: 89).

Usually missing in foreign language classes are the discourse dimensions of context: the 'context of culture' and the interactional context of reader and text (ibid.: 88). Neither are foreign language learners told how *native* readers might interpret, or have indeed interpreted the text in its foreign cultural context, nor are they shown how their own personal experience as *non-native* readers might help them understand the experience conveyed by the narrator.

So the pedagogical question posed above has to be rephrased into two separate questions:

First: 'What textual knowledge is necessary for students to reconstruct the narrator's experience of events?' We have just seen how the grammatical and lexical choices of the author can be linked to the conveyance of meaning. Making students aware of this is the main challenge for teachers used to minimizing the role of grammar in developing oral communicative competence. It requires a shift of attention from the grammar of face-to-face interaction to the grammar of written discourse.

Second: 'What personal experience can the students draw on to respond to the text?' Besides the general background knowledge mentioned above, each reader brings to the text his or her experience with other texts: bedtime stories and school textbooks, personal letters and commercial advertisements. These prior texts affect the way the written word is understood and integrated into the learner's current state of knowledge.

## Drawing on prior textual experience

The psycholinguistic research devoted to uncovering the influence of 'prior texts' on the ability of learners to read in a foreign language has generally focused on prior information, cultural sensitivity, and general education. It has been less concerned about the influence of prior reading experience—that is, the way learners have been trained at home and in school to retrieve knowledge from written texts. Ethnographers like Heath (1983) provide dramatic examples of such influences.

From observing the reading habits of families from three different communities in the Piedmont Carolinas over a number of years—a black working-class, a white working-class, and a white and black middle-class community—Heath was able to identify differing ways in which children are taught to interact with texts, from bedtime stories to other reading events.

In the black working-class community of Trackton, children were not read to nor taught directly to read. They were mainly left to their own devices, 'growing into knowing' when they were ready to know; observing and imitating adults; getting to understand their global environment through indirect analogic, associative thinking; participating in community literacy events, such as letter reading, church events, group story-telling, and so on — where the meaning of texts was negotiated orally among many readers. In Trackton, reading was very much a social activity.

In Roadville, the white working-class children were read bedtime stories, and taught early on to read texts and read them correctly. Reading was an individual achievement. Parents were anxious to break down reading tasks, such as street signs or cookie labels, into manageable units of meaning, making sure the children followed a path of hierarchical difficulty in the understanding of the written word. As they read to their children, parents asked mostly *what*-questions, inculcating habits of accuracy and attention to detail and a respect for books. In Roadville, however, reading was an activity that had little to do with the needs of everyday life.

In Maintown, children of middle-class families were exposed to written texts early on and the stories read were purposely integrated by the parents into the rest of their children's lives. Ducks swimming on a pond were related to the story of the ugly duckling read the night before, a stray dog encountered on the street was identified as the possible incarnation of the character in a familiar story. Maintown children were asked *what* and *why* questions as they read and were read to from books; they were trained to organize and classify the information retrieved, to give running commentaries, and flights of fiction were encouraged.

For Maintown children, the school reinforced habits acquired at home and they performed well. Roadville children did well at first, but were quickly out of their depth when interpretation skills were required. Trackton children never had a chance of using their inductive, analogic way of learning and were poor achievers from the start.

As we present learners with foreign language texts, it is good to remind ourselves that they bring different talents to bear on their understanding of these texts: some are good at grasping the total meaning of a text, at making unexpected analogies, at discovering metaphors and symbols; others are good at close readings, at collecting information, at making lists; yet others excel at making thematic links, at grouping ideas, at organizing what they have learned. Some are used to evaluating and expressing personal opinions, others have been trained to refrain from any personal response to the text. The former can be encouraged to go beyond personal opinions and pay attention to how the text is put together to convey deeper meanings; the latter can be encouraged to go beyond the signs on the page and put them in relation with their own experience. A pedagogy of text-in-context should allow all these different styles of learning to bloom, while at the same time easing learners into styles different from their own.

## Understanding the silences

Literacy in a foreign language includes the capacity to perform both efferent and aesthetic reading. However, aesthetic reading more than efferent reading has to pay attention not only to what is said but to what is left unsaid. Each word chosen by the author is selected at the expense of others that were not chosen. Understanding a text's silences is the most difficult task of the foreign language reader, for the decision of the author to leave things unsaid is based on his or her confidence that the readers will be able to read between the lines.

To what extent are foreign cultural readers entitled to fill those silences as they wish? Fowler remarks: "Literary competence" is not one single skill but is variable relative to cultural circum-stances' (1986: 176). Are, for example, Indian readers, who have a totally different family structure than a Jewish German family in the Prag of 1913, entitled to 'read' Kafka's *The judgment* as the just punishment of a son by his father (Krusche 1985)? Is a Ghanaean student, unable to identify with the Christian protest-ant ethic underlying Dürrenmatt's play *The Visit*, entitled to the interpretation that the main character, Ill, only got what he deserved?

A reader-response approach to reading must take into account the cultural relativity of the reader. As we will see in the next chap-ter, it is precisely those moments of discrepancy between the cul-turally intended reader and the culturally foreign reader that the language teacher should value the most. Rather than be the object of correction or even ridicule, these moments should be exploited as a unique mirror to the particular reader's perspective and con-trasted with the response of other readers at other times under other circumstances.

## Conclusion

In this chapter, we examined some of the differences between spoken and written language. As we moved from the spoken language to the written language, the voice of the social community gave way to the particular voice of the individual relating his or her unique experience in particular ways. Our attention was drawn from the mere story level of what was written to the discourse level of how it was written.

As we explored the six dimensions of particularity identified by Becker, we saw how writers shape the medium, structure their experience by means of grammar and vocabulary, negotiate the interpersonal relationship they wish to have with their reader, draw on background knowledge and refer to prior texts, and decide what to leave unsaid. Writers can choose a more orate or more literate mode of writing that will in turn affect the distance they want to establish between the text and their readers. The readers are of course free to read the text as they wish, but the text structure has been chosen by the writer so as to elicit either a more efferent or a more aesthetic kind of reading.

Although each of these dimensions was discussed separately, it is of course impossible to do so without implicating the others. Thus, as writers shape the medium, choosing their degree of distance or involvement, they are obviously also engaged in defining their relationship with their reader and using grammar to do so. Similarly efferent and aesthetic reading are affected by text genre and the kinds of structural expression chosen. In all its dimensions at once, a foreign language text invites the learner to discover both the personal voice of a foreign author, and the cultural voice of a speech community.

This would be a daunting task indeed for a foreign language reader, if the text did not, at the same time, appeal to his or her personal response and to the cultural voice he or she in part represents. Particular meanings in a text can only be discovered if readers are ready to engage their own particular response to the text. The next chapter will attempt to show how communicative activities can elicit these responses and enrich the universe of meanings available to language learners.

## Note

1 'To write is already to organize the world, it is already to think. It is therefore useless to ask the other to rewrite himself, if he is not ready to rethink himself.'

# 5  Teaching the literary text

We read on, caught up in the discourse, involved in creating a world with language, and learning language at the same time as we use it in the realization of another reality. Far from being diminished, human experience is extended.
(Henry Widdowson 1981: 213)

The major difficulty encountered by language learners when they deal with written texts stems from the passage from a more orate to a more literate mode of speech. A frequent complaint from students, as they enter the intermediate level, is: 'The first year was fun, we could talk about ourselves and our daily lives. Now that we are reading these texts, I have nothing to say'. From the here-and-now communicative activities of the elementary levels to the more text-bound discussions of the intermediate and advanced, students feel a lack of continuity that is both disappointing and frustrating.

They thought they understood what it meant to talk like members of French or German speech communities: all you needed was to abide by their grammatical and lexical rules. Now it appears that the rules in the use of written language are of a different order. Speakers and writers make choices that are not always predictable and codifiable. There is a difference between the generic reality of the dictionary and the particular reality of written texts. How can students be led to see that particularity is something that can be pleasurable, and that it is jointly achieved between them and the text? How can the spoken skills they developed in the first year to express general meanings be now put to use to express particular meanings?

Many arguments have been made in recent years for including literary texts in the readings taught in language classes. More than any other text, it is said, the piece of literary prose or poetry appeals to the students' emotions, grabs their interest, remains in their memory and makes them partake in the memory of another speech community. In my view, the main argument for using literary texts in the language classroom is literature's ability to represent the particular voice of a writer among the many voices of his or her community and thus to appeal to the particular in the reader. After years of functional approaches to language learning that helped learners approximate the voice of the target speech community, there is a renewed interest for the individual voice and the creative utterance. The literary text is the epitomy of the double-voiced discourse Bahktin attributes to the writer: 'The writer is a person who is able to work in a language while standing outside language, who has the gift of indirect speaking' (1986: 110).

In this respect, as J. H. Miller (1992) has said, literary and non-literary discourse differ in degree but not in kind. The newspaper article, the essay and the short story are on a continuum from single-voiced to double-voiced discourse. Foreign language learners have to be exposed to different types of texts, from the most conventional to the most particular, but if they are eventually to find their own voice in the foreign language and culture, literary texts can offer them models of particularity and opportunities for the dialogic negotiation of meaning.

I will first report on some current practices in the communicative teaching of literary texts and suggest ways in which they can be reoriented toward a pedagogy of dialogue that elicits and values diversity and difference.

## Current practices

Communicative language teaching has inspired a host of interactive activities to teach literary texts at the intermediate level. Two examples will show the potential and the limitations of such activities.

## Example 1

The class is an intermediate German class at an American university. Eighteen undergraduates between the ages of 18 and 22 are sitting in a circle. They are of various ethnic backgrounds: two Japanese men, three Chinese women, one Pakistani, one Greek, the others are Anglo-American. The teacher, herself of Anglo-saxon origin, opens the lesson by asking in German: 'Has anyone of you ever run away from home?' Two or three Anglo-Americans raise their hands. The teacher asks each one: 'Tell us about it. Why did you do it? How old were you? How long did you stay away?'. The answers vary. After having generated interest in the topic, the teacher then breaks the class into groups of three and gives them five minutes to interview each other. Their task is given to them on a slip of paper:

> Did you try to run away from home? How old were you? Did you leave your family a note? Where did you want to go? (to a friend? to Africa? to the circus?) What did you want to take with you (your savings? photos? your teddy bear?) How long did you stay away? Did your parents have to call the police? What was the reaction of your family? (your friends?)

The Anglo-American students talk readily in German, some know the situation well ('I was bored', 'My mother kept nagging at me', 'I felt kind of constrained'). The non-Anglo-Americans listen: for them, running away from home is a rather foreign concept.

The teacher now announces that they are going to discuss the reading for the day—a short story by the Swiss author Peter Bichsel entitled *San Salvador* (1964). They are to open their books and read the two pages silently. The story shows a man trying out a new fountain pen he has just bought. He first scribbles on a piece of paper to test the pen, then takes a new sheet of paper and writes a note to his wife: *Mir ist es hier zu kalt. Ich gehe nach Südamerika* (I'm too cold here. I am going to South America), signs his name, and sits there. He thinks of going to the cinema but it is too late, his favorite pub is closed on Wednesdays, he thinks of palm trees, thinks of his wife singing in the church choir, and . . . just sits there. The last sentences of the story read:

> Und um halb zehn kam Hildegard und fragte: 'Schlafen die Kinder?' Sie strich sich die Haare aus dem Gesicht.

> [At half past nine, Hildegard came back home and asked: 'Are the children asleep?' She pulled her hair from her face.]

The simple story of an aborted attempt to 'leave home'. The extremely detailed description of the fountain pen and of Paul's attempts to write the note, as well as the amount of things left unsaid, suggest that, as in many of Peter Bichsel's stories, the paraphrasable content conceals an indictment of the unspoken constraints of petty-bourgeois life, the lack of communication even among intimates and the isolation of the individual.

The students have now finished reading the story. Rather than asking the traditional 'comprehension questions on the text', the teacher decides to have a student actually perform in front of the class the detailed gestures depicted in the story. As the teacher reads the story aloud, each sentence comes to life, illus-trated by its theatrical equivalent: *(Er) nahm seine Feder zur Hand . . . schraubte die Kappe auf die Feder . . . entleerte seine Feder und füllte sie wieder* (He took his pen . . . screwed the cap on the pen . . . emptied the pen and filled it up again . . .). The students seem interested, the teacher has no difficulty in getting them to volunteer to act out the scene.

After the text has been acted out, and as the lesson draws to a close, the teacher then asks the class: 'Why do you think Paul decided not to leave for South America?' Students express their opinions: 'Because he doesn't want to leave his children / because he is afraid of the unknown / because he doesn't want to upset his wife . . .'. The teacher accepts all interpretations as equally valid, calling them *interessant*. Thus ends the lesson. As students pack their books to leave, one Japanese student turns to another Japanese student and says: *Es ist eine gute Ehe; er liebt seine Frau* [it's a good marriage; he loves his wife]. This interpretation is hardly the one a Swiss reader would give to the story and yet the Japanese student's response was not unjustified considering that Paul thinks repeatedly about his wife through-out the story.

## Example 2

In another intermediate German class in the United States, the teacher, a Chinese teacher of German from Beijing, is discussing with her class a short story by Paul Maar entitled *Die Erfin-dungsmaschine*, that had been assigned as overnight reading (Maar, 1973). The story tells of an inventor who, short on ideas, ends up inventing an 'invention machine' that gives him ten ideas to invent, such as 'walking stick with kilometer count', 'slippers with built-in heating device', and 'chocolate-tasting spinach'. The teacher asks a few comprehension questions on the text. The students find that the inventions in the story are not very exciting, so the teacher suggests brainstorming other, perhaps more relevant or innovative, ideas. Students come up with: 'a pill that would replace eight hours of sleep', 'an essay-writing machine', 'an essay-correcting machine'. Everyone has a good laugh. The teacher then breaks the class into groups of four, and asks each group to make a list of the five most important inventions in the history of mankind. After five minutes, representatives of each group are sent to the board to write their listings. Two of these lists read:

| | | | |
|---|---|---|---|
| 1 | automobile | 1 | telephone |
| 2 | aeroplane | 2 | clock |
| 3 | television | 3 | aeroplane |
| 4 | light | 4 | printing press |
| 5 | wheel | 5 | computer |

Students justify their choices: 'We selected the automobile because we need it to move around; the aeroplane, to travel long distances; the telephone, to talk with our families . . .'. The teacher then asks each student in turn to rank order the inventions listed on the board. 'Light' (electricity?) gets three votes, 'wheel' gets three more, one vote goes to 'telephone', another to 'clock'. Teacher and students find these results *interessant* and leave it at that. The lesson ends.

## Discussion

The first thing the outside observer notes is the diversity of communicative activities offered by both teachers. Students are encouraged to voice their personal opinions and experiences in pairs, small groups, and whole class configurations, at a level that is both relevant to their lives and adapted to their linguistic means. In the first class, the pre-reading activity has provided a personal, experiential content schema for the reading of the literary text. In the second class, personal reactions to the text have been solicited, the readers have been encouraged to get involved in 're-writing' the story. However, we are left wondering to what extent the texts enabled the students to discover new meanings for themselves—what Widdowson (1981: 211) calls 'alternative contexts of reality'.

Let us reconsider example 1. If the story is told to express the experience of petty-bourgeois stuffiness and paralysis, then bringing the readers in touch with their own experience and similar feelings is indeed a good starting point, but this personal experience needs to be linked to the *what* and the *how* of the narrative in order to be expanded and enriched. The reasons some of the students might have had for running away from home are expressed in a new way by the narrator through the written medium. The situation of the readers in the class is different from that of the character in the story, but their feelings might be similar, if not identical, to those evoked by the text.

The answer to the question posed by the teacher ('Why did Paul decide not to leave home?') is not explicitly stated in the story. It is, however, to be found in the discourse of the narrative. The point of departure established by the first sentence, 'He had bought himself a fountain pen', is rather unusual for someone who wants to leave for South America; one would have expected him to buy an airplane or a boat ticket! The exiguous spatial frame of reference filled with definite articles, concrete objects (the fountain pen, the ashtray, the desk, the paper), and petty concerns ('the ink dried up . . .') suggests a finite materialistic world in which imagination and fantasy dry up like the ink on the page. The exaggerated text space devoted to the writing equipment and procedure (one-third of the story) reinforces the feeling of Paul's powerlessness and the stifling of free will by materialistic concerns. The story is told exclusively through the eyes of Paul, leaving no escape for the readers and not allowing them to see the situation from the point of view of, say, his wife. The intended effect on the readers must be to make them experience by proxy the stuffiness of a petty-bourgeois Swiss family.

The adolescent Anglo-American students can empathize with the feelings of constraint expressed by the text, but the teacher has to establish a more explicit link between the text and their experience when they themselves wanted to leave home. By analyzing how the text conveys a certain experience and by describing that experience, adolescent learners might realize that their reasons for leaving home were slightly different from the conditions suggested by the middle-aged Swiss narrator. The non-Anglo-American students in the class can add to this discrepancy by relativizing the response of the Anglo-American readers. Thus the alternative context of reality offered by the text can be discussed in the light of the alternative contexts of culture present in the class; the cultural relativity of the theme itself can be highlighted by comparing the reactions of the Japanese and the Anglo-American students in the class.

For example, the way Paul thinks of his wife suggests less love than habit and the orderliness of family life. That might be precisely the point of cultural discrepancy among different students in the class about what constitutes conjugal 'love'. By discussing this point across generations, social backgrounds, and national cultures, classroom dialogue gives depth and breadth to the original text.

In example 2, the creation by the students of a parallel text with alternative 'inventions' is a good point of departure for a comparison of the different world views expressed by the students and by the text. The inventions listed on the board, reflecting the lifestyles and concerns of American students in 1993, can be usefully contrasted with the inventions mentioned in the story, that correspond to a certain world view expressed by the author in 1973 in Germany. However, the communicative activities devised by the teacher risk reinforcing the learners' stereotypes rather than opening their minds to alternative world views, if these activities do not take into account the discourse of the narrative itself. That discourse is as ironical and distant from the character as the students should be vis-à-vis their own 'inventions'.

The fact that the teacher herself is not a native American could help bring yet another perspective on the topic. Whereas the priorities listed on the board reflect the concerns of students living in the United States, what in the teacher's experience would have been the priority lists of Chinese learners of German in the Republic of China—or of native Germans in Germany? To what extent would they reflect the concerns and aspirations of their respective societies?

In both examples, the teachers used the text as a springboard for having the students express themselves and relate the storyline to their own experience. They seemed reluctant, however, to ask students to look at their experience critically in light of the text. As we saw in Chapter 3, there are several reasons for this.

The first is partly a response to the expectations of their students at the intermediate level. For most of these, there is a disturbing gap between the teaching of face-to-face communication in familiar contexts, and that of literary texts in seemingly distant and unfamiliar contexts. Teachers are naturally keen on reducing the gap by having the students talk about reality as they perceive it. What students do not realize is that these texts express a 'reality beyond realism' (Widdowson 1981: 211) based on a common human experience that is eminently relevant to their lives; however, in order to discover that reality, they must read the texts in a different way.

The second reason is the fear of 'indoctrinating' their students if they make their own response to the text explicit, or of promoting stereotypes when relating to the particular world view of foreign language writers. They realize that they have to take into account the context in which the text was written and read by its intended readers, but they hesitate to make generalizations about 'cultural' characteristics. For example, German short stories have common themes (e.g. criticism of the petty-bourgeois) and common ways of dealing with these themes that are different from those of English short stories, but many teachers of German in the United States would hesitate to describe to their students German petty-bourgeois attitudes for fear of stereotypes. The concerns about indoctrination and cultural stereotyping are the two most frequently cited reasons for refraining from interpreting both the particular and the general cultural meanings conveyed by written texts.

A third, less frequently cited, reason is to be found in the feelings of inadequacy of non-native teachers when interpreting foreign literary texts, even if they have been trained in literary studies. Many of them still bear the marks of a graduate training that discouraged any meaningful reader participation. They therefore often confuse reader response with free associations and reactions of the reader's mind.

All these factors account for the fact that many teachers refrain from exploring either their own response to the text or that of their students. The non-committal pluralism of opinions that ensues does justice neither to the text nor to the students' search for meaning. In order to teach literature as dialogue between a text and a reader, teachers must first get in touch with themselves as readers. They then have to make their students into readers too before they can expect them to find meaning and pleasure in the texts they give them to read.

## Defining the reader

The kind of readers teacher and students decide to be will determine the extent of their involvement with the text and the nature of the meanings their dialogue with the text will generate. If they read the text as a paradigm for certain grammatical structures, that meaning will be purely grammatical. If they read the story in an efferent manner, it will be given a purely referential meaning. If they choose to give it an aesthetic reading, multiple layers of meaning will emerge from their personal response to the text. The following are suggestions for teachers about to teach literary texts in language classes.

## Pre-teaching activities

*Choice of text.* Rather than selecting a text exclusively on the basis of thematic interest and linguistic simplicity, the teacher may wish to consider other criteria:

—Does the text lend itself more to an efferent or an aesthetic
   kind of reading?
—Is the narrative structure predictable or unpredictable?
—Are the cultural allusions clear or unclear to foreign readers?
—Are the silences in the text understandable to foreign readers?

A linear, predictable narrative structure on a familiar theme with easy-to-fill silences elicits more readily a response from a foreign reader, but it can also be deceptive and tempt students into reading only on an efferent level. A linguistically easy text might present a narrative sophistication that is unfamiliar to the students, thus raising their aesthetic curiosity.

*Reader reaction.* Before teaching a text, the teacher may wish to examine his or her own reaction as reader: what is it that he likes or is touched by in the text? What is it he does not like? Whatever the reasons (emotional resonances or personal contexts of experience, aesthetic pleasure or intellectual satisfaction), the teacher's initial reaction to the text will be his most valuable asset in teaching it. Ideally, a teacher should never have to teach anything to which he or she is totally indifferent; even hating a text can be the best incentive to find out something about that text and oneself as a reader.

*Personal experience.* It is important to develop a personal response by understanding the experience expressed through the text. Beyond the paraphrasable content, what human experience or theme is the text trying to express in words? For example, Paul's attempts to write the note to his wife rather than discuss the matter with her, and his final decision not to leave, convey a feeling of incommunicability and powerlessness. Language teachers are sometimes afraid to identify and have their students respond to such general human themes, and yet, more often than not, what a literary text puts into words are elemental experiences of life and death: love, fear, loss and alienation, wonder, motion and stillness. Once the teacher has allowed the text to make sense for him or her, he may want to find out how other readers have interpreted that text (colleagues, friends, literary critics). It is also a good idea for the teacher to enrich his or her reading of that particular text by comparing it with other texts by the same author, and by gathering information about the biography of the author, the period, and so on.

*Textual clues.* The teacher will want to identify the main textual features that convey the theme of the text. For example: the feeling of pettiness and confinement in *San Salvador* is rendered by the short static sentences describing minute details of objects on Paul's desk and by the repeated statement *Da saß er da* (he sat there). This step is essential if the teacher wants to prevent class discussion from meandering into vague generalities that have nothing to do with the text. He or she wants to elicit students' responses to the text, not loose associations with the topic.

*Focus.* The teacher probably wants to choose no more than *two* main points he or she wants to make in class that day about the text (or section of the text if read over several lessons). These points may pertain to both the story level and the level of discourse. It is wise to free oneself from any 'coverage syndrome': what has not been covered today can be dealt with in another way another time or with another text. Furthermore, students can be trusted to discover things on their own.

*Pedagogic format.* The teacher will need to decide beforehand what classroom format best suits the teaching of the points he or she wishes to bring across: whole class discussion, individual student report, role-play, group work, or pair work (see below). It is good to be ready to switch lesson plan if the class arrives unprepared: for example, giving them ten minutes to read portions of the text silently in class, or selecting a passage to read together intensively. It is less useful to try and reconstruct what happened over ten pages if half the class has not read the text.

*Presentation of the text.* The teacher may want to practice the initial 'performance' of the text in front of the class, either by memorizing the poem, by practicing reciting the poem or reading the story aloud, or giving a paraphrase of the content of the text.

## Pre-reading activities

The following suggested pre-reading activities can be done either at home or in class. They need not be done in the order given here.

*Aesthetic reading.* It might be useful to explain in class the difference between reading for information retrieval and reading for the experience of reading. With a simple drawing on the blackboard, the teacher may want to show the students how, in the first type of reading, the eye goes back and forth, upwards and downwards and back again on the page, checking new against old information, skimming the text and scanning it for relevant items. In the second type of reading, the eye turns inward to the reader's response, rests there for a while and returns to the page; students read and pause, read and pause, letting their mind make associations, evoke prior texts, assess the effect of the choice of a word or phrase (see next section below: 'First reading in class').

*Pedagogic expectations.* It is good pedagogic practice to tell the students exactly what is expected of them when assigning them a text to read at home. The teacher may explain what type of understanding they are expected to come to class with, for instance: a word-and sentence-level grasp of *what* the text is about, and a story-level comprehension of *why* events and actions take place. The teacher may explain what will be discovered together in class, for example: a discourse-level understanding of *how* the text expresses a certain experience; the relation between the text and their own experience as foreign readers, what the text means for native readers.

*Presentation of the theme.* Either through personalized questions, writing activities, or parallel texts, it is a good idea to sensitize the students to the experience thematized by the text. For example, the teacher may have students in groups discuss their desire to run away from home or have them write (in the foreign language) a short paragraph or a poem expressing that experience. The teacher may then want to compare the discourse features of these students' texts, and identify characteristics that are similar to, or that contrast with, those of the original. He or she may extract from the activity some key concepts that capture aspects of the theme in the foreign language—for example, *Kleinbürgerlichkeit, Einsamkeit, Kinder/Kirche/Küche, es ist mir kalt* [petty-bourgeois, loneliness, children / church / kitchen, I am cold].

*Readers' expectations*. Students' structures of expectation or schemata need to be activated in order for them to comprehend the story:

1 Content schemata. Students might need help setting the story in its appropriate logic: motives and intentions, plans and expectations might be different in their society and culture. Some background knowledge should be given beforehand to avoid needless misunderstandings.
2 Genre schemata. Without indulging in literary terminology, it is useful for the students to know whether this is a fairy tale, a satire, a tragedy, a comedy, or a parable.

## First reading in class

Whether the text is taught in one lesson or over several lessons, the opening lines, or the first paragraph of the narrative should be read (and re-read) together in class. Either the teacher reads the passage aloud, or assigns a student to do so, or the class reads it silently within a given time limit. The teacher can then dramatize for the students the difference between efferent and aesthetic reading. Once most of the syntax and vocabulary have been clarified, the teacher rereads the passage out loud, stopping after each phrase to encourage any member of the class to inter- polate—also out loud—possible meanings / associations / com- ments / questions, which are then continuously cross-referenced with each other as the reading goes on. The teacher first models these 'responses' by conducting a dialogue with him or herself.

Here is, as an example, the transcription of an intermediate German class starting to read Kafka's *Metamorphosis*. The stu- dents have not read the text beforehand; their books are open in front of them.

Teacher (recites from memory): 'Als Gregor Samsa .. eines Morgens .. aus schwe:ren Träu:men erwachte .., fand er sich . . . in seinem Bett . . . zu einem UN::geheuren UN::geziefer verwandelt'. (Looks at the text and reads it aloud once more.) Tja, das ist in der Tat ein ungeheurer erster Satz. Der skanda- löseste Satz der ganzen deutschen Literatur. Zuerst mal: Wieso heißt es sofort 'Gregor Samsa'? Der Erzähler nimmt

an, ich kenne ihn, aber ich kenne ihn nicht!; mit diesem ein-
fachen Satz, zwingt mich der Erzähler daran zu glauben,
daß ein gewisser Gregor Samsa so plötzlich übernacht ein
Ungeziefer geworden ist. Er läßt mir auch gar keine andere
Wahl. Nichts von 'Es war einmal ein Mann, der hieß Gregor
Samsa. Eines Morgens . . .'. Da würden wir wenigstens
wissen, aha, das ist ein Märchen . . . aber so einfach brutal
mit der Tür ins Haus: 'Als Gregor Samsa eines Morgens aus
schweren Träumen erwachte, fand er sich in seinem Bett
zu einem ungeheuren Ungeziefer verwandelt'—als ob das die
natürlichste Sache der Welt wäre!

[Teacher recites from memory: 'As Gregor Samsa woke up
one morning from heavy dreams he found himself transformed in his bed into a monstrous beetle'. (Looks at the text
and reads it aloud once more.) Well, that is really a monstrous
sentence. The most scandalous sentence of the whole of
German literature. First of all: Why does it say right away
'Gregor Samsa'? The narrator seems to assume that I know
him, but I don't know him at all! With this first simple sentence, the narrator forces me to believe that a certain Gregor
Samsa became a beetle just like that overnight! And he doesn't
leave me any choice either. Nothing like: 'Once upon a time,
there was a man and his name was Gregor Samsa. One morning . . .'. At least we would know that it is a fairy tale. Just
abruptly like that: 'As Gregor Samsa woke up one morning
from heavy dreams, he found himself transformed in his bed
into a monstrous beetle'. As if it were the most natural thing
in the world!]

The teacher then reads the rest of the paragraph aloud, helping
students interpolate their comments. The types of comments
students are likely to make have been observed by psycholinguists (e.g. Horiba 1990, Faerch and Kasper 1987) using
think-out-loud protocol procedures, called also 'concurrent
introspection', to tap the content of readers' immediate
awareness during reading. They include: predictions ('Will he
turn back into a human being?'), questions ('How big is
he?'); comments on structure ('That is an unusual beginning');
comments on own behavior ('I just don't understand'); confirmation on predictions ('So I was right'); references to ante-
cedent information ('Yes, that's true, he was lying on his
back'); inferences ('His boss is sure to be angry at him');

general knowledge and associations ('That is interesting, I often feel like that too').

Cazden (1992), who has used such a think-aloud approach in English composition classes, describes this process as a 'minimal example of externalizing interpretation'—a secondary dialogue that grafts itself onto the text and elicits the kind of reader response necessary for active interpretation. Other techniques for prompting readers' responses are described below. They provide a contrastive backdrop of a more orate type to the more literate mode of a literary text. They respect the orate mode of the reader's voice and the more literate mode of the literary text, but have both interact as the reader adds his or her voice to the voices in the text, and participates thereby in the construction of its meaning.

## Teaching the narrative

As with any literary text, the dialogue between reader and text will orient itself to the two levels discussed in the last chapter: that of the story and that of the discourse structure of its narration.

### Exploring the story

Many excellent suggestions have been made to activate the readers' cognitive processes while reading and make the text relevant to students' lives. Let me just mention a few.

Isenberg (1990) offers information-processing techniques to explore the when? what? why? how? of the story-line:

—formulate questions
—establish logical and analogical relationships
—select/reject information
—group/regroup, organize/reorganize facts and events
—generalize
—rank in order of importance
—explore consequences of actions, generate alternatives, predict outcomes
—evaluate.

Rankin (1989), van Eunen (1987) suggest various ways of enlisting these different cognitive operations when teaching the German short story or fairy tale. In ESL classes, di Pietro (1987) has students rewrite story-lines through strategic scenarios. Collie and Slater (1987) offer a host of communicative activities to bring the story to life when teaching novels, short stories, drama, and poetry. They generally entail:

—gathering the facts (linguistic and referential)
—brainstorming plans and intentions
—relating both to the readers' personal experience.

Most of these activities exploit the referential aspect of texts for the language learner.[1]

However, if reading literary texts in language classes is meant not only to reinforce students' personal experiences, but to expand the range and the depth of those experiences, these activities are not sufficient. The following example, taken from Collie and Slater (1987) will illustrate the limits of story-based activities.

The class has finished reading William Golding's *Lord of the Flies*. An 'Inquest on Board Ship' activity is suggested. This activity has three parts:

> *First part:* a general brainstorming session with the whole class. Imagine that on the way home, the Chief Officer decides to investigate what really happened on the island. What questions would he need to ask? What answers would be given by Ralph? Jack? Roger?
>
> *Second part:* role-play/improvisation. Roles are distributed: the presiding officer, his panel of inquiry, five boys. With the help of the recorded questions and answers, they enact the inquest scene.
>
> *Third part:* the verdict. The class is divided into groups of four or five, representing the presiding officer and his panel of inquiry. They have just witnessed the questioning of the five boys, and their task is now to arrive at a verdict, and to write a report on the incident, which includes recommendations for the treatment of the boys when they return to England.
>
> (Collie and Slater 1987: 161)

By encouraging the students to remain on the level of referential or efferent reading, this activity leads them to look for a clear-cut, moral solution or interpretation for the tragic events depicted in the story. But the discourse structure chosen by the author at the end of the novel hardly allows such a clear-cut conclusion. Indeed, it puts in question the value of devising activities that might distinguish between 'good guys' and 'bad guys'. Let us take a closer look at the text:

> The officer nodded helpfully.
> 'I know. Jolly good show. Like the Coral Island.'
> Ralph looked at him dumbly. For a moment he had a fleeting picture of the strange glamour that had once invested the beaches. But the island was scorched up like dead wood — Simon was dead — and Jack had . . . The tears began to flow and sobs shook him. He gave himself up to them now for the first time on the island; great, shuddering spasms of grief that seemed to wrench his whole body. His voice rose under the black smoke before the burning wreckage of the island; and infected by that emotion, the other little boys began to shake and sob too. And in the middle of them, with filthy body, matted hair, and unwiped nose, Ralph wept for the end of innocence, the darkness of man's heart, and the fall through the air of the true, wise friend called Piggy.
> The officer, surrounded by these noises, was moved and a little embarrassed. He turned away to give them time to pull themselves together; and waited, allowing his eyes to rest on the trim cruiser in the distance.
> (Golding 1964: 186)

The staging of this final confrontation of Ralph and the naval officer has a shock effect on the reader. On the one hand, fourteen lines of tears, sobs, great shuddering spasms of grief, shaking and emotion, a sudden understanding of the human condition, the depths of despair; on the other hand, in four sobering lines, the realization that for the adult, all these are merely embarrassing noises that only slightly detract from the established social conventions and war games. While Ralph 'gives himself up' to tears, the officer 'allows his eyes to rest on the trim cruiser in the distance'. This business-as-usual attitude is emphasized by the rather pedestrian rhythm of the last three sentences, that stand in stark contrast to the long cadenza and the repeated triple chords that sum up Ralph's experience. The semi-colon, rather than a comma, that separates the penultimate and the ultimate sentence of the novel introduces a pause of respectability while the officer 'waits' for things to return to their proper order. But what is this proper order? If ever the question arises as to why Ralph weeps at that point in the novel, we only need to look at the text. Caught between the social superficiality illustrated by the officer's remark, on line 2 ('Jolly good show. Like the Coral Island.') and the visual link between the officer and military power on lines 18–19, Ralph has no hope that his experience will ever be understood and his tragic knowledge passed on. The cruiser in the distance seems to say it all.

Through this ending, Golding could not give a stronger indictment of adult society. As he says himself in an interview with James Keating,

> Of course, the cruiser, the adult thing, is doing exactly what the hunters do — that is, hunting down and destroying the enemy — so that you say, in effect, to your reader, 'Look, you think you've been reading about little boys, but in fact you've been reading about the distresses and the wickednesses of humanity'.
> (Golding 1964: 194)

By remaining on the level of the story, the activities in Collie and Slater (1987) encourage students to distribute blames and praises, and to maintain a social order that Golding's novel puts precisely in question. We have to go beyond the story and devise activities that will explore the interaction between the discourse structure and the responses of the readers in the interpretation of the text.

## Exploring the discourse

In a variety of imaginative and creative ways, students can be shown how to explore the narrative options at work in the creation of the text: medium and genre, narrative structure (e.g. point of view and text time), audience, referential world of the story, and the various voices and silences in the text. Their attempts at identifying and varying any of the six dimensions of difference explored in the previous chapter can serve to highlight the particularity of the dialogue in which the text invites its readers to engage. We will take each of these dimensions in turn (for further suggestions, see Kramsch 1984, 1987b; Ozzello 1987; Nutting 1987; Roth 1983; among many others).

## Varying the medium or the genre

To illustrate the way the medium itself shapes meaning, it can be useful to translate the text into a kinetic or visual medium or into another language. In the first example given at the beginning of this chapter, the instructor had intuitively felt the need to dramatize the gestures of the character as he tested his new fountain pen. Such an activity can highlight the relative size and shape of objects, the frequency and amplitude of movements, the place and value of characters relative to one another, and illustrate how these factors contribute to the overall meaning of the passage. Particularly appropriate for such a spatialization would be, for instance, in Kafka's *Metamorphosis*, the scene in which the family sees Gregor come out of his room for the first time: the clerk, one hand against his open mouth, the other staving off the danger, slowly retreats; the mother, with her hair still down from the night, looks at the father, clasps her hands, makes two steps towards Gregor and falls unconscious, her face buried in her vast petticoats; the father, clenching his fist toward the son, gives him an angry look as if wanting to throw him back into his room, but then casts an uncertain glance around the room, shades his eyes with his hands and weeps (Kafka [1916] 1960: 14). The freezing and eventual shrinking of the family's physical space as the cockroach Gregor starts invading their psychological space can be highlighted by varying the medium from written to gestural.

Besides a kinesic representation, a text can be given a visual form on paper. The following exercise is suggested by Collie and Slater (1987) to capture the story of *Lord of the Flies*: 'Choose the book's most powerful "pictures". Write the description of one of these images (a paragraph, plus title)' (ibid.: 161). I would suggest reformulating this activity as follows, to focus the students' attention on discourse forms: 'Provide a design for the book's paperback cover that captures the theme of the novel as you understand it'. As students justify their choices of motifs, shapes, colors, and space allocation, they get a sense of similar choices the author had to make with words, sentences, and paragraphs on the page.

The same activity could be done by having the students express the theme of the novel through texts taken from other genres: a 'concrete' poem, or an epitaph for Piggy, or a press release, or a letter written by Ralph to his English teacher—with whom he might even have read R.M. Ballantyne's *Coral Island* (1857)—upon his return to Britain.

A third way of highlighting the discourse value of the author's choices is to compare it with its translation into another language. For instance, as can be seen by contrasting the opening lines of Kawabata's classic novel *Snow Country* ([1947] 1971) with its English translation, the Japanese language can depict actions and events that have to be expressed quite differently in English. For example, it can recount the experience of someone travelling to another country without having to use a verb of motion. The first paragraph of the novel consists of three short sentences, which amount to a single line of Japanese text:

> Kokkyo no nagai tonneru o nukeruto Yukiguni de atta.
> Yoru no soko ga shirokunatta. Shingoojo ni kish ga tomatta.

Seidensticker's (1956) translation reads:

> The train came out of the long tunnel into the snow country. The earth lay white under the night sky. The train pulled up at a signal stop.'

By contrast, a literal translation would be: 'Border range / of / long tunnel / dir. obj. marker / upon exiting / Snow Country / it was'. The Japanese text has three words indicating the location: 'snow country' (*yukiguni*), 'tunnel' (*tonneru*), and 'border range' (*kokkyo*). It has no mention of a 'train coming out' nor of a 'train pulling up'. While the English rendition reads like the beginning of a linear narrative, the Japanese language can set the stage without any verb of motion, border ranges can be crossed, tunnels can be driven through in total motionlessness, sequentiality of events disappears, boundaries between spaces dissolve.

The words 'snow country', 'border range' (or boundary between two foreign countries), and 'tunnel' can be interpreted to suggest separation of the world before and the world after the tunnel. After the tunnel, the world is white, unreal, and distant from everyday life. This world is not accessible by train, but by the jump over the time and space in the mind of the readers themselves (Jackson 1989). Thus the Japanese text inscribes the theme of the whole novel—motion in stillness, stillness in motion—in the grammar and the discourse structure of its first three sentences. We will return to this theme when we consider the teaching of poetry.

## Varying the point of view

Requesting students to recast a text in another form often dramatizes for them how the point of view chosen by the narrator affects their understanding of the story. For example, asked to summarize 'in their own words' the first chapter in Kafka's *Metamorphosis*, one student wrote: *Der Vater gab Gregor einen wahrhaftig erlösenden Stoß und Gregor flog blutig in sein Zimmer zurück.* [The father gave Gregor a truly redeeming kick and Gregor flew into his room, covered with blood]. The words 'a truly redeeming kick' are lifted directly from the text, but as such, they heavily bear the mark of the point of view of the narrator which happens also to be that of Gregor Samsa. In the story, Gregor is the one through whose eyes all events are seen, even though this is a third person narrative. The teacher wrote in the margin of the student's summary the following remarks: 'Whose point of view? Does this present participle express your evaluation of the situation or that of the narrator?' To which the student answered: 'Now for the first time I understand what you mean by point of view.'

Point of view can be brought to consciousness by varying the following commonly used pedagogical technique. Student A is in charge of summarizing the reading for the day. As he or she does this orally at the beginning of the lesson, three or four students are sent to the blackboard and are asked to each write in their own words the summary given orally by the student, possibly adding missing elements or questioning some potential misunderstanding. The class as a whole then examines the four different renditions of the summary (see Chapter 3). As this was done, for example, for the beginning of *Metamorphosis*, it was interesting to compare how one student had written: *Gregor Samsa war in ein Ungeziefer verwandelt* [Gregor Samsa was changed into a beetle], another *Gregor Samsa wurde in ein Ungeziefer verwandelt* [Gregor Samsa had been changed into a beetle], and another *Gregor hatte sich in ein Ungeziefer verwandelt* [Gregor Samsa had changed himself into a beetle]. This was a unique opportunity to reflect on the conscious choice by Kafka of a fourth—

rather unusual—lexical and grammatical option: *er fand sich
. . . verwandelt* [he found himself changed] and on the different
impact this linguistic choice has on the reader.

Rewriting the story from the point of view of another character is one of the best ways of diversifying the students' context
of reality. For example, a favorite text for beginning German
learners is the parable 'Before the Law', a story told by a priest
to the main character K. in Kafka's novel *The Trial*. Textbooks'
reading selections reproduce only the story itself, severing it
from its narrative context, which includes also the commentaries
by the priest. The students, like K., generally feel pity for the
man from the country who sits all his life before the law without
ever being let in. They too feel the doorkeeper has deceived the
man by letting him believe that one day he would be allowed to
go in. But, in the novel, the priest who tells K. the story also
shows him how attentively one must read a text before hastening
to unwarranted conclusions: 'Do not adopt the foreign opinion
without examining it . . . You don't have enough respect for the
scripture and you are changing the story . . . You should not
rely too much on opinions . . . One need not hold everything
for true, one needs only to hold it for necessary' (p.264, my
translation).[2] Over seven long pages, the priest proceeds to show
him how one could read the same story with quite a different
interpretation and even feel sorry for the doorkeeper. This is
precisely the type of multiple perspective teachers of literary
texts should develop in the language classroom (see, for
example, Roth 1983).

### Varying text time

There are several ways students can be made aware of the effect
on the reader of the sequencing of events, for instance by paying
attention to the amount of text space relative to real time of
events or to the sequence of events itself. Students can be asked
to tell the story starting from another point in time, to continue
the story, to fill the 'zero textual spaces' within the narrative
(what happened between chapter one and chapter two of
*Metamorphosis*?) (see, for example, Nutting 1987).

Many of these activities are well-known in the pedagogic
literature, but they are often performed as pure linguistic
exercises, with the aim of merely using the low-level grammar

forms in the most accurate way possible. Here, they are meant to trigger a conscious reflection on the discourse value of the sequencing of events. For example, students in a beginning German class can be asked to tell the story of the frog king starting when the princess comes back to the palace. 'Relate the loss of her golden ball and her encounter with the frog in the pluperfect. Start with *Es war ein furchtbarer Tag gewesen . . .*, [it had been a horrible day. . .,]; end with *Aber jetzt war alles in Ordnung. Die Prinzessin stieg die Treppe zum Schloß und lächelte ihrem Vater entgegen.* [But now everything was in order. The princess went up the steps to the castle and smiled as she saw her father]. Then the class has to be asked: what is the difference in terms of its effect on the reader between your text and the Grimms' text?

## Varying the audience

To sensitize them to the notion of audience, students can be asked to write, like Dürrenmatt in his novel *Grieche sucht Griechin* (1976), different endings for the same narrative: for example, one for junior high schools, one for parish libraries, one for university students. They can then compare the intended and the achieved effect on the various populations of readers.

They will notice that tailoring one's story to a specific audience changes all the other dimensions of discourse, and requires the narrator to choose also between a more orate or more literate mode of writing.

Students can also be asked to cast themselves in various readers' roles for the duration of the reading. For example:
As you read Golding's *Lord of the Flies*, imagine that you are any of the following:

—a feminist
—an officer in the British navy
—a priest
—a schoolboy
—an avid reader of adventure stories
—a Marxist
—a boy scout.

Adjust your reaction/interpretation accordingly.

## Varying the referential world of the story

To appreciate the process of schema construction that goes on during reading, students should be able to compare their emerging schemata with the expectations they have as readers and the expectations the text builds up through its discourse structure. Withholding from them the end of a story and asking them to write it can offer a nice point of comparison between their logic and the logic the text was inviting them to develop.

For example, considering the crucial role played by the last paragraph of *Lord of the Flies* in forcing the reader to reconsider the meaning of the whole story, one approach is to withhold that last paragraph from the students and to ask them to write their own three sentences. Having collated all the endings on a common sheet of paper, including Golding's ending, the various texts are then read and discussed by the whole class or in small groups. Students are to respond to each and assess its comparative effect on the reader as well as its retroactive impact on the general meaning of the novel.

Cultural differences are likely to emerge from such an exercise, as the following example, taken from another language class in the United States, will show. The activity described above was conducted in Japanese with the classic story by the author of *Rashomon*, Ryunosuke Akutagawa, called *The Spider's Thread*, a Buddhist variation on a familiar religious theme (Akutagawa 1918). The bandit Kandata, condemned to the Buddhist version of Hell, is drowning in the Pond of Blood when Buddha, remembering how this Kandata had once saved a spider's life, decides to return the good deed. He lowers a spider's thread down to the floor of Hell to save him. But, at the last minute, Kandata, fearing that the thread might break if too many of his fellow men try to be rescued too, cries: 'Here, you sinners! This spider's thread is mine. Who on earth gave you permission to come up it? Get down! Get down!' And the narrator continues:

> Just at that moment, the spider's thread, which had shown no sign of breaking up to that time, suddenly broke with a snap at the point where Kandata was hanging. So he was helpless. Without time to utter a cry, he shot down and fell headlong into the darkness, spinning swiftly round and round like a top.

The teacher had read the story with her students until the

passage cited above. She then asked her American students to imagine what could have happened that hurled Kandata right back into the Pond of Blood. There were four different versions.

*Version 1*: Other sinners followed Kandata up the thread. He shouted: 'It's mine, I saved the spider', and shook the thread. This caused it to break.

*Version 2*: The spider, whose web Kandata was climbing, appeared above him. Kandata brushed the spider aside, casting it down into hell. Buddha disapproved of this and hurled Kandata back into the pond.

*Version 3*: Buddah wasn't pleased that Kandata took his deliverance as a personal success and he punished him for it.

*Version 4*: Kandata himself accidentally cut the thread with the knife he used in his previous life to kill people.

The teacher then asked the students to give a name to each of these causes and wrote them down on the board:

1 the physical action of shaking the thread
2 Buddha's punishment for yet another crime
3 Buddha's punishment for his arrogance
4 consequences of Kandata's sinful past.

They compared the wording of their stories and the wording of Akutagawa's story. They contrasted in particular the Christian views of retributive justice (versions 2 and 3) or the fatal causality of egoistic actions (versions 1 and 4) with the Buddhist view of punishment expressed in the Japanese story. They were then given to read the last lines of the story, which are indicative of a 'karma' beyond fatality or the notion of an angry God:

Standing on the brink of the Lotus Pond of Paradise, the Buddha watched closely all that happened, and when Kandata sank like a stone to the bottom of the Pond of Blood, he began to saunter again with a sad expression on his face . . .

But the lotuses in the lotus pond of Paradise cared nothing at all about such things.

The pearly white flowers were swaying about the Buddha's feet. As they swayed, from the golden pistils in their centers, their ineffable fragrance ceaselessly filled all the air.

It was near noon in Paradise.

(Akutagawa [1918] 1970)

## Teasing out the voices in the text

Several suggestions have been made to help students identify the different voices that make up the texture of a story or play. Following up on reader's theater techniques (Coger and White 1973, Peterson 1985, Ratcliff 1985, see also Chapter 3), Cazden (1992) suggests scripting non-scripted texts for oral presentation, with or without spatial arrangement and bodily movement. The principle is simple: in small groups students have to decide who will give a voice to which word or cluster of words as the group reads the text aloud. Separating voices in a text without changing anything to the text fosters greater reflexivity about interpretive and composing processes. 'Scripting expository texts that are monologic in published format, makes particularly interesting interpretive work', Cazden writes (ibid.: 70). For example, scripting a classic short story as Wolfgang Borchert's *Das Brot*, still frequently read in first-year German classes in the United States, allows students to decide which sentence or group of sentences will be read by the wife, the husband, the wife's narrator, and the husband's narrator, according to whether the event is seen through the eyes of the character, the omniscient narrator, or the characters' perceptions of each other. It allows them to distinguish between the voice of facts and the voice of speculations, voices of the present and voices of the past or future. It makes them experience a story that they traditionally have difficulty relating to, given their ignorance of postwar conditions in Germany.

Other interactive techniques can make more silent voices heard. A press conference with a student or an empty chair representing the narrator, or a debate between two narrators, can give visibility to an omniscient perspective and make it more easily discussable. For example, a confrontation of the two narrators of Berthold Brecht's *Leben des Galilei* and Hermann Hesse's *Demian* respectively could lead to a public debate, first between the two narrators then with the whole class, on the question 'Can one hope to change the world if one has not first changed oneself?'. *Demian*'s narrator argues, of course, that the main thing is to 'let the bird out of the egg' in the process of self-metamorphosis; Brecht's narrator argues that it is not psychoanalysis but social action that will save the world (see Teacher's diary below).

A similar activity can be used with William Golding's *Lord of the Flies*. An inquest on board ship can be fruitful, but only if the narrator is put aboard the ship too. He could then sow the seeds of sedition among the boys and the course of the trial might be reversed. For Ralph could point to the fact that they are being brought home on a cruiser of the navy and he could question the moral right of the officer to put them on trial. The boys might want to try the officers themselves for crimes against humanity. Conceivably, both trials would end in a stalemate—which would be a good way of having students grasp the essence of the tragic, which Golding expresses throughout the novel.

A simulation activity devised by Morgenstern offers yet another way of raising the students' discourse consciousness in intermediate Spanish classes. Most American students find Latin-American stories depressing. Do the characters have no way out? Latin-American 'fatalismo' clashes with the American view of the pursuit of happiness. In a third semester Spanish class, at the end of the term, the instructor had his seventeen students read a short essay on happiness. He then wrote on individual cards the names of various characters encountered across the stories read over the semester in the textbook (Crow and Dudley 1984, *El Cuento*), and on another set of cards outside events or situations referring specifically to each of the characters.

Students at random drew a character and its matching event, and had to think of how his or her character would react to that event, whether this event would make the character happy, and how they would have to change the story in order to accommodate the role of the character in this new context. They wrote their story as homework assignment and read it to three different 'judges' the next day in class. These judges were played by three students: the first was to evaluate whether the new story fitted into the general plot; the second was to assess the verisimilitude of the character's reaction to the new events; the third was to appreciate the aesthetic quality of the new story—for example, symbolism, narrator's perspective. The best student in the class was to play the role of 'arbiter'. He or she went from judge to judge and listened in on the stories told and on the evaluations by the judges, serving as moderator against differing views and offering suggestions when ideas were lacking.

The narrators had to use all the strategies of persuasion and all the arguments they could think of to make their case before the judges. Each judge gave a number of points on a scale of 1 to 5. The debriefing session served as an open forum for the comparison of various story-lines and discourse forms; it easily took place in the foreign language, even at that level. It was interesting to see who received the most points and for what reason. Some students said afterwards that they understood for the first time what it means to interpret a text and negotiate its meaning (Morgenstern 1989).

In the previous chapter, with Tammy's 'Mother's Day' story, we saw what dramatic differences in meaning a simple story can communicate when it is told by different narrators. In this chapter's first section we have stressed the need to go beyond the plot and character description and into the way the story is narrated. We turn now to the teaching of poetry, using some of the same pedagogic principles to show students how form and content reinforce one another in the creation of particular meanings.

## Teaching poetry

By virtue of their iconicity and their obvious formal aspects, poems are ideally suited to have learners experience early on the two main features of aesthetic experience: distance and relation. Poetry first detaches the readers from their usual frames of reference by immersing them in a world of sounds, rhythms, stress, and other formal features of speech. It then sensitizes them to the relationship between what linguists call the referential and the expressive aspects of language, or what cognitive scientists call 'content space'—that is, ideas, facts, and beliefs—and 'rhetorical space', or mental representation of actual or intended text (Scardamalia and Bereiter 1985). This rhetorical space is based on new ways of forming sounds, new ways of shaping words, phrases, sentences, of structuring discourse, of relating to other texts, and of conceptualizing experience.

I will suggest three ways of encouraging the aesthetic reading of poetic texts. One seeks to 'celebrate' poetry by giving it its full physical form; the second strives to understand poetry by exploring multiple meanings and perspectives; the third attempts to create poetry by having the students experiment themselves with new relationships of form and meaning. Let us take each of these steps in turn.

## Celebrating poetry

In the early stages of language learning, when the foreign words are still like freshly minted coins, full of the strangeness of their sounds, shapes, and meanings, it is easy to appreciate new combinations of sounds, new metaphors, new values given to silence. 'Far from being subordinated to meaning (as is usually the case in ordinary use of language), in poetry sound plays a leading role, operates in full partnership with meaning, and even helps to create meaning' (Waugh and Newfield 1986: 32, cited in Hiraga 1990). 'Celebrating' a poem means drawing conscious pleasure from its visual and prosodic features, without at first analyzing their nature or their impact.

Traditionally, the teacher distributes printed copies of the poem to the class; the poem is then read once by the teacher, once by the students, and analyzed for its vocabulary and grammar. With such a procedure, each reader remains an island unto him or herself, each word is decoded in isolation and examined only for its referential content. By contrast, celebrating poetry is a group experience that foregrounds the pleasure of form *as* content.

The teacher may wish to first recite the poem in front of the class, with appropriate gestures, facial expression, tone of voice, even graphic representations on the blackboard. Several educators recommend memorizing the poem: as a pianist studying someone else's music begins by memorizing it and then slowly comes to understand it, they suggest that memorizing a poem helps to make the poem one's own (Stevick 1988: 67). Furthermore, being able to recite it from memory enables the teacher to keep eye contact with the students, to anticipate their misunderstandings and to respond to their facial responses.

The teacher can then write the poem (or portions of it) on the board or the overhead projector, and the students copy the text in their notebooks. This procedure, too, allows for comments, explanations, and clarifications by the teacher and the group, as they write along. It allows both for personal and for group response. The fact that the poem is in each notebook in the students' handwriting is the initial step to 'making it one's own'; the text on the board, visible by everyone and everyone's property, enables each student to keep both text and fellow students in the same field of vision.

Teachers cannot overestimate the importance of letting the poem grow on the students as they become more and more familiar with it over time. Referring to Ortega's concepts of exuberance and deficiency, Becker (1982: 129) notes: 'One experiences (the poem) by slow self-correction of the exuberance and deficiency with which one begins . . . As you repeat (the lines), bleached, backgrounded things come to the foreground'. Whether it is concrete poetry (Krechel 1987, Krusche and Krechel 1984, Weinrich 1983), jazz chants (Graham 1978), scripted poems (Kramsch and Mueller 1991), or texts from the literary canon; whether the text is recited in chorus, individually, or in pairs—the aesthetic pleasure comes from introducing slight variations in intonation, rhythm, stress, and pace, within a predictable, familiar text. Like storytelling, variation in permanence not only brings individual pleasure, it creates also a bond among learners in the class.

A videotape by Kramsch and Mueller (1991) shows live recordings of teachers of six different languages engaged in experimenting with the sounds, shapes, and rhythms of the language through poetry. For example, the teaching of Eichendorff's 'Mondnacht' aims at creating visual, musical, and kinesic contexts of performance.

### Mondnacht

Es war, als hätt der Himmel
Die Erde still geküßt,
Daß sie im Blütenschimmer
Von ihm nun träumen müßt.

Die Luft ging durch die Felder,
Die Ähren wogten sacht,
Es rauschten leis die Wälder,
So sternklar war die Nacht.

Und meine Seele spannte
Weit ihre Flügel aus,
Flog durch die stillen Lande,
Als flöge sie nach Haus.

J. v. Eichendorff (1830)
*Gedichte*

While reciting the poem, the teacher draws on the blackboard the romantic landscape depicted in the poem, clarifies difficult vocabulary, and writes the text on the board, leaving out the title; she then has the class recite the text with various voices, like in a reader's theater script:

A (male): Es war, als hätt der Himmel die Erde still geküßt
J (female): Daß sie im Blütenschimmer von ihm nun träumen müßt
BC (together): Die Luft ging durch die Felder
DE (together): Die Ähren wogten sacht
FG (together): Es rauschten leis die Wälder
HI (together): So sternklar war die Nacht
all: so sternklar war die Nacht

ABC: Und meine Seele spannte
ABCDE: Weit ihre Flügel aus
ABCDEFG: Flog durch die stillen Lande
ABCDEFGHIJ: Als flöge sie nach Haus
all (piano): als flöge sie nach Haus
all (pianissimo): als flöge sie . . . nach . . . Haus

[It was as if the heaven had gently / Kissed the earth, / And now in blossoms' shimmer / She had to dream of him. / The air went through the fields, / Smoothly waving grain, / And softly rustling woods / So star-clear was the night. / And my soul spread its wings, / Flew through the quiet lands / As if for home.]

A kinesic alternative is to have everyone stand up, the teacher orchestrating with the students a gestural rendition of the poem with broad movements of the arms and hands.

The students then listen to Schumann's musical interpretation of the Eichendorff poem, and while they listen they have to think of a title that captures the experience it is trying to express. Some of the suggested titles have been: 'Seelenlandschaft' (soul landscape), 'Wie im Himmel also auch auf Erden' (on earth as it is in heaven), 'Sachte Nacht' (gentle night); these students' titles serve later on as a basis for gaining a deeper understanding of the emotional and religious overtones of the poem.

## Understanding poetry

The same techniques that we examined for exploring the meaning of a narrative can be used for understanding poetry. Three additional practices are, however, particularly fruitful here: capitalizing on the iconicity and metaphoric nature of poems; contrasting various translations or interpretations; and recasting one literary form into another.

### Iconicity and metaphor

Peirce defines iconicity as follows: 'Anything whatever, be it quality, existent individual, or law, is an icon of anything, in so far as it is like that thing and used as a sign of it' (Peirce cited in Hiraga 1990). These similarity relationships are used as cues to the meaning of the poem (Widdowson 1975). Let us take as an example the poem by Prévert 'L'école des beaux-arts'.

**L'école des beaux-arts**

Dans une boîte de paille tressée
Le père choisit une petite boule de papier
Et il la jette
Dans la cuvette
Devant ses enfants intrigués
Surgit alors
Multicolore
La grande fleur japonaise
Le nénuphar instantané
Et les enfants se taisent
Émerveillés
Jamais plus tard dans leur souvenir
Cette fleur ne pourra se faner
Cette fleur subite
Faite pour eux
A la minute
Devant eux.

Jacques Prévert (1972)
*Paroles*

[From a box of woven straw / The father chooses a little paper ball / And he throws it / In the wash-basin / Before his curious children / Then arises / In many colors / The great Japanese flower / The instantaneous water-lily / And the children are silent / With wonder / Never later in their memory / Can that flower ever fade / That sudden flower / Made for them / At a moment's notice / Before their eyes.]

This poem is not only *about* the unfolding of a Japanese paper flower in a water basin, it is an *icon* of this magical event. The physical shape of the poem on the page traces the contours of a flower pot and of a large flower with leaves and stem. A contradictory movement occurs during the reading of the poem between what the words say and what the reader does: as the text relates how the flower suddenly rises upward from the basin, the eyes of the reader are led down the flower into its roots. This double motion is iconic of the double meaning conveyed by the poem: as the miracle of creation unfolds in front of the child, it leaves a deep and permanent impression in the adult's memory.

The definite articles used throughout—le père, *la cuvette, la grande fleur, le nénuphar instantané*—rather than refer to previously known entities, endow their referents with mythical, prototypical properties. The man-made magic of the paper flower is a metaphor for the larger miracle of creation by God the Father. It is also a metaphor for the immortality of the poem, created by the artist and recreated by the reader every time his or her eyes go down the page.

This poem can serve as good practice for aesthetic reading by beginning learners of French. The students can be asked to draw the flower and compare their rendition with the shape of the poem. Two intriguing points of discussion could be:

—The poet speaks of a water basin (*cuvette*), but the poem shows a flower pot. What is the difference?
—The word *émerveillés* (filled with wonder) is located at the juncture between the visible and the invisible parts of the flower in the flower pot. What fills the children with wonder in each of these parts?

In more advanced classes, a brainstorming session might elicit a discussion on what distinguishes magic from miracle, the man-made from the immortal nature of art. As with concrete poetry,

such an iconic poem can nicely serve as a model for students'
attempts at writing their own poems.

Kramsch and Mueller (1991) show yet another way of highlighting the importance of form for the conveyance of meaning.
In a second-semester German class, students in groups of three
had been asked to memorize and prepare a recitation of Heine's
poem 'Die Lorelei' for a video-recorded performance the next day
in class.

### Die Lorelei

Ich weiß nicht was soll es bedeuten,
Daß ich so traurig bin;
Ein Märchen aus alten Zeiten,
Das kommt mir nicht aus dem Sinn.

Die Luft ist kühl und es dunkelt
Und ruhig fließt der Rhein;
Der Gipfel des Berges funkelt
Im Abendsonnenschein.

Die schönste Jungfrau sitzet
Dort oben wunderbar;
Ihr goldnes Geschmeide blitzet,
Sie kämmt ihr goldenes Haar.

Sie kämmt es mit goldenem Kamme
Und singt ein Lied dabei;
Das hat eine wundersame,
Gewaltige Melodei.

Den Schiffer im kleinen Schiffe
Ergreift es mit wildem Weh;
Er schaut nicht die Felsenriffe,
Er schaut nur hinauf in die Höh.

Ich glaube, die Wellen verschlingen
Am Ende Schiffer und Kahn;
Und das hat mit ihrem Singen
Die Lore-Ley getan.

Heinrich Heine (1837)
*Buch der Lieder*

[I do not know the meaning of this / And why I am so sad; /
A legend from old times / Still haunts me.

The air is cool and it is getting dark; / Softly the Rhine flows by. / The mountain peak sparkles / In the evening sun.
The most beautiful maiden sits / Up there wonderful; / Her golden jewels dazzle, / She combs her golden hair.
She combs it with a golden comb / And all the while she sings a song; it has a magical, / Strong melody.
The boatsman in his little boat / Is seized with a wild longing; / He is blind to the reefs, he only sees upward to her.
I believe the waves engulf / Boat and boatsman in the end; / And this, with her poignant singing, / The Loreley has done.]

Students had to decide who would narrate which of the six verses and how each student would stand in space to illustrate the team's interpretation of the poem. In all groups, students chose to stand next to one another facing the audience, in an A-B-C configuration. One group recited the poem as a linear narrative, student A reciting the first two verses, student B the next two, student C the last two (A-A-B-B-C-C), their eyes on the audience, with a melodramatic tone of voice from beginning to end—the popular 'romantic' interpretation.

Another group performed the text in quite a different manner. Student A recited the first verse and, moving to the end of the row, recited also the last verse; student B recited the second verse and switched places to recite also the verse before last; student C recited the two central verses of the poem. The six verses were thus narrated in the following order: A-B-C-C-B-A. The students' intention, as they explained it, was to illustrate the ironic frame in which Heine cast the legend of the *Lorelei* (recited by A), the romantic surroundings and the spell (recited by B), and in the center the two verses dedicated to the *Lorelei* herself (recited by C). A's voice was matter-of-fact ironic, B's tone was romantic, C's verses were read in a mysterious tone of voice that befitted the sorceress. It is worth noting that, while students B and C looked at the audience while they were reciting their parts, student A purposely looked into the camera, adding thereby an interesting extradiegetic dimension to the performance and creating a conscious link between the narrator and the reader/viewer.

## Multiple translations: beyond pluralism

When available, multiple translations of the same text can offer other interesting windows on interpretation in advanced language classes (Miller 1992). Below are reproduced the original and three different English translations of Rilke's poem 'Der Panther':

## Der Panther

*Im Jardin des Plantes, Paris*

Sein Blick ist vom Vorübergehn der Stäbe
so müd geworden, daß er nichts mehr hält.
Ihm ist, als ob es tausend Stäbe gäbe
und hinter tausend Stäben keine Welt.

Der weiche Gang geschmeidig starker Schritte,
der sich im allerkleinsten Kreise dreht,
ist wie ein Tanz von Kraft um eine Mitte,
in der betäubt ein großer Wille steht.

Nur manchmal schiebt der Vorhang der Pupille
sich lautlos auf—. Dann geht ein Bild hinein,
geht durch der Glieder angespannte Stille
—und hört im Herzen auf zu sein.

Rainer Maria Rilke
*Neue Gedichte* [1903] 1955

## The Panther

*Jardin des Plantes, Paris*

His gaze, going past those bars, has got so misted
with tiredness, it can take in nothing more.
He feels as though a thousand bars existed,
and no more world beyond them than before.

Those supply powerful paddings, turning there
in tiniest of circles, well might be
the dance of forces round a centre where
some mighty will stands paralyticly.

Just now and then the pupils' noiseless shutter
is lifted.—Then an image will indart,
down through the limbs' intensive stillness flutter,
and end its being in the heart.

(Tr. J.B. Leishman, 1960)

## The Panther

*In the Jardin des Plantes, Paris*

From seeing the bars, his seeing is so exhausted
that it no longer holds anything anymore.
To him the world is bars, a hundred thousand
bars, and behind the bars, nothing.

The lithe swinging of that rhythmical easy stride
which circles down to the tiniest hub
is like a dance of energy around a point
in which a great will stands stunned and numb.

Only at times the curtains of the pupil rise
without a sound . . . then a shape enters,
slips through the tightened silence of the shoulders,
reaches the heart, and dies.

(Tr. Robert Bly, 1981)

## The Panther

*In the Jardin des Plantes, Paris*

His vision, from the constantly passing bars,
has grown so weary that it cannot hold
anything else. It seems to him there are
a thousand bars; and behind the bars, no world.

As he paces in cramped circles, over and over,
the movement of his powerful soft strides
is like a ritual dance around a center
in which a mighty will stands paralyzed.

Only at times, the curtain of the pupils
lifts, quietly—. An image enters in,
rushes down through the tensed, arrested muscles,
plunges into the heart and is gone.

(Tr. Stephen Mitchell, 1982)

The various translations illustrate the difficulty of capturing
in another language the two central metaphors of the poem.
The first metaphor is that of seeing and being seen, as the
panther in the Paris zoo both sees the world and is seen by

the poet—metaphor expressed by the terms *Blick* (translated here as seeing, vision, gaze), and *Bild* (translated as image, shape). Considering that the term *Bild* in German has also the meaning of 'metaphor', it is used by Rilke to refer both to what the panther sees in the outside world and what the poet sees in the panther. In the second verse, as the movements of the panther pacing up and down in its cage become more and more concentrated into the center of its body and what Ross calls 'the still point' of the poem (1982a, 1982b), any reference to the outside world slowly becomes irrelevant, any *Bild* of outside reality 'ceases to be', as the panther becomes its own living metaphor in and through the poem. In the last line, the poem folds into itself at a still point that is both absence of noise and absence of movement. The German word *Stille* indicates both.[3]

The second metaphor is that of motion and stillness expressed by the terms *der Gang* (translated as padding, lithe swinging, pacing), *die Schritte* (translated as paces, stride, movement) and *Stille* (translated as silence, arrested). By comparing the three English translations of the last three lines

> an image will indart . . . and end its being in the heart
> (Leishman 1960)

> a shape enters . . . reaches the heart, and dies (Bly 1981)

> an image enters in . . . plunges into the heart and is gone
> (Mitchell 1982),

one can appreciate how the various translators have been more sensitive either to the content space or to the rhetorical space of the poem. Translations that use verbs of motion such as 'reaches the heart' or 'plunges into the heart' remain within the poem's story-line; they correspond to a view of bondage as lack of physical freedom; verbs like 'dies' or 'is gone' indicate the result of an action, process, or motion. We find this interpretation also in other translations of the last three lines, that express either a travelling motion:

> . . . an image enters then,
> To travel through the tautened body's utter
> Stillness—and in the heart to end.

> (Tr. Walter Arndt, *The Best of Rilke*, University Press of New England, 1989)

or an action of 'extinguishing' or 'vanishing':

> . . . Then an image enters,
> goes through the taut stillness of the limbs,
> and is extinguished in the heart.
>
> (Tr. Edward Snow, *New Poems*. Rainer Marie Rilke, North Point Press, 1984)

> . . . Then an image enters in
> Which seeps through the tremulous stillness of the limbs
> To reach the heart, where it expires.
>
> (Tr. Kate Flores, in A. Flores ed., *An Anthology of German Poetry from Hölderlin to Rilke in English translation*. Gloucester, Mass.: Peter Smith, 1965)

By contrast, the German phrase *hört im Herzen auf zu sein*, like the English 'end its being in the heart', or 'and in the heart ceases to exist' attempts to describe a change of state without a motion. Other English translators have tried to capture this stillness metaphor as well:

> . . . then one image fills
> and glides through the quiet tension of the limbs
> into the heart and ceases and is still.
>
> (Tr. C. F. MacIntyre, *Selected Poems*. Rainer Maria Rilke. Berkeley: University of California Press, 1940)

> Lets in an image as it slides apart,
> Which passes through the limbs held still and tense,
> And ceases within the heart.
>
> (Tr. H. G. Widdowson in *The Role of Translation in Foreign Language Teaching*, Paris: Didier–Erudition, 1992)

This is also what Rilke's Russian translator Bisk (1919) attempted to capture through the Russian phrase *i v serdce, daleko, zamret* [freezes far away in the heart], and Japanese translators try to express through such phrases as *Shinzoo-ni hait-te sono sonzai-o yameru* [enters into the heart and ends its existence] (Shouno 1967: 99), and *kokoro-no naka-de kie-te yuku* [goes into a (state of) vanishing inside the heart] (Fujikawa 1967: 104). These translations seek to express precisely the slow attainment of a still point, where the reader of the text, the observer of the panther and the panther as

both observer and observed become one. This fusion into one
indicates a translation from the story world to the realm of
discourse, as the poem becomes it own reference point in the
heart of the panther and in the heart of the reader.

Comparing the text of a poem across translations is indeed,
as Miller (1992: 124) suggests, witnessing each time the 'double
production of texts':

> Translation produces two texts. As translators move from
> word to word and from sentence to sentence through the text
> they produce bit by bit replicas of the original in a different
> language. At the same time . . . an original text is also pro-
> duced. A different translation produces a different original,
> by emphasizing different faultlines in the original.

Each translation actualizes in a different manner the meaning
potential of the original. In this respect, we can consider the
re-writing of a text by students in the classroom, be it in the
form of a summary, a title, or a role-play (see p.88), as the
creation of a text and the recreation of the original. Every
student production emphasizes different faultlines in the original text.

The reason I chose this poem to examine in detail what
can be gained by comparing different translations, is that
Rilke's 'Der Panther' is a favorite poem of American students
of German at the intermediate level. They usually empathize
with the animal in bondage. Identifying with its longing for
freedom, they interpret the last verse as representing the inner
death of the panther and feel reinforced in their own quest
for physical and psychological emancipation. Rather than
rejecting this interpretation, it should be used as a springboard
for opening new ways of looking at this 'death'. Students can
be asked to write down the one or two words they find most
striking, moving, or interesting in that poem. Their response
is likely to reflect personal emotional concerns that are of
great importance to them and that have to be respected.
However, the point is not to collect a plurality of interpretations that are all equally legitimate because they are all related
to legitimate personal experiences, but to show how each of
these meanings at the level of the story can be transcended
by an aesthetic meaning at the level of the poem's discourse.
Physical emancipation and aesthetic freedom are of two different logical types. To discover the emancipatory power of

poetry, personal responses have to be tied back to the wording of the text and its multifaceted manifestations across translations.

## Alternative literary forms

Besides exploring different levels of the same text and different languages' ways of expressing the same event, intermediate and advanced learners can profit from recasting the same event into different literary forms (Widdowson 1992a; see also Maley 1987: 108). For example, at a seminar for language teachers, Robert Frost's well-known poem 'Dust of Snow' was compared with the haiku on a similar theme by the Japanese poet Basho (Matsuo Basho [1693] 1972: 212).

| Dust of snow (1923) | Haiku (1693) |
|---|---|
| The way a crow | higoro nikuki |
| Shook down on me | (usually hateful) |
| The dust of snow | karasu mo yuki no |
| From a hemlock tree | (crow too snow of) |
| | ashita kana |
| Has given my heart | (morn . . .) |
| A change of mood | |
| And saved some part | [For a/the usually hateful |
| Of a day I had rued. | crow, a/the morn of snow, too ...] |

Besides the structural differences (a haiku consists of three lines of five, seven, and five syllables respectively), three main differences emerged: while in the Frost poem, the poet is at the center of the event, in the haiku it is the event itself; in the Japanese poem, that event is told in a static manner that contrasts with the dynamic narrative of the Frost poem; the Japanese haiku, moreover, has none of the cause and effect relationship that we find between the first and the second verse of the American poem.

The teachers were then asked to recast the American form into a Japanese haiku form. Below are the creations by language teachers from the United States, France, and Japan (Hiraga 1989).

### United States

A   A crow a dust of snow
a change of heart
dawns a new day.

B   The way a crow shook
Dust of snow upon my heart
To show me the way . . .

C   Crow in hemlock tree;
Snow gives me new meaning to day;
No longer mournful.

D   The crow's wings flutter
And snow—cool, white, new—powders
My black existence.

### France

E   Black crow laughing
Snow dust falling
In sorrow—peace.

### Japan

F   a crow—the dust of snow
down in light
from a tree to a heart.

In general, these remakes were faithful to the theme (all mentioned crow and snow), but had varying difficulties in replicating the static nature, the ambiguity, and the lack of logical sequence of the Japanese poem.

## Creating poetry

Many imaginative suggestions have been made to encourage students to write poetry in the foreign language—for example:

Lach-Newinsky and Seletzky (1986); Maley and Duff (1989); Graham (1991) for ESL; van Eunen (1987) for German; Ozzello (1978) for French; among many others. Many received their first inspiration from Koch's suggestions for teaching poetry to children (Koch 1970, 1983). Teachers often feel intimidated by students' productions: their authors are likely to refer to personal experiences which are dear to them, thus making error correction a particularly sensitive matter for the teacher. A good idea is to have students read their poems to one another, and have each listener write down one or two things he or she particularly liked about the poem, and one or two things he or she would have said differently. Listeners can also suggest a title for the poem according to their interpretation of what the poem is about.

Writing poetry in the language class is meant to give learners an opportunity to test the limits of available meanings within their restricted linguistic resources. It enables them to verbalize a familiar experience in unfamiliar words and thereby change the memory and the meaning of that experience. It is not intended to test their knowledge of literary forms and traditions. However, we should not underestimate the pleasure students can derive from experimenting with literary form, nor should we feel bashful, even in language classes, about discussing the craft behind the students' products.

Attention to discourse allows precisely teacher and students to capitalize on the distance between the student as narrative voice and the student as social individual. This dissociation is healthy; it is the beginning of an aesthetic and critical attitude towards language that is essential for personal and intellectual growth. It is an apprenticeship in the development of Bahktin's 'second voice' in double-voiced discourse (see Chapter 1), in which the writer consciously stands outside language in order to express particular meanings:

> To express oneself means to make oneself an object for another and for oneself ('the actualizing of consciousness') ... But it is also possible to reflect our attitude toward ourselves as objects. In this case, our own discourse becomes an object and acquires a second—its own—voice ... Any truly creative voice can only be the *second* voice in the discourse.
> (Bahktin 1986: 110)

## Post-teaching activities

The lesson comes to an end, but the work of the teacher has only begun. By reflecting on the lesson, by replaying its script so to speak, the teacher can make sense of what went on: discover individual patterns of learning, notice points that would have been worthwhile exploiting, make connections to previous lessons, spot areas of misunderstanding, formulate more precise ways of framing questions, link the remarks of one student to those of another.

If, as I suggested in Chapter 2, the language teacher is to be an ethnographer of his or her own classroom, then keeping a logbook is the *sine qua non* of good language teaching. This logbook should contain a detailed description of activities that went well, of activities that failed, a short analysis of why they turned out the way they did, and recommendations to oneself for the future. Cultural misunderstandings are particularly valuable to note and to ponder, as we shall see in the next chapters. The following is a sample entry from this author's logbook at the intermediate level of German language instruction.

From a teacher's logbook. Protocol of a fourth-semester German class (17 students). Day three of Hermann Hesse's *Demian*.

One of the key ideas in *Demian* is that sin is necessary for growth. Yesterday, I started raising the crucial question of Sinclair's 'guilt' but the students could not get away from the events narrated and kept repeating: *Er hat falsch geschworen* (he committed perjury). Today I will try and work from what they give me and raise the discussion out of the moralistic and into the mythological. I have already written down for myself possible answers to the question: 'What is exactly Sinclair's fault?' They include: he lied, he disobeyed his parents, he stole money, he abused the trust of his parents, he feels superior to his father, he has the courage to explore the other world. I can document these with specific passages in the text. I expect that some students will give me superficial sins, others, I hope, will think of some deeper ones.

The student in charge that day has written five items of vocabulary on the board before the beginning of class. I ask who has done the reading for the day: only four hands go up. So I tell them we are going to do it all together: while Joseph summarizes the plot in front of the class, two students who have read the text and I are each going to take notes on the board, the others will do so in their notebooks. In my notes of Joseph's summary, I try to use the vocabulary that is on the other side of the blackboard. Actually the student in charge recycles the vocabulary nicely, using the very sentences he has chosen as examples, so it makes my task easier. Whenever I don't understand something Joseph says, or I have a comment or question, I make myself a little asterisk in the margin or a question mark as I go along. Sometimes I hesitate between two wordings: so I put both versions and a question mark afterwards. At one point, I feel that the student has skipped some important event in the story, so I leave a blank and continue writing.

When Joseph has finished, the two notetakers and I read aloud our 'texts' on the blackboard, engaging the class in filling whatever information gaps there are. We discuss the choice of words that best reflect what goes on in the story. When in doubt, we immediately turn to Hesse's text.

I then ask the class if they know the Cain and Abel story from the Bible. Only three hands out of seventeen go up. I ask them what they know; it is like pulling teeth. I shouldn't have asked the question. So I proceed right away to the next step: I read them the story in the German Bible. As I read, I interpolate comments: Isn't it utterly unjust that God should ask Cain why he was so disgruntled, since it is said in the previous sentence that (without any reason) God had snubbed his offerings! I try, as Hesse does, to make Cain look like a hero. I explain the difference between *Zeichen* and *Auszeichnung* and that Cain's sign was both a sign and a distinction. It makes him into somebody special. Now I say: 'That brings us back to our question of yesterday: Sinclair, too, had committed something bad. But Demian doesn't seem to think that it is that bad. So: what does his sin consist of?' Each student is to write down one possible interpretation on a piece of paper. I give the class one minute. Students then go to the board and write down their statements. I number the statements for ease of reference and correct the more blatant grammatical mistakes:

1 Sinclair hat sich von Kromer in die zweite Welt bringen lassen
2 er hat dem Teufel die Hand gegeben

3 er hat falsch geschworen
4 er hat sich seinem Vater überlegen gefühlt
5 er meint, er könne dem Kromer nicht widerstehen
6 er hat sich nicht selbst von Kromers Herrschaft befreit
7 er wurde von Kromer erpresst
8 er hat die zweite Welt kennengelernt und hat sie gern gehabt
9 er hat die Versuchung kennengelernt und hat nachgegeben
10 er ist schwach gewesen
11 er hat versucht, ein anderer zu sein, als der, der er war.
    etc. . . .

[1. Sinclair has let Kromer introduce him to the second world; 2. he has reached out for the devil; 3. he has committed perjury; 4. he felt superior to his father; 5. he felt he couldn't resist Kromer; 6. he has not been able to free himself from Kromer's dominance; 7. he was blackmailed by Kromer; 8. he explored the second world and has come to like it; 9. he has learned what temptation is and has yielded to it; 10. he was weak; 11. he has tried to become another than the one he was, etc.]

I read aloud each of these 'failures', check number 1 to see if the student has another verb than 'introduced' to put in: 'verführen?'(seduce?). The student suggests the more neutral 'führen'(lead). I ask each student to comment on his or her statement. The sentences are a good starting point for clarifications, returns to the text for examples and alternative formulations. I then ask the students which failure they would rank first. When every student in the class has a number in mind, I go around the class and tabulate the answers. It turns out that 14 out of 17 students favor number 8. I remark that all the interpretations given emphasize either Sinclair's failures (weakness, dependency, etc.) or, on the contrary, his courage and boldness (attempt to break out, etc.) and that the majority of students in the class seem to favor the second aspect of his 'sin' by giving priority to number eight.

I then ask students to go back to the beginning of the first chapter and find support for their interpretation in the way the narrator presents the two worlds. How is the orderliness of the first world expressed in words? Some students stifle a yawn. I jump on the opportunity to ask students why they feel the first world is so boring. How does the paragraph show that in its structure? Students start getting interested in the detective game: one finds that all the sentences are so well balanced—a and b, c and d, e and f—that they put the reader to sleep; another finds that the number of difficult abstract nouns or principles like 'duty, rigor, model, good-heartedness' make that world difficult to understand. By contrast, the words used to depict the second world are concrete and easy to grasp: a 2-mark coin, a golden watch, a penknife.

I am glad I had time to show them how the text structure confirmed their intuition. The class seemed excited at the discovery. I will give them as an essay option tomorrow to write the story of Adam and Eve from Demian's point of view, as Hesse did with the Cain and Abel story.

## Conclusion

In the last two chapters, we have expanded the notion of context defined initially as a 'sphere of intersubjectivity' between two or several people in face-to-face interaction, to include a 'sphere of intertextuality' that encompasses texts and their readers. In our exploration of the pedagogy of literary texts, we encountered the same problems of expression, interpretation, and negotiation of meaning as in oral communication, but here, the processes through which texts are produced and received could be explored with greater leisure.

For the written word slows down the process of communication. It fosters reflection and a critical stance vis-à-vis one's own and the foreign meanings. Students have more time to make the distinction between the conventional voice of the foreign speech community and the particular voice of the author. Through aesthetic reading, they have the opportunity to dissociate their response as a member of their speech community and their response as an individual with a unique life experience. By constructing with the literary text a reality  different from that of texts of information, students are given access to a world of attitudes and values, collective imaginings and historical frames of reference that constitute the memory of a people or speech community. Thus literature and culture are inseparable. As we shall see in the next two chapters, literature has shaped the self-and other-perceptions of a people as much as have the events and experiences that gave birth to this literature.

However, in the same manner as it would not do justice to literary texts to read them only as mirrors of a given social and cultural context, so would it be reductionist to view culture as constituted only of the particular narrative voices of literary texts. As we turn now to the teaching of the larger cultural context of language, we will add to literary texts the full range of what have been traditionally called 'culturally authentic texts'.

## Notes

1 Other sources of activities for the teaching of prose and poetry are to be found in Boschma *et al.* (1987), Grellet (1987), Heid (1985), Hunfeld (1990), Kast (1984, 1985), Kramsch (1987b, 1987d), Krusche (1985), Krusche and Krechel (1984), *ELT Journal* Vol. 44/3 (1990), among many others.
2 'Übernimm nicht die fremde Meinung ungeprüft . . . Du hast nicht genug Achtung vor der Schrift und veränderst die Geschichte . . . Du mußt nicht zuviel auf Meinungen achten . . . Man muß nicht alles für wahr halten, man muß es nur für notwendig halten.' (p.264)
3 Inspiring reading, in this respect, are Ross' analyses of poems as 'holograms' (Ross 1982a,b,c) and Domin's *doppelinterpretationen* or interpretations of the same poem by the author and a critic (Domin 1966).

# 6 Authentic texts and contexts

Je te parle dans ta langue et c'est dans mon langage que
je te comprends.[1]
(Edouard Glissant 1981)

We have been concerned up to now with the ways in which
speakers and readers give meaning to utterances by shaping the
context in which these utterances are produced and received. We
have gone from the premise that meaning is not in the written or
spoken text, but in the dialogue between the learner and the
text. In both cases, social and personal voices intersect to create
what Nostrand (1989: 51) calls 'the central code' of a culture:

> The central code consists not only of customs and proprieties;
> it involves above all the culture's 'ground of meaning': its
> system of major values, habitual patterns of thought, and cer-
> tain prevalent assumptions about human nature and society
> which the foreigner should be prepared to encounter.

It is a truism to say that teaching language *is* teaching culture,
but what exactly does it mean? How can learners in the artificial
and standardized environment of a classroom have access to the
central code of another culture? The foreigner, says Nostrand,
should be prepared to *encounter* the culture's ground of meaning; but does he or she necessarily have to *understand* it? And
is it at all feasible anyway? As we attempt in this chapter to
explore these issues, I suggest taking as a point of departure the
current controversy surrounding the concept of 'cultural authenticity' because it captures much of the paradox of teaching language in classrooms.

The term 'authentic' has been used as a reaction against the
prefabricated artificial language of textbooks and instructional
dialogues; it refers to the way language is used in non-pedagogic,
natural communication. As Little and Singleton (1988: 21) point
out, 'an authentic text is a text that was created to fulfill some
social purpose in the language community in which it was produced'. In their written form, everyday texts of information

require readers to adopt the communicative reading strategies of native speakers: skim and scan for desired information, capitalize on the natural redundancy of a text and get clues from its context, recognize authorial intention and act upon it—for example, stop at a stop sign or bake a cake according to a recipe. As spoken exchanges, authentic texts require participants to respond with behaviors that are socially appropriate to the setting, the status of the interlocutors, the purpose, key, genre, and instrumentalities of the exchange, and the norms of interaction agreed upon by native speakers (see Chapter 2).

However, with the increased necessity to develop not only communicative, but also cultural competence in language teaching, the need has grown to reassess the notion of authentic text and communicative authenticity. The discussion, started in Europe during the last decades (Coste 1970, Widdowson 1979, Löschmann and Löschmann 1984, Breen 1985a) has only recently surfaced in the United States (Kramsch 1988b, Nostrand 1989). It raises some of the basic issues with which we will deal in this and the following chapter.

## What is cultural authenticity?

At least since Widdowson examined the concept of authentic text in 1979, it has become a commonplace to say that authenticity does not lie in the text but in the uses speakers and readers make of it.

> It is probably better to consider authenticity not as a quality residing in instances of language but as a quality which is bestowed upon them, created by the response of the receiver. Authenticity in this view is a function of the interaction between the reader/hearer and the text which incorporates the intentions of the writer/speaker ... Authenticity has to do with appropriate response.
> (Widdowson 1979: 166)

For example, a German menu is a genuine piece of cultural realia, but if I use it in the classroom to practice reading prices or to learn the endings of adjectives, I have not used it in the way the restaurant management had intended, nor the way native customers do when they go to that restaurant. As Widdowson comments: 'Authenticity depends on a congruence of the language producer's intentions and language receiver's interpretation, this congruence being effected through a shared knowledge of conventions' (ibid.). The teacher's task is precisely to give the learner the means of properly authenticating a text like a German menu.

Such a definition, however, raises a number of questions. Learners can be aware of the communicative conventions of German restaurants and still be interested in the differing way numbers are written in German and English, and in the way German adjectives are declined; even in a genuine restaurant, they can ask the waiter for explanations about the menu that no native speaker would ask. In other words, they can know the conventions and either simulate native-speaker behavior, or choose not to abide by native-speaker conventions and, instead, act as the learners and foreigners that they really are. Both types of behaviors are authentic, but the question is: authentic for whom?

In the enthusiasm for functional approaches to language teaching (whether they be called 'communicative', 'natural', or 'proficiency-oriented'), 'authentic' speech is often presented and read in language classes in the same uncritical way as such language is used by most native speakers—as if the classroom could ever be, or even should ever try to imitate, the natural environment of restaurants and workplaces. This applies also, as we have seen in Chapter 3, to the speech used by learners in classrooms. Either, as we saw in case 3, the students' conversational style is allowed to remain the one of their native culture, or, as in case 4, the teacher insists that they adopt a behavioral style more congruent with the conventions of the target society. In both cases, the language is used in an authentic manner, but we have to ask ourselves: authentic of what? As Widdowson perceptively remarks, 'Uncritical acceptance of the need to present learners with "authentic" data can lead to an avoidance of pedagogic responsibility' (ibid.: 171). What exactly *is* our pedagogic responsibility?

Let us examine what the issues are. If authenticity is a relational concept—that is, a characteristic of the context in all its dimensions (see Chapter 2), then we need to reassess the common usage of the term. According to the *Oxford English Dictionary* (1989 2nd edn.), the term 'authentic' has at least four meanings:

1 in accordance with a socially established usage or tradition (= from a duly authorized source);

2 entitled to acceptance or belief, as being in accordance with fact (= real, trustworthy);

3 the result of a recognizable communicative intention (= sincere, not specious);

4 compatible with an identifiable, undisputed source or origin (= original, genuine).

This cluster of dictionary meanings, that considers established conventions, facts, intentions, and sources to be undisputed and socially agreed upon, has to be flagged for social and cultural differentiation in four respects.

### Representative usages

Firstly, how do we determine which socially established usages or traditions are representative of the native speaker's speech community? If, as I suggested in Chapter 2, the notion of a generic native speaker must be put in question both from a linguistic and a pragmatic perspective, then to what extent should we continue to teach generic contexts of use? To what extent should language teaching retain as its sole point of reference the national characteristics of certain communities of native speakers?

The question of cultural authenticity was raised for example in an interesting manner by two German foreign language educators from the (then existing) German Democratic Republic (GDR). Commenting on the misrepresentation of their country in an American textbook,[2] they write:

A report by a journalist [f.] from the Federal Republic [FRG] on a trip through the GDR cannot be considered an authentic text for the GDR, even though it is written by a native speaker of German. Not only is the point of view of the observer [m.] different, but also the quantity and quality of his [sic] cultural knowledge and in many respects his [sic] use of the language are different from those of a journalist [m.] from the GDR. However, such a text can be quite authentic of the perspective of FRG journalists [m.pl.] on the GDR. This example shows that authenticity is always socially determined; it always means 'authentic of . . .'.

(Löschmann and Löschmann 1984: 41, my translation)[3]

[The notations [f.] and [m.] indicate the gender chosen by

the authors for the respective words in the German text, a potentially significant cultural fact in itself.]

This statement stresses the importance of readers'/writers' perspectives in the debate about authenticity. Too many textbook publishers believe that there is a universally 'German' link between the German language and any German speech community, and that any speaker of German is automatically representative of any given German society. As Saville-Troike (1992) points out, the link between a given language and the communities that speak that language can vary a great deal. Let us note that the fact that West-Germans might consider the language of the article itself sexist and therefore culturally different from an article written in the West, is yet another illustration of the serious cultural problem identified by the authors of the article.

## Cultural competence

Secondly, does cultural competence include the obligation to behave in accordance with the social conventions of a given speech community? Should we, as Santoni insists, 'ask students to try as hard as they can to be someone else, to plagiarize as well as they can all sorts of linguistic and behavioral patterns from observed "authentic materials" (even to the point of caricature) [because it] is the best way to feel and understand the culture' (cited in Nostrand 1989: 52)? Or should we not rather, as Nostrand (1989) and Valdman (1992) strongly recommend, separate knowledge about the culture and experience of the culture—cultural competence and cultural performance? The ability to 'behave like someone else' is no guarantee that one will be more easily accepted by the group who speaks the language, nor that mutual understanding will emerge. A tragic illustration is provided by the many Asian or Hispanic immigrants or native Americans in the United States, whose sociolinguistic skills may help, but in no way guarantee, their social integration.

## Critical understanding

Thirdly, should it really be our goal to develop in our students the same uncritical insider's experience of the target culture as those who are instrumental in forging it in a given society?

Should we not give our students the tools for a critical understanding of the target culture and its social conventions? As already discussed in Chapter 2, is it not the privilege of the language learner to understand and poach on the target culture without automatically contributing to its construction?[4] The ability of the learner to behave both as an insider and an outsider to the speech community whose language he or she is learning, depends on his or her understanding of the cultural situation.

## Authentic language *learning*

Ultimately, such critical understanding is an educational issue. As Breen (1985a: 62) suggests, 'the learner will re-define any text against his own priorities, precisely because he is a *learner*', and in this respect the learner is not any different from any other language user. The fourth question is therefore: should we not, as teachers, be concerned less about '[authentic] language-using behavior' and more about 'authentic language *learning* behavior'? Breen (ibid.: 65) argues the point forcefully:

> Perhaps one of the main authentic activities within a language classroom is communication about how best to learn to communicate. Perhaps the most authentic language learning tasks are those which require the learner to undertake communication *and* metacommunication.

I fully share Breen's conviction, but I am also aware of how this view of learning stems from an educational culture and intellectual tradition that have strong roots in the European enlightenment. This tradition might not be shared by teachers from other educational systems, such as, for example, most foreign language teachers in the United States who value action and communication *rather than* metacommunication (see, for example, Omaggio 1986). Breen's view is again different from the German hermeneutic tradition in language education, currently advocated by Hunfeld (1990). This tradition stresses not so much the benefits of critical analysis in language learning as the difficult process of putting the other in relation with self. Hunfeld writes:

> What does the foreign language *mean* for the foreign language learner? Many things. For example, the obligation to adapt,

to repeat the conventionally sanctioned phrases, to play a role, to identify [with members of another group]. But it also means being able to compare one's own world of language with that of others, to broaden one's experience with language and language use, to insert some uncertainty into ways of speaking one had hitherto taken for granted; it means border crossing, blockade, disturbance—in sum, to use Humboldt's words, it means 'acquiring a new way of viewing the world.'
(Hunfeld 1990: 15, my translation)

These three intellectual traditions, the critical, the pragmatic, and the hermeneutic, are not incompatible—for example, self-discovery can be furthered by metacommunication and hands-on experience—but it is up to the teacher to set the ordering of educational priorities.

Cultural relativity stops at the threshold of the teacher's classroom. Not because the educational culture of the language class reflects by necessity the dominant culture of the institution, but because teachers could not teach if they did not make pedagogical choices. Indeed, I would argue that the seeming lack of educational vision among some language teachers is a sign not of eclectic choices but of the uncritical acceptance of the dominant educational culture of their society.

Breen concludes: 'Perhaps all other questions of authenticity in language teaching may be resolved if the potential of the classroom [as a classroom] is fully exploited' (1985a: 68). Is educational authenticity then just another word for pedagogic effectiveness? After all, do not these various educational cultures have that much in common that they all seek to contrive the most effective conditions for learning a foreign language? Do they not all want language learners to be able to:

1 communicate appropriately with native speakers of the language;
2 get to understand others;
3 get to understand themselves in the process?

As with most matters cultural, it is a question of emphasis. A pragmatically-oriented educational culture stresses the first goal and measures the effectiveness of language learning against the ability of learners to participate in socially appropriate verbal exchanges with others. A critical pedagogy stresses the second goal and searches for evidence of effective language learning in the insights gained by the learners about foreign attitudes and mindsets. A hermeneutic approach weighs effectiveness in terms of the learners' discovery and understanding of self through others. In the way the hermeneutic approach defines itself, one can already see the difference in emphasis it establishes between it and, for example, what it calls the 'pragmatic-communicative' approach:

> The [hermeneutic] approach ... carries the hermeneutic skepsis into the foreign language learning process. It insists that the opportunities for understanding are always also liabilities of non-understanding ... The principle of this approach is neither to adopt nor to reject the thinking of others, but to relate it to one's own.
> (Hunfeld 1990: 15, my translation)

In this sense, all pedagogy is an artifact of educational discourse. Widdowson (1990: 46) has written recently: 'The difficulty with [Breen's] conclusion is that one can claim authenticity for anything that goes on in the classroom, including mechanistic pattern practice and the recital of verb paradigms, on the grounds that it may be conducive to learning'.

Mechanistic pattern practice, however, is not bad or ineffective *per se*, but only as measured against the communicative or cognitive goals of an educational culture that uses such metaphors as 'meaningful communication', 'negotiation of meaning', and 'creative uses of language' to express its vision of human relationships. We have to commit ourselves to a set of metaphors, but we have to remain aware that these metaphors are the very culture we live by and that in other educational cultures people might live by other metaphors. The difficulty—and the perils of cross-cultural understanding— stem precisely from trying to express one metaphor in the language of another and to judge the pedagogic effectiveness of one in terms of the other.

I will therefore leave aside questions of 'authenticity' and 'effectiveness' and try instead to describe the educational metaphors that underpin different educational traditions in their use of non-pedagogic texts for the teaching of foreign languages. I will first examine the communicative proficiency approach prevalent in the teaching of English as a second language and of foreign languages in the United States.

## The communicative proficiency approach

### Focus on talking and doing

Communicative approaches to language teaching, whether they be of the functional-notional type of the seventies or of the proficiency orientation of the eighties, expose learners as much as possible to spoken or written texts that have not been fabricated for pedagogic purposes. It is hoped that, by making communication more authentic, learners will be able to better *understand* the speaking customs and ways of life of the target country, and thus behave more appropriately in native-speaker environments. Such an approach is inspired by much of the pedagogy developed for teaching ESL to immigrants in English-speaking countries. I will therefore take as an example the use of non-pedagogic texts to teach American culture.

### Reading the media in the ESL class

One of the more attractive recent publications for teaching ESL reading in the United States is *TIME — We the People. Authentic Readings for Students of English* by Linda Schinke-Llano (1989). This reader offers real-life *TIME* magazine articles collected under different rubrics. The format and layout of the articles reproduce those of the genuine magazine. Background notes precede the readings. Students are encouraged to put their understanding into action through comprehension/discussion questions and communicative activities. As an example, Article Four, entitled 'Trapped behind the wheel' under the rubric 'Lifestyles', is reproduced in Appendix II.

The linguistic and cultural apparatus given to the readers is meant to help them understand what the text says and what actual facts it refers to. The post-reading questions and activities encourage them to relate this factual information to other factual information from their own country and culture. These facts are authentic in the sense of 'trustworthy', since the cultural world of bald eagles, car pools, rush hours, and Egg McMuffin™ has reality and credibility, and since learners of English in the United States find this reality confirmed as soon as they step out of the classroom.

However, because the textbook gives no explanations relating to the social meaning of these facts for native speakers in the United States, foreign readers are forced to be readers they

cannot be. Many American readers of *TIME* magazine themselves may not be consciously aware of the political leanings of
the magazine and the social and political origins of the facts
described. But they are sure to recognize explicitly, because they
have *lived* in the country for a while, the cultural connotations
related to the automobile, the appeal to cleverness to cope with
problems, the threat of the American dream turning into an
American nightmare. Foreign readers, on the other hand, unfamiliar with the codes of either the American dream or American
journalistic prose, cannot possibly authenticate this piece without help.

How are they to understand the very title: 'Trapped behind
the wheel' if they do not understand its cultural connotations?
In a society that values efficiency and 'living in the fast
lane', where the automobile is the very symbol of American
'get-up-and-go' freedom and individualism, traffic congestion
and the obligation to live in the slow lane are more than just
traffic problems. They put in jeopardy the very fabric of
the American way of life. Hence the strong and purposeful
contradiction in terms implied in the title and in the caption
'Going nowhere on the Long Island Expressway'. Hence the
appeal, by the American writer to her American readership,
to the American way of dealing with social and political
problems through individual inventiveness and creativity. In a
culturally specific way, the article sets traffic problems on the
personal plane, as a challenge to individual ingenuity and
'adaptive behavior', as a way of learning how to 'accept that
you are where you are, and there is nothing that you can do
about it' except change your attitude.

American readers can identify with this appeal. Foreign
readers may not. For example, they might not understand why
public transportation is not better developed around large urban
areas, why the government does not better curb the power of
the automobile industry, why people live so far from their workplace. And they might not understand why the writer takes such
an apolitical stance towards what they perceive to be a societal,
not a personal problem. An authentic reading of the text by
foreign readers would need explicit clarification of all these
points. However, such a critical stance itself goes against the
grain of the culture as it is 'lived' by the average American citizen. Indeed, it goes against the grain of a whole educational
culture.

As I have shown elsewhere (Kramsch 1991), the teaching of foreign and second languages in the US bears the mark of American educational history. Whereas in most other industrialized countries, the primary aims of education have traditionally been general intellectual discipline and development of the mind, predicated on the idea that the acquisition of a body of knowledge, of a mind culture or intellectual training, are good both for higher education and for life, American education since the First World War has had different priorities. Schools are to prepare students for the duties of life, educate citizens for their responsibilities in the community, and increase their chances of employment. Public education, and within it the teaching of foreign languages, has been traditionally based on utility, democracy, and scientific measures of progress.

Whether it be English as a Second Language or foreign languages taught in the schools, language education is seen primarily as a means of socially integrating foreign immigrants into US society on the one hand, and integrating the US into the world's 'global economy' on the other. It is not seen as a tool for critical thought, for citizens' enlightenment, or aesthetic education. Most learners of English as a Second Language in the US are less interested in gaining a critical understanding of American society than in gaining as quick an access as possible to the technological and economic benefits they have come to the country to seek. The current push to learn foreign languages in schools also stems from economic concerns and from the desire that the US regain its lost competitiveness on world markets. It represents a push to link education more closely with business and industry.

It is in this light that we have to understand some of the statements made in the US about the teaching of culture in foreign language classes. Despite recent voices in favor of a relational pedagogy that takes into account various perspectives on self and other (e.g. Byrnes 1991, Swaffar 1992), most teachers see culture as a fifth skill on the ACTFL proficiency scale (American Council 1986). They view cultural competence as a knowledge of foreign facts and a general acceptance of the foreign culture. Cultural acceptance is a matter of ethics and democratic attitude; cultural knowledge can be administered in appropriately paced building blocks. For example, Richardson and Scinicariello (1989: 52) write about the use of television material in language classes:

> Novices, as defined by the ACTFL proficiency Guidelines, have a particularly hard time understanding authentic language. They need very short (1–2 minutes) action-oriented segments in which there is visual support of the meaning . . . The subject matter should be limited to everyday needs and vocabulary . . . Intermediate students are not yet ready for abstraction, so the best choices remain action-oriented segments about everyday events and programs about topics of personal interest, e.g. sports and music.

Such a statement shows that educators are quite aware that the difficulty of real-life materials is not only a linguistic one, but a matter of discourse style and choice of topics. 'Abstract' topics such as ethnic minorities, the environment, women's rights are less interesting for American students than are personal stories and life-styles. But what if the average foreign viewer is interested in precisely those topics? Should not that be reason enough to select them?

Nostrand (1989: 51) remarked recently that a coherent *understanding* of another culture includes 'the central code of (that) culture plus an awareness of its socioeconomic and regional variation'. What if sports and music are not part of the central cultural code of those viewers whom French television constructs or intends to cater to, but rather, vocabulary and arithmetic contests, like in *Des chiffres et des lettres?* (Mouchon and Vanoye 1982) or even 'abstract' political debates and literary discussions like in Bernard Pivot's *Apostrophes* (Gschwind-Holtzer 1986, Abastado 1982b)?

The issue that is raised by the use of real-life materials is that culture is a reality that is social, political, and ideological and that the difficulty of understanding cultural codes stems from the difficulty of viewing the world from another perspective, not of grasping another lexical or grammatical code. Richardson and Scinicariello (ibid.) realize this as they admit: '[by watching foreign television,] students will certainly be exposed to political ideas different from those that dominate American society . . . It is to be expected that students, parents, and even other members of the community will question its value'. However, basing themselves on a study that shows that 'understanding of program content depends . . . on the pleasure the viewer experiences from watching the program and the degree to which the viewer's own opinions match those expressed', Richardson and

Scinicariello (ibid.: 63) recommend: 'The television materials used for comprehension activities in the classroom should be entertaining and challenging, but the intellectual content cannot be radically different from the students' view of life'.

In the face of the double meaning of the term 'challenging' (see Chapter 1), I would like to argue that our main responsibility in the teaching of real-life materials should be not only to entertain and challenge—i.e. test—the students' individual ability to learn the language, but also to challenge—i.e. put in question—their traditional intellectual style. This latter challenge has been picked up by another educational tradition to which I will now turn. It is the French tradition in teaching French as a Second Language, which takes a discourse analysis approach to media materials.

## The discourse analysis approach

### Focus on saying

French linguists and language educators (e.g. Abastado, Beacco, Compte, Zarate, and others), stress what Claude Hagège (1985: 204) calls *l'ordre des mots* by contrast with *l'ordre du monde*. They make it clear that what French television shows is not how the French live, but how French television chooses to portray them living. In their teacher training seminars, they initiate teachers of French as a Second Language not only to the cinematic discourse of television, but also to its social discourse or 'bardic function' within French society (Fiske and Hartley 1978).

### Demystifying television discourse

Abastado (1982a: 11) demystifies the discourse of television as having the following three main characteristics:

1 Television discourse is assertive, rarely tentative or hypothetical. Even when it presents dissent, television is not self-critical like, say, a postmodern work of literature would be. It presents itself as one with the fabric of life itself. French television viewers, like Americans, understand analogies of details that make sense as a whole across other societal events in which they live. For example, a literary debate like Bernard Pivot's *Apostrophes* on Antenne 2

asserted itself within a network of cultural phenomena that include eighteenth century *salons littéraires*, baccalaureat literature essay topics published in *Le Figaro* and discussed by large segments of the population, and the high social status of literature professors (Abastado 1982b). In other countries like Germany, literature is in fact still the major legitimation of TV itself in educated bourgeois circles, hence the large number of literature-related broadcasts on German TV (Geisler, personal communication). Such topics are presented as so natural and obvious that native viewers are very often not in the best position to deconstruct or demystify them.

2 Television discourse is redundant, both across the various programs and broadcasts and with the rest of society. Its message is repeated in newspapers, on posters, over the radio; images are reinforced by captions. This redundancy increases the sense of total immersion and the authentic-slice-of-life feeling.

3 Television discourse is hyperbolic, sensational, commercial. In France, it is characterized by typical mannerisms such as the stress on first syllables that goes against normal prosody:

La PLUS grande salle de concert de France pour une Assemblée GÉnérale des ACtionnaires . . . Le TORtion-naire NAzi REfuse d'être CONfronté Avec ses victimes.

[the BIGgest concert hall in France for a GEneral Assembly of TRUSTees . . . the NAzi TORturer REfuses to be CONfronted WITH his victims]

and the use of clichés:

Ouragan sur la Bretagne: six morts, des dizaines de blessés, tel est le bilan de ce caprice de la nature . . . Les terroristes tombent dans les filets de la police lyonnaise . . . Lundi noir à la bourse New Yorkaise: une page se tourne brutalement— une dure leçon.

[Hurricane in Brittany: six dead, tens of wounded, such is the death toll of this whim of nature; terrorists fall into the nets of Lyon's police; black monday at the New York stock exchange: a page is brutally turned—a hard lesson.]

What we see, is not the *culture directe* of France itself, but France's *culture médiatique*.

## Reading cultural codes: 'mosaïque des culturèmes français'

French foreign language educators realize that 'the teaching of culture has been limited by the acquisition of a foreign cultural content, an informative and factual type of knowledge that the learner must accumulate with precision and accuracy' (Zarate 1983: 34, my translation). They further uncover, beyond the conventions of television discourse, the tenets of French cultural ideology: *culturèmes français* (Abastado 1982a) or *savoirs sociaux* (Beacco 1984), that underlie the seemingly disparate topics and events. They show that the choice of information and topics covered is related to societal parameters: problems that French society has to face, its hopes and fears, its memory of past humiliations and past prides.

For example, Mouchon and Vanoye (1982) analyze the discourse and the cultural symbolism of the all time favorite game *Des chiffres et des lettres* watched by millions of viewers every week on Antenne 2, despite its incredibly slow and cerebrally demanding style. They suggest that the game is so successful because it evokes in the cultural imagination of French viewers early childhood memories of compulsory elementary school literacy classes and a certain acculturation into French society through its public school system—what Mouchon and Vanoye call 'les charmes discrets du certificat d'études' [the discrete charms of the certificate of primary education]. They conclude:

> In essence, the success of *Des chiffres et des lettres* is directly in line with the French school tradition, taken at its source, where a knowledge of words and the possession of as large and varied a vocabulary as possible as well as the ability to perform rapid mental computation was a guarantee for obtaining the basic diploma: the certificate of primary education. Little wonder then if certain of the most classic elements of schooling reappear here. The school ritual is respected in its various manifestations. The 'master of numbers and the master of letters' behave just like in school, praising and chiding and evaluating the difficulty of the test . . . The modalities of learning are fixed in a clearly established ritual. The master is expected to commit himself totally to his pedagogic mission and to efface himself as much as possible as an individual made of emotions and sensitivity; the rare moments where he

breaks that mold are limited by the time and by a certain conventional behavior.
(ibid.: 53, my translation)[5]

This analysis reveals, in a seemingly anodine TV show—selected, by the way, for screening by American students at the intermediate proficiency level to teach them words and numbers—the power of nostalgia and the conservative values at work in French society. It would be interesting to compare this analysis with an analysis of the American equivalent *Double Jeopardy*, that also challenges the candidates' literacy skills, but where the premium is put on quick thinking, quick output, and quick monetary gains.

## Reading filmic codes

Discourse analysis of filmic material needs to be familiar with the tools of the medium. Like the author of a written text, the film-maker has three main choices when using 'the sign and syntax of film language' (Monaco 1977: 119):

1  what to shoot;
2  how to shoot it;
3  how to present the shot, well aware that any shot will carry both denotative and connotative meanings.

The first two decisions relate to the *mise-en-scène*, the third requires montage or editing of the sequence of shots.

### *The* mise-en-scène *or composition*

Decisions have to be made on five counts:

*Shot.* The shot is the filmic equivalent of the word in written texts. Events can be shot in close-up, mid-shot (from the waist up or head-and-shoulder shot), or long-shot. Typically, a close-up of a person gives more importance to the person herself, a long-shot of that person reduces her individual importance and places her in her surrounding context.

*Frame.* A frame can be open or closed, according to whether there is any movement of persons leaving and entering the frame. A closed frame can give the viewer a sense of tighter film-maker's control. Significant features of frames are also: proportion of persons relative to objects and to other persons, proximity or persons and objects to one another, choice of colors and shapes.

*Focus*. The relative importance given to foreground and background is also carrier of meaning. The more depth there is — that is, the more equal importance is given to foreground and background — the more choice the viewer has to direct his or her attention to various features in the frame.

*Angle*. High-angle, eye-level, low-angle are some of the options of the film-maker. The choice of a low-angle shot generally has the effect of aggrandizing the person in the frame.

*Sound*. In addition to speech, decisions have to be made as to what musical score to use and what noise to include. The source of this sound, whether on- or off-screen, has to be identified.

## Montage or shot sequences

The two major decisions to make when assembling shots and sequence of shots to tell the story are:

*Order of narration*. Will it be linear chronological, or make use of flashbacks, flashforwards, etc.?

*Transitions from one sequence to another*. Types of cut: plain cut, jump cut, dissolve, fade in/fade out. Frequency of cuts.

Let us take an example. One of the broadcasts from Antenne 2 selected for export, depicts the gathering of truffles in the Périgord. This three-minute documentary opens and closes with long shots of Périgord landscapes. At the beginning, long-shot sequence of misty hills and vales, cut to a typical stone farmhouse in the regional style, farmers passing by the house, opening bars of *Gone with the Wind*. The connotation is: 'retour à la terre' with a touch of nostalgia. Out of the landscape emerges the voice of a young woman, with a distinct high Parisian accent:

> Le décor? Bien sûr, le Périgord. Les acteurs? Les hommes. Mais ils ne peuvent pas la trouver sans les animaux. Il y en a trois: d'abord le cochon.

> [The setting? Of course, Périgord. The actors? Men. But they cannot find it without the animals. There are three of them: first the pig.]

Follow a series of mid-shots and close-ups of several farmers with their respective truffle hunters. An older man in his seventies, wearing a beret and leading his pig on a string, explains how he makes his pig find truffles and prevents it from eating them; a younger man, Pierre, in his twenties, shows how he uses his dog Sultan to dig up the truffles; two men in their forties or fifties claim that the fly is the best. All four men speak with an unmistakably southern French accent, in sharp contrast to the Parisian French of the woman reporter, who appears only once on screen, but whose voice is heard as a running commentary to the whole narration. Only once, as the grandfather turns to someone off screen and emits a surprised 'Eh beh . . .' [well] does she echo his expression of surprise, and imitates the local accent and intonation in her commentary: 'Eh beh, c'est aussi s(e)mple que ça!' [well, it is as simple as that]. The effect on the viewer is ambiguous: it is not clear whether the woman is making fun of the Southern French accent or of those who use it, or whether she admires it. A fifth man in his twenties enters the scene, he too in a head-and-shoulder shot in front of an oak tree, to explain, also with southern accent, how the truffle is a fungus that grows on the roots of oak trees. The voice of the woman picks up on his explanations while the camera pans trees and bushes. Then as the musical theme of *Gone with the Wind* reappears, the female voice recites the following closing statement: 'Le champignon, la terre, l'arbre, l'homme, l'animal, le soleil—c'est la plus belle histoire d'amour' [the mushroom, the earth, the tree, the man, the animal, the sun—it is the most beautiful love story]. The final shot is a long-shot of Pierre and his dog walking away in the distance along the furrows of his well-ploughed field.

The way this *histoire d'amour* is told reinforces all the codes of French cultural self-perception to which French television viewers cannot but be sensitive. This is not just a documentary feature on truffles in the Périgord. It is a hymn to the traditional values of *le terroir français*, to the sensuous attachment of the French to French soil and French history. The roles are distributed according to this manifest destiny of France: five male characters rooted in their soil like the oak tree; the voice of modern woman woven around three generations of men, like the truffle that interweaves its filaments onto the roots of the tree. The symbolism is clear: the only time the young woman appears on screen, wearing a fashionable leather jacket, she is kneeling and holding a truffle in her hand; this is also the first time the trufffle is actually shown on the screen. Other details reinforce the sexual connotations of the truffle story: the flirtatious comment made by another female voice off screen as the young farmer smells the earth around the truffle ('Oh ce Pierre, il se délecte!' [Ah this Pierre; he is savoring it]); the sexual vocabulary used to describe the symbiotic process known as mycorrhiza ('l'union du chêne et de la truffe' [the union of the oak tree and the truffle]); the combination of male and female agents in French: (man, pig, dog, and oak tree of the masculine gender—fly, earth, truffle, and the female voice of the feminine gender). The rephrasing of these agents in the closing statement into the more generic terms: 'le champignon, la terre, l'arbre, l'homme, l'animal, le soleil' [the mushroom, the earth, the tree, man, the animal, the sun], reinforces the natural, organic order of things and gives it mythical dimensions beyond time and space.

This style of presentation is familiar to television viewers born and raised in France. It reinforces their feeling of permanence and rootedness in French soil; it confirms their belief in the superiority of natural, biological processes like food and sex over such ephemeral goods as money and success. The fact that the musical soundtrack is taken from an American classic could be seen as ironical in this context. It shows, if anything, that the appeal to traditional values and to the love for one's home country is universal, whether we are dealing with the French or the American South.

A discourse analysis approach to teaching this documentary goes beyond giving the learners the dictionary meaning of *truffe*, *mouche*, *chêne*, and *mycorrhize*, and even cultural notes such as the fact that truffles are expensive (3500F/kilo), that they are used for sauces and pâtés and that they were believed to have aphrodisiac properties. It attempts to expose the cultural and filmic codes of the text in order to understand better how the media both reflect and create the way the French view themselves and the world.

Such an approach responds in part to Breen's plea for a critical pedagogy of culture. It extracts from the documentary the important factual information; it attempts to understand the intentions behind the words of the characters; it makes explicit the social and historical tradition which accounts for the French style of presentation of the facts. However, it does not take into account the fact that this documentary is now screened by a non-native viewer, who is not familiar with the world perspective dramatized by this documentary. Although more complete than the proficiency approach, discourse analysis is not sufficient to develop cross-cultural competence because it too focuses only on the transmission of cultural information or meta-information, not on its negotiation by the learner.

In addition, it tends to focus on national characteristics and thus reinforces the quaint myth of 'le Français moyen', normative, typical of all French speakers. 'By the sheer fact of having been selected by the author of the textbook, by the teacher, by the media, the testimonies presented are given official legitimacy, they confer a representative character to whoever claims to speak for the group' (Zarate 1983: 34, 39, my translation).

How can we create the conditions under which learners can themselves put cultural events in relation with one another, find their hidden patterns, interpret their links, and have enough diversity of perspectives available to avoid stereotypical generalizations? Recent developments in video and computer technology attempt precisely to help students achieve on their own the relational learning necessary to make sense of real-life materials. Besides offering hitherto undreamed-of possibilities, these technologies raise a host of epistemological questions that should be of interest to language teachers and researchers, whether they actually use the technology or not. I will therefore turn to these in the remaining portion of this chapter.

## The challenge of multimedia

### Thinking and solving cultural problems with language

The development of multimedia, a combination of video and computers, is likely to revolutionize the way we use real-life materials including television broadcasts for pedagogic purposes (Compte and Coste 1983, Underwood 1988, Rogers 1988, Lyman 1988). This technology is based on the principle of 'hypertext'. As Jim Noblitt points out, the concept of hypertext was coined in the mid-sixties by Theodor Nelson to refer to texts which are non-sequential in form.

> Just as there are many parallel associations in human consciousness, there are many interconnections between texts and ideas within a text. The computer is seen as offering a way to make a record of links between associated items and to permit

the user to move about in a multi-dimensional space of related material (the fundamental characteristic of a relational database).
(Noblitt 1989: 56)

Multimedia or hypermedia uses not only written texts, but material in various media, including text, sound, and visual material as its relational database.

Multimedia technology affords the learner the following ways of learning a language from real-life material.[6] Students are given multiple points of access to the same material and multiple potential paths through the material. For example, a conversation with a French person can be viewed at normal speed, as a native speaker would; it can be run with French subtitles or with English subtitles, or with an English summary; it can be interrupted at any point, and with a click of the mouse on a particular word or phrase, the appropriate help can be made to appear in a sidewindow (relevant dictionary entry or grammatical reference, translation, drawing, photograph, or film); it can be instantly matched with other material illustrating analogous features of speech (e.g. all occasions in which French characters greet or take leave from one another, shrug their shoulders or use the expression *bon*); it can be played at natural speed or in slow motion. Students can explore the material at their own level of proficiency, understanding, and interest.

Through a system of windows on the computer screen and the user's control of speed, direction, tracks, and scripts, learners can get as much lexical, grammatical, and informational help they need; they can browse, explore, trackback on the material, make observations and make decisions on their own, and in general interact with the program by asking the computer for information (via a keyboard) and reacting to that information. The program is, in computer parlance, learner- or 'query-driven'. Through immediate and random access to any part of the videodisc, learners can restructure, reorganize, and edit the material as they wish; different learners can explore different aspects of the same material and compare notes. In short, multimedia is a powerful blend of computers, video, photography and sound, that has been rightly called 'a new kind of imaginary playground for the mind' (Rogers 1988: 44).

How does multimedia operate for the teaching of culture? It can do so in two forms: interactive narratives or interactive documentaries. Multimedia can offer explorations in a narrative mode. The most well-known example is the interactive videodisc narrative that has been developed at the Massachusetts Institute of Technology in the framework of the Athena Language Learning Project (Murray *et al.* 1989, Furstenberg 1988). *A la rencontre de Philippe*, filmed in France with French actors by French filmmakers, starts when a young Parisian named Antoine turns to the camera and invites the students to go with him to a café where they are to meet Philippe. As they arrive, the student witnesses a fight between Philippe and his girlfriend Elisabeth. Elisabeth is visibly angry. She suddenly gets up and storms out of the café shouting 'J'en ai marre des parasites!' [I am sick and tired of parasites!]. In the following conversation between Antoine and Philippe, we learn that Philippe has been living for three months in Elisabeth's flat, that their relationship is in shambles, and that she has asked him to leave. Antoine, as a good friend, gives Philippe some advice on how to find a flat in Paris. After Antoine leaves, Philippe sits there looking rather gloomy, when he suddenly turns to the camera and asks the student to help him. This is the beginning of the involvement of the student who will help Philippe find a flat and a job in Paris and get reconciled with Elisabeth.

By clicking on one or the other of the possible responses to Philippe's questions on the French menu—'Will you help me?', 'Do you want to look into the job ads or the housing ads?', 'Were there any messages for me on the answering machine?', 'Who called?', 'Do *you* know where the check is?', 'How did you like the flat?', 'What should I do?'—the student can influence the course of events that are stored on different tracks on the disc. He or she can type in and receive messages 'on the telephone', ask for a re-run of portions of the film, for a transcript, for subtitles. Then, while Philippe goes to a job interview, the student can call up on the screen various documents: a plan of Paris, of specific districts, of newspaper ads that she circles; she can click on a specific quartier and the camera leads the student to the local grocery store, bakery, or real estate agency for inquiries; she can click again on a specific street and the camera goes and visits specific flats, leads her up the stairs and into the different rooms. No decision by the student is wrong, it only leads down a different path to a different ending.

Multimedia can also operate in the interactive documentary mode. Suppose you are a student assigned to learn about Brittany. Instead of plowing through dense newspaper articles packed with unknown words and facts, or even viewing television broadcasts spoken at top speed and taken out of their sociocultural context, you are about to take a video adventure. You sit in front of two video monitors, a computer and a new multimedia program. On one screen, an animated film introduces Monsieur Dupont, who invites you into his office in a small town in Brittany. Meanwhile, on the other screen, a color film shows Brittany farmers dumping truck loads of artichokes on the roads. On the first screen, Monsieur Dupont, the préfet, confides that the farmers are discontent and he needs you to help find the reason. The evidence is in his notebooks and cabinets, on the screen in front of you.

Using the computer's mouse to move the on-screen image of a tiny hand, you 'open' a file cabinet, take out a folder marked 'Interviews'. Suddenly, the other screen fills with the image of a real farmer, talking about the prices of artichokes, the eating habits of the French, and complaining about the central government. The file cabinet turns out to contain a dozen similar interviews with immigrant day laborers, retailers, grocers, housewives, trade-unionist, folk singers—along with animated maps and articles about regionalism, stereotypical pictures of 'La Bretagne' and 'Les Bretons', and the history of those stereotypes (Bertho 1980). You also have access to endless vocabulary dictionaries, transcriptions, subtitles, and so on. Using the mouse, you browse through the films, text, and photographs, letting your curiosity lead the way. As Meinhof aptly remarks: 'The events in the C2's public life are not presented as given facts to be learned but as conflicting discourses' (1990: 608, my translation). Based on these various discourses, students fashion a theory of what regionalist claims are about. This simulates real life: there is no single right answer, they have to interpret the facts. But what the computer does is activate the process of students' relational thinking.

The advances in multimedia technology have brought about a revolution in the transmission of knowledge that has been compared with the Gutenberg invention of the printing press.

Through the exploration of microworlds, they afford a type of learning that replicates non-pedagogical ways of acquiring knowledge that are radically different from traditional textbook learning.

## New ways of learning

The computer offers an exploratory, learner-driven type of learning that differs from traditional schooling in five important ways. This learning is:

*Non-linear.* Students are usually schooled to acquire knowledge in a linear fashion, structured by chapters in books, days on the syllabus, items to be tested, and curricular requirements to be checked off. By contrast, real-life materials provide a world of knowledge that is non-sequentially organized and that invites relational thinking and hierarchical structuring of the phenomena observed.

*Context-bound.* What textbooks tell you to learn are rules and items of grammar or vocabulary that are right or wrong. But what learners really have to learn is how to put this knowledge to use in varying situational contexts for varying purposes, for the benefit of varying interlocutors or readers. Real-life materials impose right away a global domain of cultural knowledge that has to be learned across different contexts.

*Recursive.* Students have been schooled into a building-block, bottom-up mentality of learning, that promises a whole body of knowledge from the sum of its itemized parts. Discrete-point mastery of these parts is supposed to ensure understanding of the material. But real-life materials have not been made according to building-block principles of learning: they invite the learner to reinterpret, reorganize, and reconstruct prior knowledge in light of the new, to recognize the traces of prior texts and events as they appear in new contexts, endowed with a new value.

*Constructivist.* Schools have tended to imbue written texts with ultimate authority and to promise academic success to those learners who can 'unlock' their meaning with dictionaries, grammars, and others reference books. Students do not generally view themselves as 'constructing' meaning as they read: they believe they 'find' the meaning enclosed in the text. Yet, the meaning of real-life materials, accessible in almost unlimited quantities in the computer, is not encoded only in the lexical and grammatical structures used by the speakers/writers, or in the cinematic language of shots, sequences, and the like. It also lies in the construction of a certain social reality by a society in dialogue with itself. Non-native learners of the language eavesdrop, so to speak, on that dialogue and have to construct or reconstruct its meaning.

*Learner-directed.* Students traditionally leave it up to the teacher and the textbook to tell them what they need to learn. Real-life materials, by contrast, require students to explore various levels of understanding and to be conscious of their own knowledge assets and deficits.

Computer technology, in particular multimedia, offers possibilities of teaching context itself in a way that teachers have always dreamed of. By opening up microworlds to play with, by providing opportunities for autonomous, exploratory learning, for analyzing, synthesizing, interpreting social phenomena, these technologies, born from the spectacular advances made in cognitive science, not only are attractive to use, they also encourage teachers to devise ever more refined procedures for the organization and presentation of knowledge. The question is: what knowledge?

## Discussion

The enormous educational potential of the computer is confronting teachers with their pedagogic responsibilities as never before. Never before have teachers so urgently needed to know what knowledge they want to transmit and for what purpose, to decide what are the more and the less important aspects of that knowledge, and to commit themselves to an educational vision that they believe in. Each of the five features of learning discussed above presents a formidable educational task for the language teacher:

1 The computer encourages learners to make connections between items, to discover patterns, make inferences. However, the teacher must first decide which data can be put in which relation with which other to yield which meaning. This is a matter of judgment and judgment does not emerge from the data. The new multimedia databases will be only as effective and educational as the teacher's understanding of the subject matter.

2 It provides opportunities for varying the contextual frame in which knowledge is organized and presented. But where will the teachers get the necessary interdisciplinary back-

ground to view cultural events and phenomena from a variety of frames, to interpret events from higher-level constructs?

3 It offers paths of exploration that are neither right nor wrong, but just have different logical consequences. How can the teacher find place for that type of learning in an educational culture that promotes quantitative and normative measures of effective learning?

4 It invites the learner to construct meaning using the associative network of the database. But a database made of foreign real-life material is assembled according to selection criteria that are likely to reflect the cultural mindset of the programmer. The subjectivity of the programmer is as unavoidable as that of the textbook author. But where will programmers get their crosscultural understanding from?

5 Finally, but most importantly, the computer enables the learners to direct their own learning, to develop their own interpretation of events, to set their own educational priorities. But how can we prevent the microworlds of the computer from becoming solipsistic playgrounds for the mind?

It has been said that the computer develops a 'secondary orality' among users (Noblitt 1988), via and around electronic channels of communication. It has also been pointed out that the computer is a mere tool or conduit that can, in fact, enhance and enrich contacts between people and help foster the self-in-relation pedagogy I proposed in Chapter 1. However, the culture of the computer is imposing on this pedagogy its own ways of relating, that cannot but influence the way learners perceive themselves and others. The medium is still too new to know exactly in which ways it is affecting our use of language in the creation of meaning, but it has already brought about a revolution with which teachers cannot but concern themselves.

The new computer and video technology, in sum, brutally confronts the teacher with the fundamental paradox of language teaching: how to teach foreign cultural phenomena via an educational culture that is part of the learners' native culture; how to give learners access to as large a context as possible, but at the same time help them constrain that context to make it meaningful; how to use the computer not as an instrument for single-voiced discourse, but as an enrichment for a double-voiced discourse among learners.

Hypermedia leaves intact the problems encountered with the proficiency and the discourse analysis approaches. It does not in itself lead to intercultural understanding. Thus, what has been proposed more recently is a cross-cultural process or 'démarche interculturelle' that builds on the three approaches discussed above, but places them in an interactionist perspective and in a constant tension between native and target culture. This approach clearly distinguishes intercultural discourse from the transmission of cultural information or even from mere cultural awareness. It will be the topic of the next chapter.

## Notes

1 'I speak to you in your tongue, but it is in my language that I understand you.'
2 'Moeller, J. and H. Liedloff. 1979. *Deutsch Heute. Grundstufe*. Boston: Houghton Mifflin, p.398.
3 'Ein Bericht einer Journalistin aus der BRD über eine Reise durch die DDR kann nicht als authentischer Text für die DDR angesehen werden, obwohl er von einem Muttersprachler Deutsch abgefaßt ist. Nicht nur der Standpunkt des Betrachters ist ein anderer, auch Quantität und Qualität seines landeskundlichen Wissens und in mancher Hinsicht auch seine Sprachverwendung sind verschieden von denen eines Journalisten aus der DDR. Authentisch kann ein solcher Text jedoch durchaus sein für die Sicht von BRD-Journalisten aus der DDR. Das Beispiel verdeutlicht, daß Authentizität immer sozial determiniert ist; immer bedeutet es "authentisch für . . .".'
4 'The question is being raised in interesting ways by educators who are conscious of the outsider's bias imposed on the foreign reality as it is presented through textbooks. For example, Keller (1987) questions the one-sided treatment of race in German textbooks of English, that tend to focus the teaching of American culture exclusively around the position of Blacks in US society, thus offering in his view a much too simplistic picture of the complex issue of race in American society. A similar problem is depicted in Fricke (1983) concerning the teaching of French culture in German schools with regard to the period of the German occupation of France between 1940 and 1944. Which view should be presented? The official view of heroic France resisting German occupation, or the much

more ambivalent view as presented in such films as Max Ophüls' *The Sorrow and the Pity*? The problem is particularly sensitive for those German teachers who wish to depart from official interpretations of history.

5  "En somme, le succès des chiffres et des lettres s'inscrit dans le droit fil de la tradition scolaire française, considérée à ses sources, où connaître des mots et avoir du vocabulaire dans les domaines les plus variés possibles et savoir compter vite assurait l'obtention du diplôme de base: le certificat d'études primaires. Rien d'étonnant alors si l'on retrouve certains des éléments les plus classiques de l'école. Le rituel scolaire est respecté dans ses différentes manifestations. Le "maître des chiffres et le maître des lettres" se comportent comme à l'école en donnant des satisfecits ou des blâmes, et en jugeant de la difficulté de l'épreuve . . . Les modalités d'apprentissage sont figées dans un rituel clairement établi . . . Le maître doit se donner tout entier à sa mission sociale et s'effacer le plus possible comme individu fait d'humeur et de sensibilité, les rares moments où il déroge sont contraints par le temps et par un côté "convenu".'

6  For more information on hypermedia technology, see: Patrikis *et al.* 1990; Noblitt 1989; Batke 1991; and Garrett, Noblitt, and Dominguez 1989.

# 7 Teaching language along the cultural faultline

Ein-und ausschlüpfen
in Sprachen, aus Sprachen,
Pendelfahrt zwischen den
Welten.[1]
(Jean Apatride 1982)

Traditional thought in foreign language education has limited the teaching of culture to the transmission of information about the people of the target country, and about their general attitudes and world views. The perspective adopted has been largely that of an objective native culture (C1) or target culture (C2). It has usually ignored the fact that a large part of what we call culture is a social construct, the product of self and other perceptions.

During the last decade or so, a general rethinking of the role of language as social practice has taken place that suggests new ways of looking at the teaching of language and culture. Four lines of thought emerge in particular:

1 *Establishing a 'sphere of interculturality'.* The link between linguistic forms and social structure is not given, it has to be established. Similarly, understanding a foreign culture requires putting that culture in relation with one's own. As we have seen for social interactions as well as for the interaction with written texts, meaning is relational. Thus, for example, an intercultural approach to the teaching of culture is radically different from a transfer of information between cultures. It includes a reflection both on the target and on the native culture. This process is seen as an eminently educational process (e.g. Zarate 1982, Porcher 1986, Kramsch and McConnell-Ginet 1992a).

2 *Teaching culture as an interpersonal process.* If meaning emerges through social interaction, then it is pointless to try and teach fixed, normative phenomena of language use.

Rather we should, as many educators advocate (e.g. Abdallah-Pretceille 1983, Müller-Jacquier 1986), replace the presentation/prescription of cultural facts and behaviors by the teaching of a process that applies itself to understanding foreignness or 'otherness'. As we have seen in Chapter 1 and as the French educator Zarate (1986) advocates, teachers should be encouraged to recognize the rupture points in the logic of the explanations brought forth by their students in order to bring cross-cultural aspects of communication to the fore.

3 *Teaching culture as difference.* With the recent revival of nationalism, and as, at the same time, national identities are being questioned around the world, the temptation is great to view culture only in terms of national traits: the French do this, Germans do that. However, traditional questions like 'what does it mean to be French / to be German?' become increasingly difficult to answer considering the growing multiethnicity and multiculturality of French and German societies. Not that national characteristics are unimportant, but they cannot be adduced without further specification of other cultural factors such as age, gender, regional origin, ethnic background, and social class. National traits are but one of the many aspects of a person's 'culture'.

4 *Crossing disciplinary boundaries.* Many educators (e.g. Debyser 1981, Kramsch 1988a, Byram 1989) link the teaching of culture or (Fr.) *civilisation* to the academically recognized disciplines of anthropology, sociology, and semiology. They encourage language teachers to broaden their readings to include, besides literature, studies by social scientists, ethnographers, and sociolinguists on both their society and the societies that speak the language they are teaching.

These lines of thought lay the ground for a much richer understanding of the teaching of culture than heretofore envisaged by the majority of language teachers. In this and the next chapter, I will examine how language can be taught along those lines. Although I will draw mainly on persons from different national cultures, and will take C1 and C2 to represent one's own and another person's membership in the 'imagined communities of nation-states' (Anderson 1983), the cross-cultural approach I will describe here applies also to the crossing of any boundary between generations, ethnic groups, and social classes.

## Cultural reality and cultural imagination

On the reality of facts and events that constitute a nation's history and culture is superimposed a cultural imagination that is no less real. This cultural imagination or public consciousness has been formed by centuries of literary texts and other artistic productions, as well as by a certain public discourse in the press and other media. American social scientists like Riesman (1950), Marx (1964), Bellah *et al.* (1985) have analyzed the myths about America that populate American public imagination. French sociologists like Bourdieu (1967, 1975, 1980), LeGoff (1978), Lebras and Todd (1981), and Nora (1986) have studied how French national self-perceptions have been formed, how stereotypes about regions have been constructed over the last two centuries through literary texts, travelogues, illustrations, almanacs, jokes, and the media.

The teaching of culture is all the more difficult as myth and reality both contradict and reinforce one another. The Germans like law and order? For the traveller in Germany, that stereotype has proven to be false again and again, and yet most Germans will be convinced that 'Ordnung muß sein' and so will many foreigners insist that Germans are a very disciplined people. The French—individualists? Any trip to Paris will show the visitor how conformist the French can be in dress and fashion. And yet, everyone believes that 'il n'y a pas plus individualiste que le Français'. That myth is tenacious and will explain the perception many French people have of the gregariousness of Americans, whereas Americans might feel that it is they who belong to an individualistic, the French to a collectivist society (Triandis 1989). As in a prism, perceptions and counterperceptions bounce images back and forth often based on the polysemy of language itself (Bredella and Haack 1988). And yet, myths cannot be discarded, for they affect the way learners of a foreign language see others in the mirror of themselves, despite all evidence to the contrary from 'objectively' transmitted facts.

Thus the teacher of culture is faced with a kaleidoscope of at least four different reflections of facts and events, that replicate on a larger scale the hermeneutic configuration we examined in Chapter 2 for interpersonal interactions. Granted that C1 and

C2 are themselves aggregates of a multifaceted reality, representing many different subcultures (generational, occupational, educational, regional, age, race, or gender-related), these reflections can be summarized as shown in Figure 1.

*Figure 1*

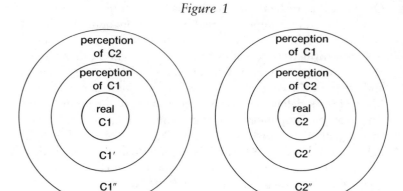

C1′ = C1 perception of self
C1″ = C1 perception of others
C2′ = C2 perception of self
C2″ = C2 perception of others

For example, German learners of American English and immersed in a German C1 carry in their heads an image of the United States that corresponds to the German dream of America, nourished in part by the German literary imagination of the nineteenth century, the novels of Karl May, the role of the American army in Germany since the Second World War, and the new German Cinema (C1″). This German image of America, of which Americans are unaware, has deep roots in the way Germans perceive themselves, their hopes and fears, their dreams and aspirations (C1′). Indeed, it is often an anti-image of themselves. It has only indirectly and partially to do with American reality (C2). For example, as we can see in Wim Wenders' films like *Paris Texas*, *The American Friend*, or *Stroszek*, German film-makers with a social conscience feature the United States as a place of desolation and alienation that most Americans do not recognize as their own. It has certainly little to do with the way Americans dream of themselves (C2′). In another example, Keller (1987) studying auto- and heterostereotypes among

German and American high school students found that while 46 per cent of Americans view 'race-consciousness' as central to their self-image, only 28 per cent of Germans stated 'rassen-bewußt' as part of their image of Americans, despite the heavy emphasis placed by English textbooks in Germany on racial problems in the US. To be sure, the terms 'race-conscious' and 'rassenbewußt' might be semantically equivalent, but they have quite different social connotations in each country.

Conversely, German self-perception can be quite different from the way Americans view German reality (C2″). This American perspective on German C1 is partial and filtered through the Americans' view of themselves (C2′). It is often filled with the romantic view of castles and old traditions that they miss in their own culture.

## An example: open vs. closed doors

For an American visitor to Germany, one of the noticeable facts about German way of life is the fact that many Germans keep their doors closed when they are in a room or office. By contrast, Americans will often leave their doors open (Moeller and Liedloff, 1979 ch. 8). This mere observation is insignificant in itself. However, given that foreigners to a culture will try and make sense out of phenomena they do not readily understand, they will construct the open vs. closed door phenomenon according to their own C1′ and C1″. Mainstream Americans and Germans are likely to construct this cultural event roughly along the lines of Figure 2.

Since Americans interpret their own custom of leaving the door open as a sign of American friendliness, they will be tempted to view closed doors as a 'typical' sign of German discipline or unfriendliness. This perception is not shared by the Germans themselves, who see in closed doors a sign of order and human respect (see Chapter 1). Conversely, given the orderly perception they have of themselves, Germans might view American open doors as a sign of disorderliness and disrespect that they might find distressing. Depending on their own social and cultural background, they may relate this disorderliness to the anti-authoritarian upbringing of American children, to the uncurbed pursuit of private interests in a capitalistic society, and to the alarming lack of governmental regulation in many aspects of American life. How do we get out of this cycle of perceptions and misperceptions?

| cultural event | United States<br>open doors | Germany<br>closed doors |
|---|---|---|
| meaning (value): | friendliness | order |
| constructs:<br>(what does this<br>value mean to an<br>American?<br>to a German?) | friendly vs. don't like you<br>trust you vs. exclude you<br>sociable vs. conceited<br>helpful vs. bossy | order vs. disorganized<br>in control vs. chaotic<br>structured vs. amateur<br>professional vs. not serious |
| range of<br>convenience:<br>(what other<br>examples of this<br>American value?<br>of this German<br>value?) | no hedges<br>glass doors<br>smile<br>informal parties<br>'call me Bill'<br>'dear friend' | hedges and fences<br>full doors<br>handshake<br>role of hostess at parties<br>'Sie,' 'Frau Doktor,' 'Herr X'<br>'Sehr geehrter Herr' |
| superordinate<br>construct:<br>(what do all these<br>examples have in<br>common?) | open to all/public<br>  vs. private | official/professional<br>  vs. private |
| common aspect:<br>(where is the<br>emphasis in both<br>cases?) | person in community | individual in society |

*Figure 2: Personal constructs (Kramsch 1983: 444)*

The only way to start building a more complete and less partial understanding of both C1 and C2 is to develop a third perspective, that would enable learners to take both an insider's and an outsider's view on C1 and C2. It is precisely that third place that cross-cultural education should seek to establish.

The following will sketch a four-step approach to cross-cultural understanding:

1 Reconstruct the context of production and reception of the text within the foreign culture (C2, C2').
2 Construct with the foreign learners their own context of reception, i.e. find an equivalent phenomenon in C1 and construct that C1 phenomenon with its own network of meanings (C1, C1').
3 Examine the way in which C1' and C2' contexts in part determine C1″ and C2″, i.e. the way each culture views the other.
4 Lay the ground for a dialogue that could lead to change.

## C2, C2': reconstructing the C2 context of production and reception

Let us take as an example an American television commercial for Coca-Cola that has been suggested to teach English to Russian learners (Garza 1990). This advertisement was found particularly appropriate for Russian learners of American English because of its rich cultural connotations and its potential differences with the (then) Soviet cultural imagination. I showed it in summer 1991 to fourteen American teachers of Russian in the United States.

The teachers viewed the commercial twice. They were then asked to brainstorm what lexical and cultural facts a Soviet learner of English would need to know in order to understand this commercial. Only after this period of brainstorming were they given the following script:

**American television commercial**

Running time: 1.08'

0.00 Newspaper ad: 'HELP WANTED. Prepare, season and cook Italian food 40 hours, $250 per week, 3 years experience. Must speak English.'

0.07 Early morning sun. Mid-shot of back of youngster looking for a job. In the background a diner. On the roof in big letters: BENDLY DINER. Brown station wagon and red sedan parked in front of diner.

0.11 Red sign with white letters: 'HELP WANTED. Short order cook.'

0.12 Close-up face of youngster, looking down at the sign. Shy but smiling.

0.14 Inside the diner. Mid-shot of cook and waitress arguing over a sandwich. Cook: 'Please, Debbie!' Waitress to cook: 'I don't want it! You try it first!'.

0.16 Cut to boy holding the red sign and saying: 'Excuse me sir'. On-looking customer in the background.

0.17 Close-up of cook. Cook looks up: 'What is it?'

0.18 Cut to boy, pointing to sign (white letters on red background): 'I was just wondering if the job is still available?'

0.19 Close-up of cook's face bringing a can of Coke (white letters on red background) to his lips, eyes turned upward: 'Any experience?'

0.20 (voices off) 'Oh come on Bert!'

0.21 Close-up of boy's face saying to cook: 'Please!' Voices off: 'Give the kid a break. Bert, come on!'

0.24 Close-up of cook's face looking at the Coke can with a sigh of satisfaction.

0.25 Three men at the bar: one white manager (tie), one black (tie), one white truckdriver. Black man holds a large cup of Coke. Voices off: 'Give the guy a chance!'

0.27 Cut to mid-shot of cook and waitress. Cook, looking at the men, throws his arms up in the air in a conciliatory manner. 'OK. All right.'

0.29 Close-up of cook. 'All right, kid.'

0.30 Cut to the 'kid' catching the white apron.

0.32 Cut to the cook saying, with a magnanimous and somewhat ironical tone: 'It's all yours.'

0.33 Mid-shot of boy: 'You won't regret this, sir'. On-looking man in the back.

0.34 Cut to two girls, one of whom is drinking a large cup of Coke.

0.35 'Oh, he's nice!', looks at the boy as she drinks her Coke.

0.36 Cut to four hamburgers frying, a hand covers each one in turn with a bun.

0.37 Cut to sizzling fat on the pan.

0.38 Cut to two hands breaking two eggs and dropping them on the pan.

0.39 Cut to the three men at the bar.

0.40 Faces slowly turn toward the viewer.

0.41 Chorus 'Coke is it!' Mid-shot of cook, arms crossed, looking on. Back of boy at griddle. In the foreground: a ketchup bottle, box of eggs.

0.42 Boy turns around, disposes egg, bacon, parsley on plate.

0.43 Cut to a customer looking up to viewer in disbelief from behind his magazine.

0.44 Cut to boy standing in front of cook. Chorus: 'The taste that stands alone'.

0.46 Cut to two hands cutting four sandwiches in half with amazing efficiency. Chorus: 'What you find when you get where you're going . . .'

0.48 Close-up of cook and waitress facing each other in amazement.

0.49 Mid-shot of boy.

0.50 Cut to flipped pancake in mid-air.

0.51.0 Two, three, four pancakes in mid-air. Chorus: '. . . is the biggest cola taste of all'.

0.51.5 Sixteen faces at the counter and in the diner (4 blacks 12 whites): 'Oh!'

0.52.0 Large plate with two pancakes on it.

0.53.0 Three, four, five pancakes landing on the plate.

0.53.5 Cheers from customers. Sports atmosphere. Applause. Chorus: 'Oh, Coke is it!'

0.56 Close-up of the boy, shy but beaming. Chorus: 'Coke is it!'

0.57 Mid-shot of cook slapping his hands. Behind him, the waitress laughing. Chorus: 'It's the one you grow up with'.

0.58 Cook opens his arms . . .

0.59 and embraces the boy. Chorus: 'Coke!'

1.01 Cook takes off his cap and gives it to the boy.

1.02 Mid-shot of the two 'men' (for the first time in same frame): cook and boy wearing the cook's cap and holding a Coke.

1.04 Cheers from the crowd. Four cups of large Cokes are raised to a toast (held by white men, white women, black men).

1.06 drinks Coke from can facing left (same direction as in 0.19). Cook looks into camera, points to him, laughing.

1.08 Across the screen: COKE IS IT!

What would Russians find particularly difficult to understand in this American ad? The American teachers first decided they would have to explain the following lexical items:

*Diner.* A roadside short order restaurant that has a long counter and usually booths and that is often a remodelled railroad dining car. Serves any meal 24 hours a day. Food is fast and good.

*Help wanted.* In the US jobs are advertised in a special section of the newspaper and through signs in the window bearing these words.

*Short order.* An order for food that can be quickly cooked.

*Coke is it!* The Russian equivalent would have to be 'Coke is everything'.

At this point, the group felt a growing dissatisfaction with pure vocabulary glosses. The 'it' in particular referred to a host of features that were implicit in the TV spot and that would not be covered by linguistic definitions alone. For example, Russians might not understand the reason for the euphemism 'help' instead of 'work'. The passive phrase: 'Help wanted' might be perceived as too impersonal and cold by Russians who were used to signs in shopwindows reading 'You are invited to work here'. The Americans wanted to explain that the use of the impersonal phrase in English had the double connotation of (1) efficiency (what is important is that there is a job to be done, and anyone can do it, provided he or she is efficient enough; (2) human need (work is represented as helping other human beings, and thus becoming part of a community).

## Cultural codes

It is obvious to any American viewer that the commercial is a parody of the twenty seconds American success story, a celebration of American values, with all their traditional codes:

—friendliness, camaraderie, and social bonding;
—the diner as the great equalizer of class and race;
—individual courage and initiative compensating for inexperience of youth;
—opportunity to prove oneself;
—life as a ballgame: the cheers from the crowd of on-lookers sound like the cheers of teams at a football game;
—team spirit: the kid gets the job because of support from the team;
—help of the underdog ('Give the kid a break!');
—the food, advertised as Italian, is in fact all-American: American breakfast (eggs, bacon, and pancakes), sandwiches, hamburgers.

By turning this success story into a parody, Coca-Cola of course presents to the American viewers an image of themselves that they can both identify with and take with a grain of salt ... or a bottle of Coke. Coca-Cola picks up where American reality has become a myth that makes people smile. Note that it is not Coke that gives the youngster the credibility needed to get the job nor the energy to do it well, as would magic potions in other national myths. Coke is only part of the environment: so invisible at first that it is hard to perceive the commercial as a commercial at all and not as a documentary. The importance of Coke grows as the success story grows, due to human entrepreneurship and flair. It interweaves itself so pervasively into the very fabric of the American way of life that the statement 'Coke is it' acquires the meaning 'Coke is the American way of life'.

Both *mise-en-scène* and montage underscore the role of Coca-Cola in this human life story. The visual link between scene 0.18 and 0.19 subtly associates the traditional colors of the can of Coca-Cola and the HELP WANTED sign; the social bonding expressed by the link between the logo 'cook' and the logo 'Coke' of the men at the counter through Coke, the invisible Greek-like chorus commenting and interpreting the events in Coca-Cola language, celebrating both individual autonomy ('The taste that stands alone') and competitiveness ('Is the biggest cola taste of all'), both individual quest ('What you find when you get where you're going') and natural fulfillment ('It's the one you grow up with'). Growth into a life with Coke is presented as an organic growth into manhood, where the son grows into the father's role and takes over: a modern fairy tale. Coke solves the generation conflict like the young boy solved the conflict at the workplace between the cook and the waitress. By identifying itself with youth, Coca-Cola reaches into the very essence of American cultural imagination. It tries to export that imagination together with its product.

Understanding this commercial in its context of production requires taking into account also its political connotations. The cleverness of the ad is precisely that it does not look like an ad at first, that the motto 'Coke is it!' is purposely ambiguous. It coaxes the viewer into accepting a mainstream American myth, by presenting it tongue-in-cheek. A more explicit appeal to the viewer as consumer, more open forms of persuasion would probably defeat Coca-Cola's commercial goals. And that is where a foreign viewer would have to understand the political power of multinational corporations, and contrast the self-perceptions depicted in this ad (C2') with facts of American reality (C2).

Yet it is important for non-Americans to understand that large corporations not only sell products, they also sell myths and group identities.[2] In a country where it is not history that holds the people together, and not only geographical origin, but to a large extent the ideology of the American dream, such stories as this Coca-Cola ad take on an inordinately more complex role than just any other commercial in any other country.

## Generic codes

The commercial as genre is a logo in itself, familiar to American television viewers. A logo is something like the synthesis of an advertising image and a brand-name. The video commercial is characterized by its fragmentation, its speed, that make memory and critical distance impossible. It is full of allusions to animated films and implicit quotes from other commercials ('Give yourself a break today, go to McDonalds'). Different cultural signals intersect with others, thereby acquiring a new value; for example, the classical theme of the fairy-tale quest, the challenges the hero has to overcome, are all themes on which COKE superimposes itself.

Constructing the cultural context of production of this television text would require examining other texts that have a similar meaning in the American imagination. A collage of such texts might include other publicity such as other TV commercials (Nuts n' honey, Coors beer), or magazine ads (Fortune 500, McDonalds), political speeches, and children's books (*The Little Engine that Could*), or even magazine articles such as the one discussed in the previous chapter. The link between all these texts would not be their propositional content, but their social value. They might be contrasted with other American voices, that have a different perception of what C2 is about and try to counter mainstream American myths (alternate C2').

## C1, C1': constructing a context of reception in the learner's native culture

Besides trying to understand the foreign culture on its own terms, learners have to be aware of their own cultural myths and realities that ease or impede their understanding of the foreign imagination.

The commercial was shown therefore to two other groups of teachers. One group was composed of ten recent immigrants from the (then) Soviet Union to the United States who were teaching Russian at various high schools and colleges in the US. The second group consisted of twenty Soviet teachers of English from various Soviet republics, on a short visit to the United States. They too were asked what would be difficult for a native speaker of Russian to understand in this American advertisement.[3]

The immigrants to the United States identified several aspects of the story as being totally incomprehensible for a Russian speaker. First, the cinematic style: the fast pace, the excitement, the narrative gaps or seeming lack of continuity in the narrative, the brashness (why are pancakes swirling in the air?) are all techniques which, for an American, are codes for efficiency, success, and prowess, but for many Russians are merely gratuitous and bewildering acrobatics.

This foreign style of presentation is coupled with a totally foreign view of human relationships. The initial suspicion of the American cook vis-à-vis the lack of experience of the young boy is likely to be interpreted by Russians as the usual antagonism between employer and employee: what the boy is to be admired for is not that he has grown into a man, but that he has got the better of the boss! Siding with the underdog is something foreign to Russians, who would interpret the cheer 'Give the kid a chance!' as an appeal to let the boy enter the boxing ring and show the cook that he can do better than him.

Thirdly, the American 'job' concept is not easy for former Soviet citizens to understand. Anyone applying for work had better be clean-cut and clean-shaven, so many would not understand the middle-class connotations of such an appearance, but even if they did, they would not understand why a middle-class 18- or 19-year-old school or college student would want to work 40 hours a week. Should he not be in school or doing community service? And what is the reward? Flipping hamburgers all day long? Who would want that? Drinking a can of Coke? Strange reward—the cook might have given him at least a whole case of Coke! And then, drinking Coca-Cola is perceived as a waste of money: at that age, proper youngsters do not drink Coke!

However, some aspects of this advertisement are easily accessible to native speakers of Russian. They can identify with the sports atmosphere, the cheering of fans in the diner; rooting for the team is a phenomenon that is close to their heart. They can understand the initial suspicion of the employer vis-à-vis a prospective employee. They can side with the youngster making it despite the distrust of the boss. They are also sensitive to the fairy-tale atmosphere of the story and the magic at work. But then, what does all this have to do with Coca-Cola and the fact that this ad is meant to make you buy the product?

All three groups were then asked to rewrite the ad for Russian viewers. What equivalents in the Russian culture would help sell Coca-Cola in Russia? What should be the Russian equivalent? The American teachers devised the following scenarios:

*Scenario 1*. A tired, exhausted man is going along the street. He is thirsty. It is very hot. He stops and wipes his forehead. Suddenly a car stops in front of him. The car is red. The driver is prosperously clad: white suit and red tie. On the front seat: cans of Coke. 'Hello, Vanya. Haven't seen you for ages! How are you? — Couldn't be worse. I feel terrible. My heart . . . I have a splitting headache. My wife left me and I am thirsty. And to crown it all: the kvas has run out. I've been standing in line for a hour and a half.' — 'Don't worry! Coke is it!'

*Scenario 2*. Empty store. A shipment of Coke is just being delivered. Customer enters the store, buys the lot and waits for cab. Impossible to get a cab in Moscow. The man finally bribes a cabdriver with a can of Coke. He arrives at the birthday party — lots of hugging, kissing. The birthday boy drinks a can of Coke with relish. Coke is it!

*Scenario 3*. Long line in front of the store. What are they selling? — Chicken. The man decides to wait. All of a sudden a can of Coke lands at his feet. The man opens it, brings it to his lips and . . . the line shrinks miraculously, he finds himself at the head of all the others and gets his chicken. Coke did it again!

*Scenario 4*. Two Russian businessmen enter the 'banya' (steam baths) in coats and ties, carrying briefcases. They give the usual bribe at the entrance. Viewers think it is vodka. Cut to the men in towels, talking animatedly about what's in the briefcase (viewers still think it is vodka). They then pull out a can of Coca-Cola and drink it happily, with gusto.

The remakes by the American teachers pick up on the well-known frustrations of everyday life in the former Soviet Union (lack of private cars, difficulty of getting taxicabs, shopping lines, bribes) and show how Coca-Cola can 'miraculously' alleviate these frustrations. In so doing, they capitalize on the ability of Russians to make fun of their daily difficulties and on the properties of Coca-Cola to make things happen, including quenching thirst. These rewrites do not, however, attempt to reach equivalent deep layers of cultural consciousness as does the American ad for American viewers. By selling its miraculous properties as an 'outsider' to the Russian scene, it risks alienating those who do not care to be taken over by Western capitalism.

The ten Soviet teachers of Russian living in the United States, by contrast, suggested the following scenarios. Scenario 5 is from a Russian who emigrated to the United States before 'perestroika', the others from more recent immigrants.

*Scenario 5.* Tired unshaven man along a dusty road. No money. No work. Suddenly, a very attractive restaurant alongside the road, with a large sign on its roof: THE PARTY IS EVERYTHING. In somewhat smaller letters: Drink Coca-Cola. A very small sign in the window: 'Pryglachaia rabotu' [You are invited to work here]. The man enters. Suspicious glance from the boss. Pity and curiosity from the men at the counter. They encourage the man: 'Yes, show him!'. The cook takes the challenge. The man straightens his hair, wipes his dirty hands, puts on the apron and starts preparing lunch orders. Thick blinis slowly pile up on plates. Cheers from the all-white, all-male crowd. The boss recognizes that his employee has superseded him. Respectful handshake from man to man. The cook gives the man a brand-new cap and a large case of Coke. The man proudly drinks a can of Coke, while the motto appears on the screen: *Coca-Cola eto vsë* [Coca-Cola is everything].

*Scenario 6:* Coke is winning over!

Shot 1. A group of relaxed cooperative members in imported sneakers and brand-new T-shirts, puffing at Marlborough cigarettes and sipping Coke on a sunny beach in the Caucasus.

Shot 2. In a traditional Russian village: an elderly peasant couple sitting in front of their untidy cabin drinking Coke.

Shot 3. A woman crane operator up in the air drinking Coke.

Shot 4. Setting up a new joint venture: Shaking hands, making toasts, raising cans with Coke.

Shot 5. Mother soothing her crying baby with Coke poured into a baby bottle.

Shot 6. Smiling Boris Yeltsin with a can of Coke clasped in his hand.

Shot 7.   Launching of an all-union anti-Coke campaign. Official ban on the distribution and drinking of Coca-Cola.

*Scenario 7.* Far away countryside. A shepherd looks with a sad expression on his face at his very thin cows, thinking what to do. Cut to a railroad extending to the horizon. There is no one around for miles. Suddenly the sound of a train approaching but instead of a train we see a real cowboy (American type, nice, good-natured, smiling in typical 'Colorado' dress). The sound we hear is not the train but his spurs. He is carrying a can of Coke. Cut to fat, well-bred cows, carrying necklaces of empty Coke cans around their necks, dancing and listening to the American cowboy playing the balalaika and singing Russian music. Both he and the Russian shepherd sit around the campfire and drink Coke. Cut to the two men embracing and watching the herd walking down a hill toward the sunset. The Russian steppe looks like the American prairie. *Koka Kola eto vsë* Coke embraces both.

In their content and their style of presentation, these three scenarios (numbers 5–7) by Russian teachers living in the United States show a sensitivity to both the American and the Russian cultures. They attempt to show different facets of Russian culture and to tap deep commonalities between the American product and its potential Russian consumers: the class consciousness (implicit in the American, explicit in the first Russian scenario), the railroad, the vast expanse of land, the rural concerns are indeed elements of both the American and the Russian cultural imaginations. Moreover, the Russian teachers chose to write these scenarios using techniques and shots familiar to viewers of Soviet films: the opening shot of scenario 5 is reminiscent of the classics of Soviet cinema; the montage technique used in the two others (6 and 7) echoes prior Soviet films rather than the narrative form more common to American films. These teachers tried to weave Coca-Cola into the fabric of the country's social and historic tradition as the American commercial had done.

The same task was now asked of the second group of Soviet teachers, those who were on a visit to the United States from various parts of the Union, including Russia, the Ukraine, Georgia, Siberia, Uzbekistan, and Lithuania. While those from Moscow were able to generate on the whole quite imaginative

scenarios, a large number of teachers from more distant prov-
inces found the task culturally so implausible, indeed so incomprehensible, that they could not even imagine what such a commercial could be like. Why, they asked, would such an ad be
necessary? If Coca-Cola were available, it would sell automatically. And if not, that would be because there already existed
some perfectly adequate local cold drinks! Indeed, the resistance
of some of the teachers to even speculate on the need for publicity made it clear that the proposed task was forcing them to
adopt a genre that was culturally so foreign that all imagination
froze dead in its tracks.

This interesting failure to recast one society's product into
that of another shows the limits of cross-cultural role-plays, but
it makes the need for metatalk all the more imperative. The
American teachers were hard put to explain why publicity is
necessary, market competition useful, hidden persuaders desirable. They had never even had to ask themselves the question.

The same ad was then presented to several native speakers of
other cultures and their reactions solicited. Germans thought
that the football atmosphere in a restaurant was 'low-class', they
thought the food could not be good if it was cooked so fast;
Japanese found the casual and informal way in which the boy
got the job quite offensive and lacking in protocol; Indians could
not understand why a seemingly well-to-do teenager was looking for a job. What puzzled most non-Americans was the indirect, 'soft-sell' aspect of the ad: what was the point of the film—
finding a job or drinking Coca-Cola? Each of these reactions
was to be understood against the backdrop of their own culture,
in the same manner as the American character of the ad had
been understood by analogy with other phenomena in American
culture.

Constructing a native-speaker and a non-native-speaker context of reception both have to occur simultaneously when
making authentic use of real-life texts. For example, only
through the misunderstanding by the Russians of breathtaking
speed as 'gratuitous theatrical effect' did American teachers of
English have the opportunity to realize that in American culture
efficiency and success are equated with speed and a certain
public display; only because Russians mistook American-style
individualism for class antagonism did Americans feel the need
to reflect on what exactly individualism means in their and
others' ways of life.

## C1″, C2″: in the eyes of others

The scenarios described above are an illustration of the well-known truth that it is through the eyes of others that we get to know ourselves and others. While trying to construct each context on its own terms, the teachers saw the foreign situation in contrast with or in analogy to their own. We have seen how American teachers of Russian recreated in their ads their own experience as visitors trying to get a cab or waiting in line in the streets of Moscow.

To explore further the way in which two more closely related cultures project on to each other the perception of their own, the same task was asked of American teachers of German and German visitors to the United States. It is namely often believed that mainstream American and German cultures are becoming so similar that teaching German culture in the United States presents no problem (however, for different opinions, see, e.g. Kalberg 1987, Kramsch 1987c).

The American teachers of German rewrote the ad according to the degree of Americanization they perceived in German society and their own American underestimation of class consciousness. They imagined victorious German soccer players drinking Coke at the end of the game, German rock 'n' roll bands drinking Coke on stage, and typical young German 'dinks' (American acronym for 'double income no kids') lying on the beach sipping Coke. For Germans, however, the idea that soccer players, who are generally from the working class, would be drinking anything else but beer is absurd; and even rock 'n' roll musicians might be seen as pretty effeminate drinking Coke when they could drink beer. The Americans designed their German ads for the same audience they would in their own country: young fans of sports and concert bands. However, in Germany, most soccer fans and fans of rock 'n' roll belong to a social class that draws its self-esteem from drinking beer, not wine or Coca-Cola.

The German visitors, by contrast, designed their ad for a middle-class viewer interested in ecological matters and belonging to the Greens political party. They situated their ad in the middle of green pastures and natural forests, named their product 'ökokola', and sold it in recycled cans for the benefit of environmental protection.

Such a kaleidoscope of C1 and C2 perspectives should be consciously assembled and critically examined. Contrary to current practice that fosters exchanges of ideas and teaching techniques either between all foreign language teachers in a given country (e.g. teachers of French, German, or Russian in the United States), or between teachers of French as a foreign language in England and in France, or teachers of German as a foreign language in the United States and in Germany, more contacts should be sought that are purposely contrastive—say, between teachers of German in English-speaking countries and teachers of English in German-speaking countries. For example, American Studies teachers in Germany should collaborate with German Studies teachers in the United States in the writing of textbooks and the design of cultural materials. Difficult aspects of both societies—such as class, status, ethnicity, private vs. public spheres, power and control, authority and anti-authoritarianism, social rights and opportunities—could profit from being apprehended from different perspectives and through different systems of thought.

This dual perspective on each other's society would bring to the fore the conceptual framework used by either educational system to make sense of the other's social construction of reality. It would also provide a conceptual framework for a critical assessment of both systems of thought on a higher level than the mere experiential illustrated in the Coca-Cola scenarios. Given the difficulty, experienced by some teachers, of changing frames of reference, one of the primary tasks in the development of cross-cultural competence should be not so much to fill one frame with different contents, but, rather, to make explicit the boundaries of the frame and try out a different one.[4]

An interesting question, however, is whether the C1–C2 duality described up to now is a sufficient guarantee of a truly critical insider's and outsider's look at both realities, given the layer of self-perception on which the outsider's look is based. The C1–C2 polarity could very well prevent one from having the necessary distance to one's own and to the other culture because of the C1′ and C2′ mirror effects. Hence the suggestion I will make in the following chapter to seek a 'third place' from where to look at both C1 and C2.

## Of bridges and boundaries

The search for points of contact between cultures, that can transform cultural barriers into cultural bridges, has been framed differently by different disciplines over the last thirty years. In the 1960s and 1970s, the most well-known scholars of intercultural communication, for example Hall (1959) Brooks (1975), Nostrand (1974), Seelye ([1974] 1984), searched for a common universal ground of basic physical and emotional needs to make the foreign culture less threatening and more accessible to the language learner. Hall distinguished 'ten primary message systems' that can be applied to any society, Nostrand identified twelve themes of French culture, Brooks formulated a list of individual and institutional key questions to understand French culture (see Hughes 1986 for various models of analysis). More recently, Robinson (1988) also seeks 'cross-cultural understanding' through consensus, and through a series of ethnographic practices to 'modify negative perceptions' and 'facilitate positive impressions' of people from other cultures.

These scholars, inspired by work done in contrastive linguistics, social anthropology, and cross-cultural psychology (see, for example, Lado 1957, Gumperz and Roberts 1978, Triandis 1977), shared a common experience of second language classrooms in which scores of learners had either to be socialized into an existing English-speaking society as rapidly as possible, or to make themselves accepted in a foreign society. In their search for bridges between the mainstream national cultures, they were convinced that the values and behavior patterns that obtain in these societies could and should be taught; they searched for structural ways in which this could most effectively be done.

In the post-structúralist era of the 1980s and 1990s, many scholars are less optimistic about the possibility of finding universal bridges of a structural nature; the notion of national culture itself has become significantly more differentiated than it used to be in the times of easily identifiable, monolithic nation states. Moreover, advances in pragmatics and in sociolinguistics have shown how unreliable our very frames of reference are. In the multiple everyday face-to-face interactions, in the daily dialogues between men and women, in the minute realization of speech acts, language is used to inform, persuade, imply, but also to misinform, deceive, obfuscate, and control peoples' thoughts and actions—that is, to create a cultural context that is both enlightening and confusing. The current contributions to the problem of language and culture by such thinkers as Byram (1989), Fairclough (1989), Tannen (1990), Lakoff (1990), show that we are no longer satisfied with structuralist solutions. Valdes' attempt to 'bridge the cultural gap in language teaching' (1986) is emblematic of the difficulty of reconciling structuralist and post-structuralist approaches in the development of cross-cultural competence. It seems that a dialogic approach can better link language and culture in an exploration of the boundaries created by language itself in the cultural construction of reality.

Before I attempt to sketch the dialogic framework in which cross-cultural understanding might eventually emerge, I will examine in turn three types of bridges that are generally proposed and that, in my view, fall short of their promise.

## Cognitive bridges or the fallacy of structuralism

It has been suggested recently that learners of a foreign language should first learn how to examine critically texts from their C1 and only then be given texts from C2. Byrnes (1991: 212) suggests first examining critically the known reality of C1:

> Under ideal circumstances initial texts could be both L1 and L2 texts dealing with C1 culture, to be followed, in reverse, by L1 and L2 texts treating the same general topic in C2 culture.

In order to 'overcome cultural distance' Swaffar (1992) suggests that students first be exposed to foreign language texts of popular literature, such as harlequin romances and detective fiction—that is, predictable texts that reaffirm particular cultural cliches, such as: 'pretty women get their man', 'hard work pays off', 'breeding tells'. Her reasons are twofold: easy stories and familiar plots give the students an incentive to read; moreover, they can easily recognize the social stereotypes on which these texts are based and thus develop a critical apparatus to perform what Swaffar calls 'a cultural reading' of any other, more sophisticated text in L2. Thus, instead of fixed typologies of isolated cultural facts, students learn to match checklists of cognitive typologies or universal networks of meaning with specific texts, for example:

| Invariant/abstract structures | Variant/specific example |
|---|---|
| enjoyment/pain | what activities constitute pleasure or pain |
| rituals | what behaviours are appropriate |
| governance | who decides what will be done |
| manners/etiquette | appropriate and inappropriate behaviors |
| class structure | what makes a class; who decides |
| dominance/legitimacy | what characteristics put people in charge |
| sustenance/survival needs | what is considered necessary for what class |

Although the contrastive aspect of both Byrnes' and Swaffar's suggestions may be a step in the right direction, as is Swaffar's attempt to find universal patterns of meaning between C1 and C2, one still has to wonder how the learner can proceed from the universal to the particular, from the categories of his or her native culture, which are deemed universal, to the other's categories. What if the categories themselves have to be weighted differently, or even abandoned and others invented? What if other, as yet unknown, meanings have to be attributed to the categories themselves? 'Survival' means different things for an American tourist in Paris, a social outcast in British society, and a Russian worker standing in line to buy food. The pedagogical failure described above with respect to the English teachers from the former Soviet Union, and their inability to rewrite the American Coca-Cola ad in their own culture illustrate well the dilemma.

All attempts to proceed linearly from the universal to the particular encounter the same difficulties as structuralist approaches to language teaching. Cross-cultural communication seems to require both at the same time: the universals can get their proper meaning (or weighting) only from the particular voice of the writer and the particular voice can be listened to and understood only through the universal. What we need is to view the two irreducible perspectives in a dialogic relationship that respects their contradictory nature and hopes for a personal resolution through dialogue.

## Professional bridges or the fallacy of expertise

As nations become more industrialized and multinational corporations increasingly put their mark on cross-cultural transactions, the culture of business and technology, claimed to be universal, is often believed to provide bridges across all other cultures. Experts, it is said, understand each other on the basis of their expertise, even if they do not know each other's language. While it is true that, for example, a certain style of doing business is exported together with the English, particularly the American English, language, it would be wrong to believe that expertise has the same social, intellectual, and emotional value around the world. As we noticed earlier, the proportion of myth and reality, and the source of national myths differ from society to society. For example, it is a fallacy to believe that because Russians now drink Pepsi-Cola, Pepsi *means* the same for them as for Americans. The very meaning of the business culture is rooted in a cultural imagination that is much older than the spread of English as an international language and an international business style.

In a similar vein, Cisterne (cited in Baumgratz-Gangl 1989: 192) shows how technological experts too are dependent on culture-bound perceptions. For example, the term 'engineer' really covers three different professional functions and social statuses in France, Germany, and Great Britain. The French *ingénieur* is a generalist with a broad general education. He or she acquires the [necessary] specialized knowledge on the job, where he occupies a leading position in both business and administration. He or she tends to solve engineering problems with a high degree of mathematical abstraction. The German *Ingenieur* is seen as a highly qualified specialist who has to solve complex scientific problems with the help of modern technologies. German engineers have to abide by the professional ethics established by the Association of German Engineers to ensure technical quality and the fulfillment of such social responsibilities as ecological protection and the improvement of working conditions. The British professional or chartered 'engineers' are technicians, directly engaged in the production process and in finding practical solutions to practical problems. Because of their close ties to the manufacturing process, and the pragmatic bend of their education, British 'engineers', according to Cisterne, have often been denied the social recognition they deserve.

However, the term in Britain covers a wide range of competency levels, as it does in the United States, where engineering schools differ widely in terms of breadth and depth of general education, even though they all share the same pragmatic orientation. Thus, cultural differences in the way engineers solve problems are rooted in different intellectual styles and schools of thought promoted by different educational cultures.

## Ideological bridges or the fallacy of democratic pluralism

In the name of cultural tolerance and democratic pluralism, some educational materials favor the horizontal juxtaposition of cultural facts when transmitting information about cultural diversity. They leave contrast and synthesis up to the learner. As Kramsch (1988b) points out, students usually have little or no systematic knowledge about their membership in a given society and culture, nor do they have enough knowledge about the target culture to be able to interpret and synthesize the cultural phenomena presented. For example, American foreign language textbooks represent an educational culture that has its own agenda, and that is often more concerned about promoting American values of non-discrimination, non-sexism, religious tolerance, and physical health than about giving an authentic representation of the foreign culture. Pluralism is often the middle solution, that only thinly conceals a conservative, ethnocentric pedagogy.

As we have seen in Chapter 2, the reluctance of young teachers to help their students interpret and construct their own social reality in the light of the other often leaves both teacher and students unsatisfied. Such a non-committal attitude undermines the search for and the negotiation of meaning that form the core of a communicative approach. It risks perpetuating the belief that beyond communication what really counts is only one's own way of life and system of thought.

What we should seek in cross-cultural education are less bridges than a deep understanding of the boundaries. We can teach the boundary, we cannot teach the bridge. We can *talk about* and try to *understand* the differences between the values celebrated in the American Coca-Cola commercial and the lack or the existence of analogous values in its Russian or German equivalents. We cannot teach directly how to resolve the conflict between the two.

Systematic training of learners in insiders' and outsiders' views of cultural phenomena should start early on with activities that require learners to adopt different ways of seeing. Beyond the activities suggested in Chapters 3 and 5, for the teaching of variation and difference in spoken and written contexts, I would like to suggest the following exercises that add a contrastive cultural dimension to well-known communicative activities.

*Personal constructs.* The way we make sense of phenomena in our own culture is by contrasting them and comparing them with other phenomena. For example, the concept of friendliness was constructed by one native speaker of American English by contrasting 'friendly' with 'don't like you', then contrasting 'don't like you' with 'trust you', 'trust you' with 'exclude you', 'exclude you' with 'sociable', 'sociable' with 'conceited', and so on (see Figure 2, page 210).

Another native speaker of English might have constructed the concept along a quite different axis of thinking. In the same manner, construct such concepts as 'challenging', 'successful', 'happy', 'work'. Choose the contrast that makes the most sense to you, then repeat the procedure four or five times. Compare your line of constructs with that of another speaker of English. Note how each one may have a socially or culturally different way of classifying the world.

*Role-play.*
a. Describe your school and your daily routine to a French student in a lycée. What points will you emphasize, *knowing what you know about the French school system and your own public or private school?*
b. You are an American salesperson in Germany. *Knowing what you know about the way many young Germans feel about nature and ecology,* compose a sales pitch for fruit, natural produce, or a beauty product for German 'green' buyers.
c. You have been offered a position as a teacher of French in the United States. You have one semester to teach the whole of French history. Which events will you stress *to help your students understand better present-day French?* How will you interpret these events for them?
   VARIANT. You have two semesters to teach this course: which periods will you cover in the first, which in the second, and where will you set the break? Which two events for each

period will you choose to discuss *because of their relevance to present-day France?*

*From City X with love.* Buy or make a picture postcard of your city which you would like to send to your foreign friend, who has never been to your country. Write a short text to it, telling your friend why you chose that particular picture for him or her.

VARIANT. Students exchange picture postcards and have to answer in the role of the addressee, *knowing what they know about each other* (biography, hobbies, plans for the future).

*Behind the looking glass.* Using slides and brochures provided by the Foreign Office of the target country, speculate what image the foreign country likes to give of itself and what it does not show. What does it tell us about the values of the people who made the cultural material? What would you like them to show that they did not show? Write a short dialogue between you and the authors.

VARIANTS. Put together a short brochure in the foreign language about your country for foreign students or tourists; or, in groups of three, prepare a short television presentation of your city or country for foreign TV viewers, *taking into account what you know about their constructs and stereotypes of your country.*

*Reviews.* Divide the class into authors and foreign reviewers. The authors write an essay on 'The American's America' for the foreign readers. The foreign reviewers have to review and edit these essays for the foreign press, *taking a foreigner's viewpoint of the United States.*

*Once-upon-a-time.* Experimenting with different outlooks on the same event. Find and read modern variants of old fairy tales (e.g. political variants of Grimm fairy tales). Students write a whole fairy tale or the end of a well-known fairy tale, giving it a psychological, social, moral, religious, or political meaning. Example: 'What became of Snow-White and her Prince after they emigrated to America because of unemployment in Germany?'

*Constructing a cultural context.* Students are given a conversation between two native speakers or a short story to read. In both texts, the outcome has been omitted. Write an ending *which is consistent with what you know* about the characters or the conversational partners and the cultural context in which the event takes place. Compare your ending with the original ending and justify the differences. How does your ending reflect your own understanding of the text? How does it reflect your understanding of the presuppositions of the persons involved?

*Film remakes.* Finally, film remakes, such as the remake of the French film *Trois hommes et un couffin* into the American film *Three men and a baby,* can be a rich source of cross-cultural comparisons (Carroll 1989).

These exercises are not easy, as they require learners to step into the outsider's shoes, so to speak, and enter what Bateson (1979) calls a 'different logical type'. Their objective is not to reach a right or wrong solution, nor even to find ways of bridging the gap, but to identify and explore the boundary and to explore oneself in the process. Such a process is more akin to aesthetic reading (see Chapter 4) than to problem-solving. The resistance encountered is often due to the unwillingness, especially on the part of teenage learners, to distance themselves from their native culture and the educational discourse with which they are familiar. It requires a gradual move from communicative to cross-cultural activities, from discourse to metadiscourse and aesthetic reflection.

This approach involves dialogue. Through dialogue and the search for each other's understanding, each person tries to see the world through the other's eyes without losing sight of him or herself. The goal is not a balance of opposites, or a moderate pluralism of opinions but a paradoxical, irreducible confrontation that may change one in the process. For example, participants in a discussion about the commercials considered above have to struggle to disengage themselves from their usual frame and see publicity from the other's perspective. In this struggle, and the back and forth of dialogue, they might find that they have more in common than they thought. For example, they may discover that in both the United States and Russia—two competitive societies in search of renewal—Coca-Cola can fulfill analogous dreams of success through sheer energy and know-how. But the two cultures will retain their different views on how this know-how gets actualized and acknowledged.

The culture that emerges through cross-cultural dialogue is of a different kind from either C1 or C2. It does not offer any certainties, nor does it resolve any conflicts. As Attinasi and Friedrich (forthcoming) remark with reference to forms of 'dialogic breakthrough' experienced during ethnographic fieldwork, cultural insights gained through dialogue, while hard to catch on the wing, can be experienced 'like startled pheasants taking off, during intensive and extensive fieldwork, or through the more or less vivid recall and reiterated reinterpretation' of the experience. As has been demonstrated repeatedly through this book, the meaning of cross-cultural encounters is hardly or rarely realized at the time. Rather, it appears at various levels of understanding at a much later date, from personal reflection and repeated attempts to bring together for oneself the various pieces of the cultural puzzle, and compare its emerging picture with that of others. In the next and last chapter, I will explore different facets of this emergence of cross-cultural understanding through dialogue.

## Notes

1 'Slipping in and out / into languages, out of languages / Commuting between / worlds.'
2 As Iyer *et al.* (1991: 36) phrased it recently, 'As much as we— and everyone else—assume that the French make the best perfume, and the Swiss the finest watches, the suspicion will continue that Americans make the best dreams.'
3 This activity took place at a seminar run by the Ford Foundation and the American Council for Teachers of Russian at Bryn Mawr College in July 1991, for American and Soviet language teachers. The Soviet Union ceased to exist as such on 25 December of that year.
4 A teacher development seminar, given by the Goethe Institute in July 1992 in Obernai (Alsace), was a first attempt to train teachers to think of foreign language study as border study. Twelve teachers from Germany, France, and the United States teaching each others' languages in their respective school systems compared self- and other-perceptions in their choice of authentic texts for the teaching of each others' languages and cultures.
5 For a description of personal constructs theory, see Kramsch (1983).

# 8  Looking for third places

For a long time you were
chased around the doorless
walls of the city.

You fell and strew
the confused names of things
behind you.

Trust, this most difficult
ABC.

I make a small sign
in the air,
invisible,
where the new city begins,
Jerusalem
the golden
out of nothing.

'Song of encouragement'
Hilde Domin [1966]
(tr. Haj Ross, 1982c)[1]


We have examined throughout this book several aspects of the relationship of texts and contexts, both on the conceptual level and on the practical level of day-to-day classroom teaching. This reflection has led us to the root of the creation of culture as a double process. Because learning a language is learning to exercise both a social and a personal voice, it is both a process of socialization into a given speech community and the acquisition of literacy as a means of expressing personal meanings that may put in question those of the speech community (Kramsch 1987a). The language that is being learned can be used both to maintain traditional social practices, and to bring about change in the very practices that brought about this learning.

The realization of difference, not only between oneself and others, but between one's personal and one's social self, indeed between different perceptions of oneself can be at once an elating and a deeply troubling experience. There are around the world an increasing number of culturally 'displaced' persons, who have grown up in one culture but, having emigrated to another country, raise their family and are active professionally in a culture that is not their own. Their many testimonies give voice to feelings of being forever 'betwixt and between', no longer at home in their original culture, nor really belonging to the host culture.

But these feelings of being on the fence, so to speak, are only a particularly dramatic manifestation of social ruptures that have always existed within seemingly homogeneous families, and other social and ethnic groups, as soon as an individual crosses the lines of race, social class, gender expectations, or sexual preferences. 'Growing into one's own' is by essence recognizing the faultlines in the social fabric, admitting for example that even though we are of the same nationality and social class, 'my' country might not be 'your' country, and your understanding of our social class might not be the same as mine. It also means acknowledging differences within oneself and seeing oneself within the historic context of one's own biography. As Hunfeld, writing for foreign language teachers, notes, 'We cannot teach an understanding of the foreign as long as the familiar has not become foreign to us in many respects' (1990: 16, my translation).

Indeed the phrase 'being on the fence' is deceptive, for it seems to suggest that we partake of only two different cultures, that of our past and that of our present, or the culture we left behind and the one we have moved into. Foreign language teaching, because of the saliency of national characteristics, is particularly prone to viewing this fence as a dichotomous boundary. But experiencing the boundary means discovering that each of these cultures is much less monolithic than was originally perceived; each includes a myriad of potential changes, as we saw in our analysis of context in Chapter 2. Thus we have to view the boundary not as an actual event but, rather, as a state of mind, as a positioning of the learner at the intersection of multiple social roles and individual choices.

The stories of such border crossings and of the 'conversion' that leads a person to realize she is no longer the person she imagined herself to be are told over and over again by those who have lived them. They are shared among people who have had similar 'border' experiences, whether through learning a foreign language, visiting a foreign country, or breaking away from traditional molds in one's own home country. These stories help the story-telling participants understand the joy and make sense of the pain these crossings have occasioned. They belong to a stock of narratives that attempt to create a third culture, made of a common memory beyond time and place among people with similar experiences. Through these dialogues, people become aware of the various frames of reference one can use to describe events. Indeed, the telling of these boundary experiences makes participants become conscious of the paramount importance of context and how manipulating contextual frames and perspectives through language can give people power and control, as they try to make themselves at home in a culture 'of a third kind'.

How are we to conceive of this third culture in foreign language education? Some language teachers have tried to minimize the discomfort of cultural difference through the reassuring thought that differences will disappear and that we will soon all belong to the same monocultural global village (Kramsch 1987c). Others have attempted to systematize the experience of cultural difference by fostering pedagogical exchanges of teachers and students across national boundaries (Baumgratz and Stephan 1987, Zarate 1990). Some scholars have made 'foreignness' into a postgraduate course of studies, a new discipline that calls itself 'interkulturelle Germanistik' and that can be intellectually researched (Wierlacher 1989, Großklaus and Thum 1989, Bolten 1989). In most foreign language classrooms, interculturality is not being taught as a systematic *apprenticeship of difference* nor is it generally integrated into a multicultural view of education.[2]

Throughout this book, as I examined the shaping of context through dialogue, the emergence of meaning between a reader and a text, the social construction of cultural myths, I adopted various disciplinary frames, from various branches of linguistics (psycholinguistics, sociolinguistics, anthropological, and educational linguistics), to literary theory. Such an interdisciplinary approach has been fruitful, but it has had its risks. It has helped us not to lose sight of the unity of knowledge and to benefit from the contexts of reference of various disciplines, but at the same time it has increased the risk of misunderstandings. For example, as we have seen, a term like 'effectiveness' can mean different things depending on whether one adopts a pragmatic, a critical, or a hermeneutic frame of reference. Similarly, the term 'universal' has different meanings for a linguist, a cross-cultural psychologist, and a politician. Crossing disciplines requires footnotes and good will on the part of the reader.

In the following, I will try to describe what that emerging 'third place' could be, that grows in the interstices between the cultures the learner grew up with and the new cultures he or she is being introduced to. I will use successively three different frames: a sociological, an educational, and a political frame. Within each of them, I will tell the same story, but from another perspective. Each will provide a different conclusion to the argument made throughout this book for teaching the interdependence of language and culture.

## A popular culture

Foreign language education has made great efforts to decenter the language teaching enterprise away from the authority of the teacher, the textbook, the literary canon, the academic ivory tower, and focus it on the actual needs of actual language learners, the *vox populi* of the language learning enterprise. But how should we define this popular voice?

The struggle of the language learner to find and carve out his or her own place within a speech community dominated by the myth of the native cultural speaker, can be compared to the live forces at work in popular culture, as it strives to carve out its place within mainstream mass or high culture. This struggle can serve as a metaphor to understand the basic dilemma of educational systems, which must both socialize learners into the social order and give them the means to change that social order.

Adopting a social semiotic perspective, I will define the learner's place as a place where he or she *creates meaning*. Learners have been seen up to now mostly as consumers, customers of various teaching methods that promise to endow them with enough native-speaker speech patterns, conversational habits, and dinner-table manners to grant them an entrance ticket into and ensure their acceptance by the target culture. The educational system is constantly searching for better ways of coopting learners' perceived needs by devising new courses for students to enroll in, developing new learning strategies for them to use, creating new materials for them to consume.

But classroom teachers know that it is a losing battle. Courses always have to be revised, research always reveals new possible ways of learning, textbooks are never totally satisfactory because foreign language learners will ever find new ways of making their own hypotheses, of understanding (and misunderstanding) cultural material, of using the foreign language to express their own unique meanings. In sum, educational thought underestimates the incredible resources, both affective and cognitive, of the 'popular culture' of the language classroom.

In his recent book *Understanding Popular Culture* (1989) the sociologist John Fiske illustrates the process through which the social order and the individual constantly trick each other, outdo each other in a fight not over commodities and facts, but over who will impose their meaning on those facts. 'In a consumer society, all commodities have cultural as well as functional values' (ibid.: 27); 'A car is not just transport, but a speech act; cooking a meal is not just providing food, but a way of communicating' (ibid.: 34). Learning a foreign language, one might add, is not just learning a new way of communicating, but a way of making a cultural statement. 'In this economy there are no consumers, only circulators of meanings, for meanings are the only elements in the process that can be neither commodified nor consumed: meanings can be produced, reproduced, and circulated only in that constant process that we call culture.' (ibid.: 27)

The French sociologist Michel de Certeau remarks that the culture of everyday life is to be found in 'ways of using imposed systems': 'People have to make do with what they have'. 'Making do' (or *bricolage*) means 'constructing *our* space within and against *their* place, of speaking *our* meanings with *their* language' (de Certeau 1984: 18). De Certeau gives an example:

A North African living in Paris or Roubaix (France) insinuates *into* the system imposed upon him by the construction of low-income housing development, or of the French language, the ways of 'dwelling' (in a house or language) peculiar to his native Kabylia. He super-imposes them and, by that combination, creates for himself a space in which he can find *ways of using* the constraining order of the place or of the language.

Without leaving the place where he has no choice but to live and which lays down its law for him, he establishes within it a degree of *plurality* and creativity. By an art of being in between, he draws unexpected results from his situation.
(1984: 30, cited in Fiske 1989: 36)

This line of thinking can be useful as we explore what the 'space' of language learners might be between and beyond the social order of their native culture and that of the target culture. Constrained by the linguistic rules of the foreign language and its rules of use, constrained also by their own socialization patterns in their own culture, language learners are indeed in a position of uncommon subordination and powerlessness. This position of subordination can be made somewhat less painful as the learners become more proficient in the language, but it can never disappear. For acquisition of knowledge and competence in a foreign language is not an additive process, but a dialectic one. Fiske describes the process as follows:

New knowledge is not an evolutionary improvement on what precedes it; rather, new knowledges enter adversarial relationships with older, more established ones, challenging their position in the power play of understandings, and in such confrontations new insights can be provoked.
(ibid.: 194)

As we saw in Chapter 1, learning to use another language for communication means leaving behind the naive paradise of native-tongue socialization. As they become more and more proficient in a second language and familiar with a second culture, language learners try to articulate their new experience within their old one, making it relevant to their own lives, one day this way, one day that way, creating their own popular culture. This popular culture will be as conservative or as progressive as each learner wishes it to be.

Learning a foreign language offers the opportunity for personal meanings, pleasures, and power. From the clash between the familiar meanings of the native culture and the unexpected meanings of the target culture, meanings that were taken for granted are suddenly questioned, challenged, problematized. Learners have to construct their personal meanings at the boundaries between the native speaker's meanings and their own everyday life. The personal pleasures they can derive from producing these meanings come from their *power* to produce them. As Fiske points out, 'There is little pleasure in accepting ready-made meanings, however pertinent. The pleasure derives both from the power and process of making meanings out of *their* resources and from the sense that these meanings are *ours* as opposed to *theirs*' (ibid.: 127).

For example, much of the value of using real-life texts to teach foreign languages may be found in the pleasure it gives learners to poach, so to speak, on some else's linguistic and cultural territory. This pleasure is akin to that of spies and actors: eavesdropping on someone else's dialogue, understanding a message that was not intended for them, using a language that is not understood by others, passing for native speakers, blending in the mass, pretending to be someone else, all these elemental pleasures make up a great deal of the fun of reading and viewing non-pedagogical materials.

*[handwritten margin note: benefits of using real-life materials for after-class reading]*

The success of communicative approaches to language teaching have been accounted for by their functional usefulness and universal characteristics, but their real potential may lie in their ability to engage the learner in the dialectic of meaning production. There will always be a struggle between the teacher whose charge it is to make the students understand and eventually adopt foreign verbal behaviors and mindsets, and the learners who will continue to use transmitted knowledge for their own purposes, who will insist on making their own meanings and finding their own relevances. This struggle is the educational process *per se*.

If there is no such struggle, it is possible that the learners are indeed accepting ready-made meanings, in the same manner as the consumers in Fiske's sociological analyses are ready to buy and wear jeans that have been pre-washed by the blue jean industry. However, it is not true that there is only one way to wash and to wear (and even to tear!) blue jeans, nor is it true that students espouse the meaning practices of the target society without challenging them. It is more the case that the teacher does not *notice* when learners express personal meanings, because teachers have been trained to see in their students' deviant utterances only aberrant native-speaker meanings.

## A critical culture

We shall now switch from a sociological to an educational frame to describe what the learner's third place might be. In this context, I will focus on the learner's ability to recognize the power of context and to adopt the critical distance that comes from this recognition.

As we left the non-controversial waters of grammar-translation or even structural ways of teaching foreign languages, and moved into more communicatively-oriented approaches, the concept of challenge-as-action (see Chapter 1) was useful to stress the fact that learners had to learn how to *act* upon their environment, not just name it in grammatically and lexically correct sentences. By teaching learners how to do things with words, how to function appropriately within a foreign society, language education was easing them into a social order and facilitating their integration into that order.

However, foreign language education, in so far as it offers alternative ways of naming and interpreting the world, has to provide also challenges of the second kind, namely the opportunity to think through and to question existing practices. An educational philosophy that stresses only doing things with words runs the risk of helping maintain the social status quo; it has difficulty dealing with the teaching of culture, because cross-cultural competence, unlike pragmatic competence, is predicated on paradox and conflict and on often irreducible ways of viewing the world, as we have seen throughout this book.

The teaching of foreign languages must be made relevant to social life, where people need to communicate with each other in order to set the stage for possible mutual understanding. However, the complexities of social contexts will always make social practice variable, unpredictable, open to multiple interpretations. Speakers need ever more refined language structures to express their personal meanings; meanings in a social context will forever elude the clarity of language structures. The constant struggle between individual and social meanings in discourse needs to be accepted and exploited, rather than ignored.

In order to maintain the tension between the two faces of the educational challenge, I would like to suggest that teachers and learners view themselves as operating within and across multiple discourse worlds. I would like to expand Edmondson's psycholinguistic model of classroom discourse worlds (see Chapter 1) to an educational view of the foreign language curriculum as a whole. For it seems to me that besides the material that textbooks tell us to teach, readers to read, and syllabuses to cover, we are engaged at all levels of the curriculum from the beginning stages of language teaching to the upper literature and culture classes, in forms of discourse that both validate the educational discourse of our schools and challenge its cultural premise. These multiple forms of discourse potentially overlap or enter into conflict with one another.

In the foreign language curriculum, the foreign language traditionally partakes of at least three different discourse worlds: instructional, transactional, and interactional. Teachers achieve lessons by presenting a certain knowledge, and by demonstrating that knowledge. But at the same time, they can subvert traditional forms of discourse and encourage their students to do the same.

In the *instructional discourse* world, teachers use the foreign language to regulate the instructional procedure of language study itself. This is the world of homework deadlines, syllabus design, grading procedures, expectations of course work: but it is also the world in which students are socialized into a certain educated behavior; initiated into a certain intellectual dialogue, a certain way of thinking; and inculcated with the unwritten rules of power, distance, and solidarity among educated people—even though all this takes place in the foreign language. It is this discourse world that forms a cultural unity between the language class and all other classes in a student's day. By giving language study the stamp of approval as a subject worth learning, academia both fosters its delivery and, at the same time, imposes on it its own intellectual style.

However, to the extent that the purpose of instructional discourse is to demonstrate a certain way of approaching a body of knowledge, of framing the questions that best further its acquisition, instruction in a *foreign* linguistic and cultural framework provides an opportunity to suspend traditional forms of instruction and experiment with new ones. For example, beyond the usual teacher-centered grammar drills and structural exercises, foreign language study has played a role in the diversification of instructional formats for the development of communicative competence. Alternatives to the traditional delivery of knowledge have included alternative teaching styles (e.g. styles that are sensitive to national or gender differences), and alternative learning styles (e.g. more or less orate or literate, contextualized or decontextualized, analogical or analytical). Instructional forms of discourse serve as the matrix in which the two other discourse worlds can be explored, and in particular, the discourse forms used for the transmission and reception—that is, for the 'transaction'—of knowledge.

In the world of *transactional discourse*, the foreign language is used to transmit and receive information about the foreign language, culture, and literature. It serves to gather and display facts about the foreign language code itself (e.g. meta-talk about grammar and vocabulary), but also about the content of readings, the gist of audio-recordings, facts and figures about the history, the society, the culture of the country, topics and ideas, characters and plots in literary texts. This knowledge constitutes the most explicit aspect of the instructional content, the one that can be listed in syllabuses and course catalogues and that can be measured and tested in the usual manner.

This type of discourse is common to all other subjects in the school's curriculum. However, more than in any other subject, facts in the foreign language class make sense only if they are linked to other facts, linguistic and cultural, of the native and of the target speech communities. The challenge is not only one of transmitting information, but of understanding the paradoxical nature of that information. Amy's example in Chapter 1 is a case in point. Like every learner, she was bringing together bits and pieces of information to make a coherent picture, not only of a poem in a foreign language, but of a mindset that she sensed was both different from and similar to hers.

In the language classroom, the foreign language is used to conduct forms of *interactional discourse* that are characteristic of the learners' or of the target culture. Thus, dyadic conversations about events related to students' lives, small group task-oriented activities, whole group discussions according to native cultural interactional norms, and also creative writing—all have meaning within the interactional discourse world of the native culture. In addition, the foreign language is used to enact and display forms of social interaction that are characteristic of the target culture. Functional and situational role-play, simulation activities, and also stylistic exercises *à la manière de*, have meaning within a target—albeit simulated—interactional world.

However, learners use the sociolinguistically appropriate norms of interaction not only to be accepted by native speakers. Here too they resist becoming 'little Germans' or 'little French'. Official pedagogy has underestimated the extent to which the use of gambits and highly 'authentic' forms of behavior by learners give them a sense of conversational power and control that the system traditionally withholds from them as non-legitimate for non-native speakers. The thrill at being able to use forms of speech that are only reserved to native speakers, such as slang or highly idiomatic gambits, are ways in which learners can gain power within a system that by its nature reminds them how powerless they really are.

Thus we see how teachers and learners use the system for their own purposes. Such an experience can signal the emergence of a third culture in the classroom if it is integrated into a critical pedagogy that applies itself to the three other discourse worlds and is explicitly reflected upon as such. It includes a systematic assessment of the situational context in the production and reception of meaning, based on observation, analysis, and personal response. It aligns itself with a larger critical pedagogy that owes much to the thinking of such educational philosophers as Paulo Freire and Henry Giroux in Freire (1970, 1985), Giroux (1988), and Aronowitz and Giroux (1991). It also echoes recent thought in what has been termed 'critical' or 'political' applied linguistics (Pennycook 1990, Kanpol 1990). Such thought seeks both to 'help [language learners] assimilate into the mainstream culture and use assimilation as a social and political tool to transform consciousness by bringing into focus the similarities within differences' (Kanpol 1990: 247).

This process of 'conscientization' can help resist traditional instructional forms of discourse. Kanpol reports, for example, how in one ESL class, the teacher set up information-gap or jigsaw tasks in the context of cooperative learning situations.[3] By having small groups of students responsible for sharing information and collaborating on a joint outcome, and *by grading the collaborative outcome rather than the individual achievement*, this teacher explicitly subverted existing instructional discourse forms. Beyond merely teaching the English language, the teacher

> downplayed individual testing and excessive competition among students [and based] a student's worth on individual and group effort rather than on . . . numerical achievement. Students learned to accept individual differences within groups yet responded as a team on issues of vocabulary choice.
> (Kanpol 1990: 246)

Critical discourse can also be applied to the transactional world of the classroom. In an ESL class that I observed, the teacher went beyond the usual transactional discourse of the classroom to question the implicit moral and ideological assumptions routinely passed on to students via the English language. After showing her students video clips from two films, *Fatso* and *Perfect* (Beckerman 1989), to stimulate group work and class discussion on the topic of good health, the teacher engaged the class into a critique of these films and of the American obsession with health and physical exercise. Some students admitted that dietary concerns and physical fitness were also in the foreground of public consciousness in their own country; others found their stereotypes about the United States confirmed. The ESL students were encouraged to find differences within the apparent similarities and analogies beyond obvious differences (see Clarke and Clarke 1990).

Finally, a critical foreign language pedagogy can help vary the usual interactional discourse of the classroom. Kanpol gives an example. In one ESL class, a short story, 'The Lady or the Tiger' (Stockton 1980), was used as the basis for a vocabulary, comprehension, and structured grammar lesson. But the story was also used to generate discussion about individual experiences. The Egyptian ESL teacher began the class by recounting her history: her entrance and the hardships she faced as an immigrant to the United States. She then encouraged small group discussion on individual differences and choice in each student's life. As the groups discussed individual choice, freedom, and the question 'what is right?', the teacher went from group to group, encouraging participants to clarify intended meanings, implicit assumptions, and world views. Interactional discourse ceased to be just a matter of using the grammatically correct phrase or the socially appropriate gambit, but became a means of entering another person's frame of reference and developing cultural and social awareness (Kanpol 1990: 247).

We can summarize the main features of a critical language pedagogy under the following aspects:

1 *Awareness of global context.* Every instance of talk or silence, participation or non-participation, is emblematic of a larger cultural context that the teacher should be attuned to and should make the students aware of. The difficulties encountered at the beginning levels of learning to speak in a foreign language are of a different degree, but not of a

different nature from those encountered at the most advanced levels. They are more often than not difficulties of interpretation, not of low-level morphology. Despite what teachers might think, the meanings that beginning learners express and convey are not simplistic just because the grammar in which they are expressed is limited. It is very often teachers' exclusive focus on low-level grammar that prevents them from understanding the discourse or cultural logic of their students' speech. It is the teachers' exclusive focus on referential meanings that can make them blind to the poetic insights sometimes offered by their students, or to their unsuccessful attempts to express one culture in terms of another.

2 *Local knowledge.* Before we even think of teaching specific forms of speech, we must be aware of the schooling habits and cultural patterns of socialization that give some learners the perception that they have greater rights to speak than others. Moreover, different learners have different learning styles, different conversational styles, different logics. Our major task is not, as some teachers believe, to find ever better ways of 'making students talk', but to understand in ever more sensitive ways why they talk the way they do, and why they remain silent: this type of knowledge Clifford Geertz calls 'local knowledge'. It is described in other terms by Ellis (1992: 171): 'Researchers [are now] seeing the classroom not so much as a place where the language is taught, but as one where opportunities for learning of various kinds are provided through the interactions that take place between the participants.'

3 *Ability to listen.* The most important and the most difficult task for the teacher is not to teach but to listen. Teacher training has focused in recent years mostly on having the teacher model as much as possible natural forms of speech and on orchestrating classrooms that are as learner-centered as possible. Teachers listen usually for nothing but the linguistic form or the propositional content of students' utterances. They are seldom trained to listen to silences and to their students' implicit assumptions and beliefs. They have also little training in listening to themselves and reflecting on their own assumptions and beliefs. Introspection and critical self-assessment are essential for the further development of any language teacher.

4 *Metatalk*. Talk about talk is what the classroom does best and yet this potential source of knowledge has not been sufficiently tapped, even in communicatively-oriented classrooms. In the days of structural pedagogies, the classroom was the locus of talk about language and its structures. Now that communicative language pedagogy has shown that there is more to learning a language than merely learning its forms, language teaching pedagogy has focused on doing things with words. Metatalk has almost disappeared from many natural and other approaches. And yet, most of the sociocultural appropriateness that communicative approaches to language teaching have shown are important in communication cannot be taught only by doing. Contexts are too varied, too changing; behaviors can only be observed, analyzed, and talked about. The classroom is the place par excellence where behaviors can be enacted and discussed as instances of the construction of meaning.

5 *Making do with words*. Rather than doing things with words, speaking in a foreign language is making do with a limited amount of someone else's words. That, not unlimited speech acts, is the reality of the language classroom. Teaching the spoken language is teaching resourcefulness, imagination, and effective poaching on all levels of meaning available.

6 *Autonomy and control*. The struggle between the desire of students to appropriate the foreign language for their own purposes, and the responsibility of the teacher for socializing them into a linguistically and socioculturally appropriate behavior lie at the core of the educational enterprise. Both are necessary for pleasurable and effective language learning. The good teacher fosters both compliance and rebellion.

7 *The long haul*. The relationship between what teachers teach and what learners learn is at best an indirect one, to be counted not in days and months, but in incidental and unexpected ways. Given the small amount of time teachers have to teach all they have to teach, they have to strive for the memorable—personal moments of dialogic insight that can bring both pain and pleasure, both shock and amazement. Rather than ask at the end of the school year 'What will my students remember from all that I have taught

them?', it might be more judicious to ask 'What will be worth remembering among the many things my students have learned?'

## An ecological culture

Finally, let us switch from an educational to a political context. In this context, I shall describe the language learner's third place as a place that preserves the diversity of styles, purposes, and interests among learners, and the variety of local educational cultures. This place has to be carved out against the hegemonic tendencies of larger political and institutional structures that strive to coopt the teaching and learning of foreign languages in the name of such ill-defined terms as 'the national interest', or 'economic competitiveness'.

In the following, I will examine the structures of dominance as they present themselves through various educational systems and the tactics of resistance that enable individual schools, teachers, and learners to build upon them, evade or resist them at the local level.

## The emergence of third places in the United States

Following the 1975 Helsinki Accords that spelled out the principles of peaceful coexistence between thirty-three European nations, the United States, and Canada, United States President Jimmy Carter nominated a special Commission to evaluate the state of foreign language study in his country. The 1978 Report of the President's Commission refers specifically to the Helsinki Agreement:

> The final act of the Helsinki Accords commits the signatory states 'to encourage the study of foreign language and civilization as an important means of expanding communication among peoples.' To help realize this goal, the President's Commission has devoted a year to an intensive evaluation of the state of foreign language and international studies and their impact on the nation's internal and external strength. (Perkins 1980: 11)

Already such a statement makes us pause. 'Nation's strength?' Admittedly, the Helsinki Agreement was signed in the middle of the cold war between the Western states and the Eastern bloc, but was not the study of foreign languages precisely meant to improve cooperation among peoples, not to serve national security purposes? The rest of the Commission's statement shows how one of the signatories, namely the United States, redefined the challenge presented by the Helsinki document. Having ascertained that 'Americans' scandalous incompetence in foreign languages explains [their] dangerously inadequate understanding of world affairs' (ibid.: 12), it goes on to make the following recommendations:

> The President's commission believes that our lack of foreign language competence diminishes our capabilities in diplomacy, in foreign trade, and in citizen comprehension of the world in which we live and compete . . .
>
> Nothing less is at issue than the nation's security. At a time when the resurgent forces of nationalism and of ethnic and linguistic consciousness so directly affect global realities, the United States requires far more reliable capacities to communicate with its allies, analyze the behavior of potential adversaries, and earn the trust and the sympathies of the uncommitted. Yet, there is a widening gap between these trends and the American competence to understand and deal successfully with other peoples in a world in flux . . . In our schools and colleges as well as in our public media of communication, and in the everyday dialogue within our communities, the situation cries out for a better comprehension of our place and our potential in a world that, though it still expects much from America, no longer takes American supremacy for granted . . .
>
> The problem is serious and complex. Yet, unlike many other public issues confronting the nation, solutions are within reach. On the basis of its study, the Commission has set forth a number of recommendations which it believes to be realistic, modest in scope, and entirely practical. We are persuaded that imaginative action, backed by a moderate investment of funds at the federal, state and local levels, and by the private sector, will yield results well beyond the sacrifices involved. The total immediate expenditure of new federal funds believed by the Commission to be required to reverse a dangerous trend is $180 million.
> (ibid.: 11)

This text is remarkable in that it brings together all the facets of the challenge ideology discussed in Chapter 1 to bear on national foreign language policy: the redefinition of the challenge of communication across cultures as a national test of strength (the name of the document is: 'Strength through Wisdom: A Critique of U.S. Capability'); the focus on competitiveness, exercise of power, achievement of superiority, eventual success. The Helsinki Accords advocated expanding and deepening the dialogue between peoples. They said nothing of citizens of nation states competing, being successful and regaining supremacy over speakers of other languages. They assumed that through this dialogue one would get to find out who constitutes one's allies and one's adversaries. By contrast, the President's Commission on Foreign Languages and International Studies seems to already know who the United States' allies, potential adversaries, and the 'uncommitted' others are, and it seems to believe that foreign language competencies are needed only to convert them more easily to its views.

To be sure, this redefinition expresses the subtext of the Helsinki Agreement. Signed at a time when the cold war showed no end in sight, there was much controversy about the desirability of such a document. One could even be cynical and take both the Helsinki and the Washington documents for political propaganda. And yet, both documents have given in their respective areas of the world an uncommon impetus to the study of foreign languages. But with the funding has come a definition of goals imposed from above. Foreign language study in the US bears heavily the mark of the 1978 Commission Report; it has given throughout the 1980s a considerable booster to the teaching and learning of foreign language across the country: at the same time, however, it has infused it with a concept of challenge that stresses international competitiveness, problem-solving, and short-term action. Applied to the foreign language classroom, it can reinforce American ideologies and impede cross-cultural understanding.

The recent Report of the Governors' Task Force on International Education echoes the 1978 President's Commission Report in its six-point challenge for foreign language education:

—Discover new and emerging international markets for American products, to become again the Yankee traders we once were.

—Bring an international perspective to our daily living—to understand foreign nations and the people beyond our borders . . . to learn the international language of business.
—Expand our research, and use our technology, to create both new products and new processes to maintain America's competitive position.
—Capitalize on the natural advantages of American manufacturers and regain competitiveness in our domestic markets.
—Improve our highways, airports, airways, and ports so we can move our people across town and our products around the globe.
—Invest in the health, education, and training of our children so they can live healthier and more productive lives.
(Baliles 1989)

Swaffar comments: 'Even beyond the crass dollar and cents level of accountability is another less tangible but certainly significant argument in favor of accepting the challenge outlined for us in the governors' report "America in Transition" (1989): Foreign language curricula have an obligation to meet the educational needs of the public domain. That is, after all, our *raison d'être'* (Swaffar 1992: 41).

The reality, however, is that there are many ways of interpreting the challenge outlined in the Governors' Report. Despite the overwhelming political pressure at work in American education, there is far from a consensus about what that education should be (Kramsch 1991). The tactics of resistance in the US capitalize precisely on the multiple facets of this 'public domain' and its 'educational needs'. Foreign language educators take the funds offered by the various funding agencies to design their own innovative programs according to their own interpretation of such concepts as 'proficiency' or 'international education'. These programs are then called 'models' that are funded for larger-scale applications. They thereby often lose their critical edge as they get coopted by funding agencies and turned into other catchwords like the current 'content-based instruction'. These terms in turn open the door to multiple interpretations and invite resistance and subversion.

A case in point is the 'Language Across the Curriculum' idea, originally developed to improve students' language skills, then to enrich students' understanding of texts, and now redesigned to engage them in a critical cross-cultural examination of the relationship of language and culture (Kramsch 1992). In the US, the concept was first developed at Earlham College, a small college in Ohio, from 1980 to 1984, and supported by a grant from the National Endowment for the Humanities (NEH) for the improvement of the students' language skills. Twenty-five per cent of the Earlham faculty with a reading knowledge of another language and teaching various subjects (European history, social sciences, law, anthropology) agreed to have their students read some of the texts in their regular courses in the original. Glossaries to the texts were provided by the foreign language teaching faculty. The texts were read by students and the professor in the original, but discussed in class in English. This led to occasional cultural simplifications. One American anthropology professor, for instance, explained the German term *Volk* in English as follows: '*Das Volk* cannot be understood merely as "the people". It is, rather, a matter of race memory and collective identity that has no counterpart in the U.S. Constitution' (Jurasek 1988: 56). As recent events have shown, the term *Volk* in German has a much more complex history than the one suggested by this definition.[4]

However, from a linguistic point of view, the Earlham experiment was considered to be a success. In 1987, it prompted the large Midwest University of Minnesota, with support from the NEH, to build upon it. It was felt that it could be improved upon by having the texts not only read but also discussed in the foreign language. At the University of Minnesota, regular courses taught in English—such as French history, Latin-American politics, Central European geography, and Spanish history—were made to include an optional one-credit-bearing 'trailer course' taught in Spanish, French, or German by the same professors who taught the main course in English. These professors, chosen among the bilingual faculty, were given one course released time from their usual teaching duties to prepare these trailer courses, which they teach once a week with the help of foreign language graduate student instructors who give the students the vocabulary they need to discuss the regular academic content in the foreign language.

In 1989, the idea was picked up and given a critical and cross-cultural perspective at St. Olaf College, a small college in Minnesota. The college received a grant from the Federal Fund for Improvement of Post-Secondary Education (FIPSE) to add to fifteen currently existing courses (e.g. European history, Social Sciences) an optional 'applied foreign language component' (AFLC) in French, Spanish, or German. This AFLC appears on the student's transcript. Three hours a week, the course is taught in English by the disciplinary faculty, one hour a week a foreign language teacher leads a discussion in the foreign language based on original texts related to the topic of the week. This opens up opportunities for the kind of discussion mentioned in Chapter 1, as students realize the degree to which language influences ideas in the disciplines and in the world of affairs. Allen and Anderson (1989) give the following examples in their description of the project:

> In a German history course, for example, students who read in the original language some of Wilhelm von Humboldt's writings on education learn that *Kultur und Bildung* carry implications much deeper than the English translation of 'culture and education' would suggest. They come to realize the enormous importance of the *Bildungsbürgertum* in German society—another term whose meaning is partly lost when translated into English as 'the educated middle class'. This additional meaning helps students understand German attitudes toward education.
>
> Students in a Russian history course who read in the original Peter the Great's 'Table of Ranks' and Ivan Turgenev's *Fathers and Sons* are confronted with the term *dvorianstvo*. They are stimulated to evaluate the applicability of the English term 'nobility' for a group whose position in society was quite different from the German, French, or English aristocracy. Students are led to ponder the general problem of according universal significance to the terminology derived from the history and language of a particular area.
>
> Similarly, in a French history course, students reading Napoleon's statement 'I am the revolution' in the original, can experience the way his choice of grammatical structure actually affected the nature of his political message. 'Je suis la révolution' was a public display of solidarity with the revolutionaries; 'la révolution c'est moi' would have conveyed despotic overtones.

The major breakthrough at St. Olaf turns out to be the dialogue it has initiated between faculty members. Foreign language teachers realize how much culture they teach as they impart grammar and vocabulary. Teachers of other subjects realize how much the discourse of their discipline is culture-determined. Exploration of the cultural connotations of words takes place among faculty members who had up to now little opportunity for professional contact.

These examples show how innovation and change take place in ways that build upon international statements of purpose and national guide-lines, but at the same time subvert their global intent by aiming for particularity and difference. I would like to turn now to other educational systems to show how, there too, structures of dominance and tactics of resistance interact to shape a language learner's third culture.

## The emergence of third places in Africa

In many African states, the cultural meaning of learning English, French, or German as a foreign language varies according to the vagaries of colonial history and current national policies. In small African states like Swaziland, Lesotho, and Botswana under the economic and currency control of South Africa, for-eign language education in schools, like any other subject, uses textbooks and methods imported from South Africa. But at the same time, it strives to use these culturally marked materials for developing a counter-cultural 'education for self-reliance'. Rather than estrange children from their roots and their native tongue and teach them the ways of English-speaking white South Africa, many teachers of English in Swaziland schools give an official voice to their cultural heritage and their own educational values through an international language like English. By inserting themselves into an international language circuit with-out letting themselves become hostage to the culture and ideo-logy of any one particular society, foreign language learners in these countries look at their local context with fresh eyes and link it to larger contexts.[5]

In the homelands of South Africa itself, the challenge of lan-guage learning poses itself in terms of a critical language ped-agogy reminiscent of Paulo Freire's *conscientizacao* (1970). The People's English Commission of the National Education Crisis Committee, established in 1985, reconceptualized the meaning of language competence as follows. For the Commission, lan-guage competence extends beyond an understanding of the rules that govern the English language and the appropriate rules of

English within South African society. It includes, among other things, 'the ability to say and write what one means; to hear what is said and what is hidden; to defend one's point of view; . . . to make one's voice heard; to read print and resist it where necessary' (cited in Peirce 1989).[6]

Thus, English is seen not only as a legitimate vehicle for the expression of native cultures, and as a window on the world, but as a weapon to be used in the struggle against Afrikaaner hegemony.[7]

We find a similar but more complex definition of the foreign language challenge in Cameroun. Until 1884, education was in the hands of mostly English-speaking missionaries, that maintained the some 240 vernacular languages at the lower levels and taught English only in the upper levels. After Germany annexed Cameroun in 1884, the German language was progressively introduced as the language of instruction in all the schools. In 1916, after the defeat of Germany, Cameroun was divided into two zones: one under the French who, according to their views on the direct civilizatory mission of the French language, made the exclusive use of French mandatory in their part of the territory; the other under the British who, according to their 'indirect rule' of colonization, maintained the vernacular languages at the elementary levels and enforced the use of English at the upper levels.

When in 1960 Cameroun became independent and both French and English were proclaimed the two official languages, the purpose of education was to 'detribalize' the country and instill in schoolchildren a sense of national identity beyond tribal and ethnic allegiance. As Vigner observes, 'The school has thus been viewed from the start as an essential tool in the building of a national consciousness and the formation of an individual citizen's identity, by contrast with the group consciousness traditionally characteristic of ethnicity' (Vigner 1991: 100, my translation). The foreign languages French and English thus served as instruments of detribalization. In so doing, however, they have become more and more inscribed in the social and cultural fabric of Cameroun and have slowly lost the status of 'foreign' languages. What role then can truly foreign languages like, for example, German play in Cameroun schools?

It seems that the introduction of a third internationally recognized language, unfettered by the painful memory of an immediate colonial past, yet part of the linguistic fabric of a more distant history, can serve as a catalyst, not for the formation of a learner's civic identity, but for the emergence of a personal identity that transcends both local ethnicities and the pragmatic needs of the nation state. Cameroun learners of German can give a universal voice to their tribal heritage through the voice of such poets as Hilde Domin.[8]

In Nigeria, an interesting role is perceived by educators for a foreign language like French. As Akinnaso (1991) points out, Nigeria has some 400 vernacular languages, three exogenous languages (French, English, and Arabic) and one official language (English). Education is carried out in English. Of the exogenous languages, French is currently the least spoken or used (Akinnaso 1991). However, contrary to what Akinnaso suggests, it is not because it has 'the least appeal to learners'. Simplistic notions of educational benefit might prompt some outsiders to infer that what has less pragmatic value on the international market has less appeal for learners. In fact, French as a subject matter features in the curriculum of every school, and is taught in every one of Nigeria's twenty-three universities. Certainly, the proliferation of departments of French was encouraged by the Federal Ministry of Education for political objectives, but for educators and students French can have another value.

Because Nigeria is 'linguistically an island in a francophone sea' (Ijoma, personal communication) and because, in addition, Nigeria is often seen by its neighbors as an anglophone 'imperialist' nation, the French language can serve to strengthen the ties between Nigerians and their West African neighbors and to gain these neighbors' trust and confidence. As in many African countries, the perceived value of Western languages has to be understood against the backdrop of their respective colonial history and in the relative emotional value that each of these languages represents vis-à-vis the other and vis-à-vis local and national African tongues. Especially in such a highly complex multilingual situation as that of African states, it is a fallacy to believe that languages are neutral commodities on the linguistic market and that it is only the practical demand that dictates their value. The symbolic value attached to French in Nigeria may offer its learners a 'third place', out of the emotionally charged dichotomies of Nigerian linguistic politics.[9]

By citing the examples of these African countries, I certainly do not wish to imply that their linguistic landscapes are analogous. Each country has its own history, its own relationship to one or several colonial languages, each has its own political reasons for furthering the teaching of French, English, or German, for example. But what I find interesting is that in each country, the uses of foreign languages far exceed the immediate global needs of national interest or governmental policies. In each case, the foreign language is appropriated by the learners to fulfill local needs related to their own search for a personal identity beyond the colonial hegemony of the target culture (for a similar situation in Morocco, see for example Adaskou, Britten, and Fahsi 1990).

## Conclusion

Foreign language learners in educational settings have been socialized and schooled to view the acquisition of knowledge in various ways, according to the values prevalent in their society. In American schools, learning a foreign language is presented as a call for action, the acquisition of a skill that will get you a better job, and help you better fulfill an American dream. In African countries, the teaching of foreign languages with wide circulation, such as French, English, or German, serves both the goals of national unity and the needs of nations and individuals to be in contact with more powerful trading partners. In all cases, foreign language teaching and learning is subservient to the goals of institutions that impose their values and their definition of the educational challenge on all subjects in the curriculum.

However, the examples of local educational initiatives in the United States, as well as those of Swaziland, South Africa, Cameroun, and Nigeria show that the link between a foreign language on the one hand and the official culture of either a school or a society on the other hand is not as essential as it seems. Language learners use the foreign language for multiple purposes that often challenge the established educational canons of both the native and the target cultures. Foreign language learners around the world have to grapple with the paradox of discovering their own national, ethnic, and personal identity through a language that is not the one they grew up with. Their teachers have to deal with the dilemma of both representing an institution that imposes its own educational values and initiating learners to the values of a foreign culture, while at the same time helping them not to be bound by either one. At every step of this complex process, the educational challenge requires both action and reflection.

At the intersection of multiple native and target cultures, the major task of language learners is to define for themselves what this 'third place' that they have engaged in seeking will look like, whether they are conscious of it or not. Nobody, least of all the teacher, can tell them where that very personal place is; for each learner it will be differently located, and will make different sense at different times. For some, it will be the irrevocable memory of the ambiguities of the word 'challenge'. For others, it will be a small poem by Pushkin that will, twenty years later, help them make sense out of a senseless personal situation. For others still, it will be a small untranslatable Japanese proverb that they will all of a sudden remember, thus enabling them for a moment to see the world from the point of view of their Japanese business partner and save a floundering business transaction. For most, it will be the stories they will tell of these cross-cultural encounters, the meanings they will give them through these tellings and the dialogues that they will have with people who have had similar experiences. In and through these dialogues, they may find for themselves this third place that they can name their own.

## Notes

1 'Lied zur Ermutigung II. Lange wurdest du um die türelosen / Mauern der Stadt gejagt. / Du fliehst und streust / die verwirrten Namen der Dinge / hinter dich. / Vertrauen, dieses schwerste / ABC. / Ich mache ein kleines Zeichen / in die Luft, / unsichtbar / wo die neue Stadt beginnt, / Jerusalem, / die goldene, / aus Nichts.' This poem by Hilde Domin is quoted here in its translation in Ross (1982). Ross uses the poem as an illustration of the experience that language learners undergo when they leave their language behind and slowly learn to gain trust in another language through the magic of words.

2 In a rather sobering study on United States undergraduates and international studies, Richard Lambert (1989) found that foreign languages and international studies are taken predominantly by humanities majors and that those majoring in economics and education have the lowest exposure to

foreign language education and international studies. He comments:

> As might be expected, the economists who, like the natural scientists, believe in universal principles rather than culture-specific phenomena offer only about four to five percent of all internationally focused courses ... and psychology just does not appear at all among international courses (p. 115) ... Especially disturbing is the relatively light exposure education majors get to internationally focused courses. The chain of education across generations is still largely parochial (p. 122) ... Nothing is more likely to perpetuate our unfortunate national devotion to monolingualism than perpetuating the tradition of a largely monolingual teaching profession (p. 69).

3 For more information on cooperative learning, see Johnson and Johnson 1987, Kagan 1989, Slavin 1983.

4 See the recent uses of the term *Volk* in East and West Germany before and after the fall of the Berlin Wall on 9 November 1989, and before German unification on 18 March 1990. In October 1989, East-Germans taking to the streets in Leipzig and Dresden were shouting such slogans as *Wir sind das Volk* ('we are the people' in opposition to the ruling apparatchiks)—a meaning pretty close to that of 'the people' in the American constitution. This was a call for revolution, not necessarily for a unification with the West. However, already in December 1989, West-Germans were brandishing such slogans as *Wir sind ein Volk* ('we are one people'), calling for unification in the name of a collective identity with strong nationalistic overtones. The phrase *Wir sind ein Volk* does indeed evoke similar statements made in darker periods of German history. The difference between *das Volk* and *ein Volk* captures the ambivalent role played by West-Germany in its recent reunification with the former German Democratic Republic.

5 I am grateful to Sarah Mkhonza from the University of Swaziland for her help in understanding the situation in her country.

6 See also the response to Peirce's article by Betty Lou Dubois *TESOL Quarterly* 24/1: 105–12.

7 I am grateful to Brian Harrison for this particular insight.

8  I am grateful to Alexis Ngatcha from Yaounde Public Schools in Cameroun for his insights on the situation in Cameroun.
9  I am grateful to Chukwuma Ijoma from the University of Nigeria for his description of the situation in his country.

# Appendix I

## Schlittenfahren  *Helga M. Novak*

Das Eigenheim° steht in einem Garten. Der Garten ist groß. Durch   *private home*
denGarten fließt° ein Bach°. Im Garten stehen zwei Kinder. Das eine   *flows / brook*
der Kinder kann noch nicht sprechen. Das andere Kind ist größer. Sie
sitzen auf einem Schlitten°. Das kleinere Kind weint. Das größere sagt,   *sled*
5  gib den Schlitten her. Das kleinere weint. Es schreit°.   *screams*
    Aus dem Haus tritt° ein Mann. Er sagt, wer brüllt°, kommt rein°. Er   *steps / bawls / rein = herein:*
geht in das Haus zurück. Die Tür fällt hinter ihm zu.   *in*
    Das kleinere Kind schreit.
    Der Mann erscheint wieder in der Haustür. Er sagt, komm rein. Na   *Na . . . bald: hurry up /*
10  wirds bald°. Du kommst rein. Nix°. Wer brüllt, kommt rein. Komm rein.   *Nix = nichts*
Der Mann geht hinein. Die Tür klappt°.   *slams*
    Das kleinere Kind hält die Schnur° des Schlittens fest°. Es schluchzt°.   *rope / hält fest: holds tight /*
    Der Mann öffnet die Haustür. Er sagt, du darfst Schlitten fahren,   *sobs*
abernicht brüllen. Wer brüllt, kommt rein. Ja. Ja. Jaaa. Schluß jetzt°   *Schluß jetzt: that's enough*
15  Das größere Kind sagt, Andreas will immer allein fahren.
    Der Mann sagt, wer brüllt, kommt rein. Ob er nun Andreas heißt
oder sonstwie°.   *otherwise*
    Er macht die Tür zu.
    Das größere Kind nimmt dem kleineren den Schlitten weg. Das
20  kleinere Kind schluchzt, quietscht°, jault°, quengelt°.   *squeals / howls / whines*
    Der Mann tritt aus dem Haus. Das größere Kind gibt dem kleineren
den Schlitten zurück. Das kleinere Kind setzt sich auf den Schlitten.
Es rodelt°.   *sleds*
    Der Mann sieht in den Himmel°. Der Himmel ist blau. Die Sonne ist   *sky*
25  groß und rot. Es ist kalt.
    Der Mann pfeift° laut. Er geht wieder ins Haus zurück. Er macht die   *whistles*
Tür hinter sich zu.
    Das größere Kind ruft°, Vati°, Vati, Vati, Andreas gibt den Schlitten   *calls / daddy*
nicht mehr her.
30  Die Haustür geht auf. Der Mann steckt° den Kopf heraus. Er sagt,   *sticks*
wer brüllt, kommt rein. Die Tür geht zu.
    Das größere Kind ruft, Vati, Vativativati, Vaaatiii, jetzt ist Andreas in
den Bach gefallen.
    Die Haustür öffnet sich einen Spalt° breit°. Eine Männerstimme° ruft,   *crack / wide / man's voice*
35  wie oft soll ich das noch sagen, wer brüllt, kommt rein.

## Fragen

1. In was für einem Haus wohnt die Familie?
2. Was wissen Sie über den Garten?
3. Was wissen Sie über die Kinder?
4. Warum weint das kleinere Kind?
5. Warum kommt der Mann aus dem Haus? Was sagt er?
6. Wie ist das Wetter?
7. Wer fährt am Ende mit dem Schlitten?
8. Warum ruft das ältere Kind am Ende den Vater?
9. Was antwortet der Vater?

## Fragen zur Diskussion

1. Der Mann kommt mehrere Male zur Tür. Welche Sätze beschreiben
   das? Was sagen diese Sätze über den Mann?
2. Der Mann geht mehrere Mal ins Haus. Welche Sätze beschreiben das?
   Was ist damit gesagt?
3. Welchen Satz sagt der Mann immer wieder? Welchen Effekt hat das
   auf die Kinder? Auf den Leser?
4. Was wird über Jahreszeit und Wetter gesagt? Welche Rolle spielt das?
5. Warum benutzt die Autorin immer wieder das Wort „der Mann"?
   Welches andere Wort könnte sie benutzen?
6. Wie meint der Mann den letzten Satz? Wie verstehen Sie ihn?

## Sledding

The private home stands in a garden. The garden is big. Through the garden there flows a brook. In the garden are two children. One of the children cannot talk yet. The other child is bigger. They sit on a sled. The smaller child cries. The bigger one says, give me the sled. The smaller one cries. He screams.

A man steps out of the house. He says, he who screams comes in. He goes back into the house. The door closes behind him.

The smaller child screams.

The man appears again in the door. He says, come in. C'mon, hurry up. You come in. None of this. He who screams comes in. Come in.

The man goes inside. The door slams.

The smaller child holds the rope of the sled tight. He sobs.

The man opens the door. He says, you may ride the sled, but not scream. He who screams, comes in. Yes, yes, yes. That's enough.

The bigger child says, Andreas always wants to ride the sled alone.

The man says, he who screams, comes in. Whether he is called Andreas or any other name.

He closes the door.

The bigger child takes the sled away from the smaller one. The smaller child sobs, squeals, howls, whines.

The man steps out of the house. The bigger child gives back the sled to the smaller one. The smaller child sits down on the sled and sleds.

The man looks up at the sky. The sky is blue. The sun is big and red. It is cold.

The man whistles loudly. He goes back into the house. He closes the door behind him.

The bigger child calls, Daddy, Daddy, Daddy, Andreas doesn't want to give back the sled.

The door opens. The man sticks his head through the door. He says, he who screams comes in. The door closes.

The bigger child shouts, Daddy, Daddydaddydaddy, daaaaaaddy, Now Andreas has fallen into the brook!

The door opens a crack wide. A man's voice shouts, how often do I have to tell you, he who screams, comes in.

## Questions:

1. In what kind of a house does the family live?
2. What do you know about the garden?
3. What do you know about the children?
4. Why does the small child cry?
5. Why does the man come out of the house? What does he say?
6. How is the weather?
7. Who rides the sled in the end?
8. Why does the older child call the father in the end?
9. What does the father answer?

## Questions for discussion:

1. The man comes several times to the door. Which sentences describe this? What do these sentences say about the man?
2. The man goes several times into the house. Which sentences describe this? What do these sentences mean?
3. Which sentence does the man repeat all the time? What effect does it have on the children? on the reader?
4. What is said about the seasons? the weather? Which role does the weather play here?
5. Why does the author always use the word 'man'? Which other word could she use?
6. What does the man mean in the last sentence? How do you understand him?

# Appendix II

## Article Four

### BACKGROUND NOTES
*for* Trapped Behind the Wheel

### Preview

*As metropolitan areas continue to grow, and as public transportation fails to expand, more workers find themselves in daily traffic jams. Many have found unusual ways to cope with this urban reality.*

### Culture

| | |
|---|---|
| **bald eagle** | the national bird of the United States, now near extinction. On the list of endangered species, the bald eagle is rarely seen in the wild. |
| **car pool** | a group of people who ride to and from work in the same car. In some locations, car pools can use special express lanes on the highway. |
| **Egg McMuffin™** [ˌɛg mək'məfən] | a product of the McDonald's fast food chain. Eaten for breakfast, an Egg McMuffin™ is a sandwich filled with a fried egg, cheese, and meat (either sausage, ham, or bacon). |
| **rush hour** | a period of time (not necessarily an hour) when people are going to or returning from work. During rush hour, streets are filled with cars, buses, and pedestrians. |
| **singles club** | an organization of unmarried individuals interested in meeting others who are not married. Singles clubs are found in most large cities. |
| **VFW** | an abbreviation for Veterans of Foreign Wars. VFW is a national organization of former military people who meet for civic and social purposes. |

### Vocabulary

| | |
|---|---|
| **adrenaline** [ə'drɛnələn] | epinephrine; a hormone produced by the adrenal gland. Adrenaline stimulates the heart and constricts the blood vessels. |
| **broker** | a financial agent who negotiates purchases and sales. Brokers work in brokerage houses. |
| **buzz** | a topic of conversation (slang) |
| **commuter** [kə'mjudə] | a person who travels (commutes) back and forth to work from home. Some commuters drive; others take public transportation. |
| **daydream** | to have dreams or pleasant thoughts while awake |
| **dummy** | a copy or imitation of someone or something |
| **entrée** ['antre] | the main course of a meal. An entrée is served after soup or salad. |
| **fetus** ['fidəs] | an unborn child. The issue of legal rights of fetuses is controversial. |
| **free-lance** | working independently and contracting with a number of people for work. Some writers and photographers prefer free-lance work to working with only one employer. |

## Lifestyles

| | |
|---:|:---|
| **gridlock** | a condition in which traffic cannot move. Gridlock is becoming a frequent occurrence in places such as New York City. |
| **laid back** | relaxed; not worried. Some people believe that being laid back fights stress. |
| **nest-building** | preparing one's surroundings to be homelike (or "nestlike") |
| **paralysis** [pəˈræləsəs] | a state of immobility; the inability to move |
| **real estate** | property; land and the buildings on it |
| **rear-view mirror** | the mirror attached to the inside center of the windshield of a car. It enables the driver to see what is behind the car. |
| **saga** [ˈsɑgə] | a long narrative about a person's adventures. The oldest written sagas date from the 12th and 13th centuries in Iceland. |
| **slurp** | to drink noisily |
| **speed demon** | a person who drives too fast |
| **stasis** [ˈstesəs] | a state of inactivity; a condition of stopping |
| **traffic** | the movement of vehicles or pedestrians through an area |
| **turnoff** | something, such as a sight or topic, that makes people react negatively or be uninterested |
| **worked over** | over-used; exploited |

## Lifestyles

**Going nowhere on the Long Island Expressway:**
"Your body releases more adrenaline, your blood vessels constrict, your pressure rises ...
You are still wound up three or four hours later."

# Trapped Behind The Wheel

*Clever commuters learn to live in the slow lane*

There are trends, all too easily discernible, in dinner conversations. The saga of domestic help is a persistent one — pretty worked over by now. Real estate is an ongoing turnoff, but the new buzz is even more boring and more inescapable. It is traffic.

In a scene replayed thousands of times each evening in Los Angeles, New York, Chicago and burgeoning suburbs nationwide, the last guests for a 7.30 dinner straggle in 40 minutes late, muttering their astonishment—but not, significantly, their apologies—that it took them 90 minutes to drive ten miles. Their woes inevitably inspire the other guests to a round of competitive traffic horror stories that continue well into the entrée.

There is the one about the drivers who sneak into the lane reserved for car pools by planting inflated dummies in the passenger seats. And the pregnant woman who successfully argued in court that she and her fetus were entitled to use the carpool lane because they were separate persons. Then there are the days that live in legend — like Oct. 29, 1986, when a single midafternoon accident on the San Diego Freeway spread gridlock along connecting freeways and surface streets from downtown Los Angeles to

the San Fernando Valley, trapping tens of thousands of motorists for eight full hours. (Survivors of such mythic urban struggles brag about them like good ole boys at the VFW bar.)

There are reasons for the quickening national paralysis: more and more people live and work in locations that are not linked to adequate public transport, millions of women have entered the work force and are new rush-hour drivers, ingenious alternatives seem to get stymied by lack of imagination or money or both, and, above all, gas is cheap. In places where gas is still below a dollar, many drivers have reverted to old habits, and in some parts of the U.S. a two-occupant car is about as common as a bald eagle.

In California the state government estimates that each day 300,000 work hours are lost to traffic jams at a cost of $2 million. On the Capital Beltway near Washington, gridlock costs employers as much as $120 million a year in lost time. But the toll on the individual commuter, usually lone but hardly a ranger, is heavier still. Without hope of release, he sits in his little cell inhaling exhaust fumes and staring blankly at the zinc sky.

Some drivers try to fight the sentence. Take Jeff Seibert, an associate professor of pediatrics

## Lifestyles

at the University of Miami School of Medicine, who finds that his 25-minute ride to work, which includes the unpredictable Dolphin Expressway, can stretch into an hour and 15 minutes. "When the radio traffic announcer advises to stay clear of a certain area, I drive right to that point," he says, figuring that the warning has cleared the congestion by dispersing most commuters onto different routes. Others, like Kathi Douglas, a recent graduate of Spelman College in Atlanta, undergo an attitude change. "I'm laid back and talkative, yet once I get on the road, I have no respect for rules and regulations," says Douglas. "You get to be really aggressive because you think it's the only way to get out of this madness."

Extreme frustration can lead to violence. Four freeway shootings have been reported in the Los Angeles area in the past eleven months. On the Santa Ana Freeway, a speed demon angered by a car that did not move from the fast lane pulled up alongside the offending vehicle and fatally shot a passenger in the front seat.

There are saner approaches to highway stasis. Ken Jenson, 28, a Los Angeles salesman, used to spend much of his hour-long commute singing with the radio. Last year he stopped the music and began studying to become a stockbroker. "I made tapes of the texts and took notes while I listened on the drive to and from work," explains Jenson, who is now a broker in the Westwood office of Merrill Lynch. "It's amazing that I didn't hit anyone." Using the rear-view mirror, many men shave with electric razors and women often apply their makeup. Some people even dress behind the wheel. Janice Conover, a Hampton Jitney Co. bus driver who regularly plies the Long Island Expressway (popularly known as the Long Island Parking Lot), has seen motorists so engrossed in the morning newspaper that they drift from one lane toward another, luckily at minimal speed.

Hungry drivers gobble breakfast, often an Egg McMuffin, from Styrofoam cartons and slurp coffee from no-slosh mugs. Others balance checkbooks, do crossword puzzles and dictate letters and grocery lists into pocket-size tape recorders. Hot summer weekends offer an opportunity for passengers to take partial charge of the car. Inching along to the approach to the George Washington Bridge between New Jersey and Manhattan, occupants of cars without air conditioning who face delays of more than an hour hold the doors open for a little circulation.

It is possible to transform an auto into a slow-rolling "home away from home." Larry Schreiner, a free-lance reporter for a Chicago radio station and several local TV stations, often lives and works in his Mercedes 560 SEL. "I have everything I need," says Schreiner, whose longest continuous stretch on wheels was 36 hours. His office supplies include five two-way radios, two cellular phones, one headset (so he can talk on radio shows while working on videotapes), two video cameras and three video recorders. That's not all. In the trunk Schreiner keeps batteries, lighting equipment, three still cameras, telephone books, road maps and a change of clothes.

For nest-building commuters, the place to go is Chicago's Warshawsky & Co., which bills itself as the largest auto parts and accessory store in the world. It offers in-dash televisions ($300), compact-disc adapters, orthopedic seat cushions, heated seats for winter, and computers with cruise control and estimated time of arrival (up to $149). Upscale drivers install $2,000 car phones (although in Los Angeles, where there are 65,000 subscribers, airwaves are jammed in rush hours). Ordinary folk can ape "techie" drivers by ordering an imitation antenna from Warshawsky for a mere $12.

Traffic is thick enough to defeat just about anything except perhaps the mating instinct. In fact, some have found that choked freeways can enhance the possibilities of finding a mate. Ruth Guillou, an enterprising Huntington Beach, Calif., widow, was idling along when she saw a "charming-looking man in a yellow Cadillac. I couldn't get him out of my mind. There should have been a way for me to make contact with him." Thus was born the Freeway Singles Club, a mail forwarding service whose participants pay $35 for a numbered decal that identifies them as members. The group has a roster of 2,000 in Southern California and has expanded to 16 states.

According to Manhattan Psychiatrist T.B. Karasu, motorists can be divided into two categories: adaptives, those who accept things as they are and understand that they cannot be in control of all situations, and nonadaptives. The nonadaptives, says Karasu, "blow their horns and irritate everybody else as well as themselves. Noise is an external and excessive stimulus that increases rather than decreases tension. When you yell or are yelled at, your body releases more adrenaline, your blood vessels constrict, your pressure rises, and you get headaches. You are still wound up three or four hours later." Karasu points out that non-adaptive behavior, or the inability to cope with freeway stress, could lead to heart attacks or strokes for some. He advises motorists to relax by thinking they are passengers in an airplane with a captain running things. "Listen to music, daydream, focus on things you normally don't find time to think about," says Karasu. "Above all else, accept that you are where you are, and there is nothing that you can do about it."

*—By Martha Smilgis. Reported by Dan Goodgame/ Los Angeles, with other bureaus*

## QUESTIONS AND ACTIVITIES

**Comprehension Questions**

1. What are the causes of the current traffic problems?
2. What are some of the negative results of such heavy traffic?
3. What kinds of things do drivers do to cope with their daily commute?

**Discussion Questions**

1. What are the different ways that people commute to work in your home culture? What do the majority of people do?
2. Is traffic a problem in your hometown or city? If so, what are its causes?
3. What solutions have people used in your hometown or country to deal with traffic problems?
4. Do you think that traffic problems are an inevitable part of the growth of cities, or can they be prevented?

**Group activities**

1. In groups of three or four, imagine that you are transportation commissioners for a major U.S. city. Identify as many solutions as you can to the traffic problems described in the article. What one solution would you recommend if the city had unlimited financial resources?
2. In groups of three or four, again imagine that you are transportation commissioners for a major U.S. city. This time assume that the city has no money to improve existing conditions. What recommendations would you make to the general population? Would you want laws passed to change people's behavior?

**Individual Work**

1. Keep a one-day record of your commuting to classes and/or work. What modes of transportation do you use? How much time do you spend in total? What is the total distance you travel? Multiply your figures for time and distance to get a figure for the week, the month, and the year. Do the figures surprise you? Why or why not?
2. Interview one other person, finding out the same information as in Individual Work 1 above. Does that person's commuting differ from yours? If so, how?

# Bibliography

Abastado, C. 1982a. 'Culture et médias'. *Le Français dans le Monde* 173.

Abastado, C. 1982b. 'Le phénomène "Apostrophes"'. Entretien avec Bernard Pivot. *Le Français dans le Monde* 173.

Abdallah-Pretceille, M. 1983. 'La perception de l'autre. Point d'appui de l'approche interculturelle'. *Le Français dans le Monde* 181.

Ackermann, I. (ed.) 1982. *Als Fremder in Deutschland*. München: dtv.

Adaskou, K., D. Britten, and B. Fahsi. 1990. 'Design decisions on the cultural content of a secondary English course for Morocco'. *ELT Journal* 44/1.

Akinnaso, F. N. 1991. 'The development of a multilingual language policy in Nigeria'. *Applied Linguistics* 12/1.

Akutagawa, R. [1918] 1970. *Rashomon and Other Stories*. Translated by Takashi, Kojima. New York: W.W. Norton (Liveright).

Alatis, J. E. (ed.) 1990. *Linguistics, Language Teaching and Language Acquisition: The Interdependence of Theory, Practice and Research*. Georgetown University Round Table on Languages and Linguistics 1990. Washington, D.C.: Georgetown University Press.

Allen, W. and K. Anderson. 1989. 'Foreign languages in the disciplines: A program of curricular integration'. Northfield, MN: St Olaf College (mimeo).

Allwright, D. 1980. 'Turns, topics and tasks: Patterns of participation in language learning and teaching' in Larsen-Freeman 1980.

American Council for the Teaching of Foreign Languages (ACTFL). 1986. *Proficiency Guidelines*. Hastings-on-Hudson, NY: ACTFL Materials Center.

Anderson, B. 1983. *Imagined Communities*. London: Verso.

**Apatride, J.** 1982. 'Ein- und Ausschlüpfen' in Ackermann (ed.) 1982.

**Aronowitz S.** and **H. A. Giroux.** 1991. *Postmodern Education. Politics, Culture, and Social Criticism.* Minneapolis: University of Minnesota Press.

**Attinasi, J.** and **P. Friedrich.** (forthcoming). 'Dialogic breakthrough: Catalysis and synthesis in life-changing dialogue' in Mannheim and Tedlock (eds.).

**Bacon, S.** 1990. 'On topic choice in oral proficiency assessment' in VanPatten and Lee (eds.) 1990.

**Bakhtin, M. M.** 1986. *Speech Genres and Other Late Essays.* Transl. V. W. McGee. Austin: University of Texas Press.

**Baliles, G. L.** 1989. 'America in transition. Report of the governors' task force on international education'. Washington, D.C.: American Council on Education.

**Barnett, M. A.** 1989. *More Than Meets the Eye. Foreign Language Reading. Theory and Practice.* Washington, D.C.: Center for Applied Linguistics.

**Barthes, R.** 1966. *Critique et Vérité.* Paris: Editions du Seuil.

**Bateson, G.** 1979. *Mind and Nature.* New York: Dutton.

**Batke, P.** 1991. 'ToolBook, windows, and hypermedia'. *IAT Briefings.* Research Triangle Park, N.C.: Institute for Academic Technology.

**Baumgratz-Gangl, G.** 1989. 'Neue Bedingungen und Möglichkeiten des allgemeinen und fachbezogenen Fremdsprachenerwerbs im Rahmen von Hochschulkooperationsprogrammen' in Wierlacher *et al.* (eds.) 1989.

**Baumgratz, G.,** and **R. Stephan** (eds.). 1987. *Fremdsprachenlernen als Beitrag zur internationalen Verständigung.* München: iudicium.

**Beacco, J.-C.** 1984. 'Savoirs sociaux'. *Le Français dans le Monde* 184.

**Beacco, J.-C.** and **S. Lieutaud** (eds.). 1981. *Moeurs et mythes. Lecture des civilisations et documents authentiques écrits.* Paris: Hachette.

**Becker, A. L.** 1982. 'Beyond translation: Esthetics and language description' in Byrnes (ed.) 1982.

**Becker, A. L.** 1984. 'Toward a post-structuralist view of language learning' in Guiora (ed.) 1984.

**Becker, A. L.** 1985. 'Language in particular: A lecture' in Tannen (ed.) 1985.

Becker, A. L. 1992. 'Silence across languages: An essay' in Kramsch and McConnell-Ginet (eds.) 1992.

Beckerman, H. S. 1989. *Inspirations for ESL*. Englewood Cliffs, N.J.: Prentice Hall Regents.

Bellah, R. N., R. Madsen, W. M. Sullivan, A. Swidler, and S. M. Tipton. 1985. *Habits of the Heart: Individualism and Commitment in American Life*. Berkeley: University of California Press.

Bernhardt, E. B. 1991. *Reading Development in a Second Language*. Norwood, N.J.: Ablex.

Berns, M. 1990. *Contexts of Competence*. London: Pergamon.

Bertho, C. 1980. 'L'invention de la Bretagne: Genèse sociale d'un stéréotype. *Actes de la Recherche en Sciences Sociales. L'identité*. Paris: Editions de Minuit, 35.

Bichsel, P. 1964. *Eigentlich möchte Frau Blum den Milchmann kennenlernen*. Olten, Switzerland: Walter Verlag.

Bilezikian, M. and M. Sarde (eds.). 1989. *Communication and Media in Contemporary French Culture. Contemporary French Civilization* XIII/2.

Bisk, A. 1919. *Izbrannoe iz Rainera Maria Rilke*. Paris: Alexander Bisk.

Blum-Kulka, S., J. House, and G. Kasper (eds.).1989. *Cross-Cultural Pragmatics: Requests and Apologies*. Vol.XXXI in the series Advances in Discourse Processes, Roy O. Freedle (ed.). Norwood, N.J.: Ablex.

Bolten, J. 1989. 'Zusatzstudium Deutsch als Fremdsprache/ Interkulturelle Germanistik an der Universität Düsseldorf' in Wierlacher *et al* (eds.) 1989.

Borkin, N. and S. M. Reinhart. 1978. 'Excuse me' and 'I'm sorry'. *TESOL Quarterly* 12/1.

Boschma, N., K. van Eunen, R. Hiuizinga, and T. Ris. 1987. *Lesen, na und? Ein literarisches Arbeitsbuch für die ersten Jahre Deutsch*. München: Langenscheidt.

Bourdieu, P. 1967. 'Systems of education, systems of thought'. *International Social Science Journal*, 19/3.

Bourdieu, P. 1975. 'Structures sociales et structures de perception du monde social'. *Actes de la Recherche en Sciences Sociales* 2.

Bourdieu, P. 1980. 'L'identité et la représentation. Eléments pour une réflexion critique sur l'idée de région'. *Actes de la Recherche en Sciences Sociales*, 35.

Bredella, L. and D. Haack (eds.). 1988. *Perceptions and Misper-*

*ceptions: The United States and Germany. Studies in Intercultural Understanding.* Tübingen: Gunter Narr.

Breen, M. 1985a. 'Authenticity in the language classroom'. *Applied Linguistics* 6/1.

Breen, M. 1985b. 'The social context for language learning—A neglected situation?' *Studies in Second Language Acquisition* 7/2.

Brooks, N. 1975. 'The analysis of foreign and familiar cultures' in Lafayette (ed.) 1975.

Burtow, G. (ed.) 1980. *Spotlight on Literature.* New York: Random House.

Butzkamm, W. 1983. 'Der kritische Moment: zwischen formbezogenem Ueben und inhaltsbezogenem Sprechen' in Heid (ed.) 1983.

Byram, M. 1989. *Cultural Studies in Foreign Language Education.* Clevedon, U.K.: Multilingual Matters.

Byrnes, H. 1982. *Contemporary Perceptions of Language: Interdisciplinary dimensions.* Georgetown University Roundtable on Languages and Linguistics 1982. Washington, D.C.: Georgetown University Press.

Byrnes, H. 1991. 'Reflections on the development of cross-cultural communicative competence in the foreign language classroom' in Freed (ed.) 1991.

Canale, M. 1984. 'Considerations in the testing of reading and listening proficiency'. *Foreign Language Annals* 17/4.

Carrell, P.L., J. Devine, and D. E. Eskey (eds.). 1988. *Interactive Approaches to Second Language Reading.* Cambridge: Cambridge University Press.

Carroll, R. 1989. 'Film et analyse culturelle: Le remake' in Bilezikian and Sarde (eds.) 1989.

Cazden, C. 1989. 'Contributions of the Bakhtin circle to "communicative competence"'. *Applied Linguistics* 10/2.

Cazden, C. 1992. 'Performing expository texts in the foreign language classroom' in Kramsch and McConnell-Ginet (eds.) 1992.

Cazden, C., V. P. John, and D. Hymes (eds.) 1972 *Functions of Language in the Classroom.* New York: Teachers College Press.

Chafe, W. 1982. 'Integration and involvement in speaking, writing, and oral literature' in Tannen, D. (ed.) 1982.

Chafe, W. 1985. 'Linguistic differences produced by differences between speaking and writing' in Olson, Torrance, and Hildyard (eds.) 1985.

Charaudeau, P. 1983. *Langage et discours. Eléments de semiolinguistique (Théorie et pratique)*. Paris: Hachette

Chatman, S. 1978. *Story and Discourse. Narrative Structure in Fiction and Film*. Ithaca, NY: Cornell University Press.

Cisterne, N. 1984. 'Ingénieurs en Europe, ou ingénieurs européens? Comparaison de la formation et du statut des ingénieurs en France, Grande-Bretagne et RFA'. *Les Cahiers du CEFI*. No. 7, juillet 1984.

Clarke, J. and M. Clarke. 1990. 'Stereotyping in TESOL materials' in Harrison (ed.) 1990.

Coger, L. I. and M. R. White. 1973. *Readers Theater Handbook: A Dramatic Approach to Literature*. Glenview, IL: Scott Foresman. (Institute for Readers Theatre. P.O.Box 17193. San Diego, CA 92117).

Collie, J. and S. Slater. 1987. *Literature in the Language Classroom. A Resource Book of Ideas and Activities*. Cambridge: Cambridge University Press.

Compte, C. and D. Coste. 1983. 'La composante télévision dans un ensemble multimédia pour l'apprentissage du français en Europe'. *Le Français dans le Monde 174*.

Coste, D. 1970. 'Textes et documents authentiques au niveau 2'. *Le Français dans le Monde 73*.

Coste, D. and J. Hébrard (eds.). 1991. *Vers le Plurilinguisme? Ecole et politique linguistique*. Special issue of *Le Français dans le Monde*.

Crow, J. A. and E. Dudley. 1984. *El Cuento*, 2nd edn. New York: Holt Rinehart and Winston.

Day, R. R. (ed.). 1986. *Talking to Learn. Conversation in Second Language acquisition*. Rowley, MA: Newbury House.

de Boot, K., R. Ginsberg, and C. Kramsch (eds.) 1991. *Foreign Language Research in Cross-Cultural Perspective*. Amsterdam: Benjamins.

Debyser, F. 1981. 'Lecture des civilisations' in Beacco and Lieutaud (eds.) 1981.

de Certeau, M. 1984. *The Practice of Everyday Life*. Berkeley: University of California Press. (from the French 1980. *L'invention du quotidien*. Paris: U.G.E., 1980)

di Pietro, R. 1987. *Strategic Interaction: Learning Languages through Scenarios*. Cambridge: Cambridge University Press.

**Domin, H.** (ed.). 1966. *Doppelinterpretationen. Das zeitgenössische Gedicht zwischen Autor und Leser.* Frankfurt: Athenäum.
**Domin, H.** 1970. *Ich will dich.* München: Piper und Co Verlag.
**Doughty, C. and T. Pica.** 1986. ' "Information Gap" tasks: Do they facilitate second language acquisition? *TESOL Quarterly* 20/2.
**Duff, P. A.** 1986. 'Another look at interlanguage talk: Taking task to task' in Day (ed.) 1986.
**Dürrenmatt, F.** 1976. *Grieche sucht Griechin.* Frankfurt/Main: Ullstein.

**Edmondson, W.** 1983. 'Kann der Lehrer Fehler erzeugen? Uberlegungen zum Korrekturverhalten im Fremdsprachenunterricht' in Heid (ed.) 1983.
**Edmondson, W.** 1985. 'Discourse worlds in the classroom and in foreign language learning'. *Studies in Second Language Acquisition* 7/2.
**Ehrlich, S., P. Avery, and C. Yorio.** 1989. 'Discourse structure and'the negotiation of comprehensible input'. *Studies in Second Language Acquisition* 11/4.
**Ellis, R.** (ed.) 1987. *Second Language Acquisition in Context.* Englewood Cliffs, N.J.: Prentice-Hall International.
**Ellis, R.** 1992. 'The classroom context: An acquisition-rich or an acquisition-poor environment?' in Kramsch and McConnell-Ginet (eds.) 1992.
**Ellis, R. and C. Roberts.** 1987. 'Two approaches for investigating second language acquisition in context'. in Ellis (ed.) 1987.
**ELT Journal.** 1990. Thematic issue on the teaching of literature. 44/3.

**Faerch, C. and G. Kasper.** 1987. *Introspection in Second Language Research.* Clevedon, UK: Multilingual Matters.
**Fairclough, N. L.** 1989. *Language and Power.* London: Longman.
**Fillmore, C. J.** 1981. 'Ideal readers and real readers' in Tannen (ed.) 1981.
**Fiske, J.** 1989a. *Understanding Popular Culture.* Boston: Unwin Hyman.
**Fiske, J.** 1989b. *Reading the Popular.* Boston: Unwin Hyman.
**Fiske, J. and J. Hartley.** 1978. *Reading Television.* London: Methuen.
**Flanders, N. A.** 1960. *Interaction Analysis in the Classroom:*

*A Manual for Observers*. Ann Arbor: University of Michigan Press.

**Flores, A.** (ed.). 1965. *An Anthology of German Poetry from Hölderlin to Rilke in English Translation*. Gloucester, Mass: Peter Smith.

**Fowler, R.** 1986. *Linguistic Criticism*. Oxford: Oxford University Press.

**Frawley, W.** and **J. Lantolf.** 1985. 'Second language discourse: A Vygotskyan perspective'. *Applied Linguistics* 6/1.

**Freed, B. F.** (ed.). 1991. *Foreign Language Acquisition Research and the Classroom*. Lexington, Mass: D.C.Heath.

**Freed, B. F.** and **E. B. Bernhardt.** 1992. 'In and around the foreign language classroom' in Kramsch and McConnell-Ginet (eds.) 1992.

**Freedle, R. O.** 1979. *New Directions in Discourse Processing*. Vol II in the series *Advances in Discourse Processes*. Freedle, R. O. (ed.). Norwood, N.J.: Ablex.

**Freire, P.** 1970. *Pedagogy of the Oppressed*. New York: Seabury.

**Freire, P.** 1985. *The Politics of Education: Culture, Power and Liberation*. South Hadley, Mass: Bergin and Garvey.

**Fricke, D.** 1983. 'Die Literatur der Resistance und Kollaboration im Französischunterricht. I und II'. *Die Neueren Sprachen* 82/2, 82/5–6.

**Fujikawa, H.** (ed.). 1967. *Rilke Shishuu* Tokyo: Kadokawa Shoten.

**Furstenberg, G.** 1988. 'Quand une technologie rencontre une pédagogie....'. *Le Français dans le Monde*, special issue.

**Garrett, N., J. Noblitt,** and **F. Dominguez.** 1989. 'Computers in foreign language teaching and research: A "new humanism"' in Graves (ed.) 1989.

**Garza, T.** 1990. 'Bringing cultural literacy into the foreign language classroom through video' in Alatis (ed.). 1990.

**Gass, S. M.** and **E. Varonis.** 1986. 'Sex differences in NNS/NNS interactions' in Day (ed.) 1986.

**Gass, S., C. Madden, D. Preston,** and **L. Selinker** (eds.) 1989. *Variation in Second Language Acquisition: Discourse and Pragmatics*. Clevedon, England: Multilingual Matters.

**Gass, S.** and **G. Crookes** (eds.). (forthcoming). *Task-based Learning in a Second Language*. Clevedon: Multilingual Matters.

Geertz, C. 1983. *Local Knowledge. Further Essays in Interpretive Anthropology*. New York: Basic Books.

Giroux, H. 1988. *Schooling and the Struggle for Public Life: Critical Pedagogy in the Modern Age*. Minneapolis: University of Minnesota Press.

Glissant, E. 1981. *Le discours antillais*. Paris: Seuil.

Gnutzmann, C., F. Königs, and W. Pfeiffer (eds.). 1992. *Fremdsprachenunterricht im internationalen Vergleich: Perspektive 2000*. Frankfurt: Diesterweg.

Goethe Institut. 1969. 'What Have I in My Bag?' Videotape. Paris: Goethe Institut.

Goffman, E. 1981. *Forms of Talk*. Philadelphia: University of Pennsylvania Press.

Golding, W. 1964. *Lord of the Flies*. Casebook edition. New York: Putnam's Sons.

Goodwin, C. 1981. *Conversational Organization. Interaction between Speakers and Hearers*. New York: Academic Press.

Graham, C. 1978. *Jazz Chants*. Oxford: Oxford University Press.

Graham, C. 1991. *Singing, Chanting and Telling Tales*. Englewood Cliffs, N.J.: Prentice-Hall.

Graves, W. H. (ed.). 1989. *Computing across the Curriculum*. McKinney,Texas: Academic Computing Publication EDUCOM.

Grellet, F. 1987. *Developing Reading Skills*. Cambridge: Cambridge University Press.

Gremmo, M. J., H. Holec, and P. Riley. 1985. 'Interactional structure: The role of role' in Riley (ed.) 1985.

Großklaus, G. and B. Thum. 1989. 'Teilstudium interkulturelle Germanistik an der Universität Karlsruhe (TH)' in Wierlacher et al. (eds.). 1989.

Gschwind-Holtzer, G. 1986. 'Apostrophes, le livre, les auteurs'. *Le Français dans le Monde* 199.

Guiora, A. Z. (ed.). 1984. *An Epistemology for the Language Sciences*. Michigan: Wayne State University Press.

Gumperz, J. J. and C. Roberts. 1978. *Developing Awareness Skills for Interethnic Communication*. Middlesex, U.K.: National Centre for Industrial Training.

Gumperz, J. J., T. C. Jupp, and C. Roberts. 1979. *Cross-Talk* . Southall, Middlesex, U.K.: National Centre for Industrial Training.

Hagège, C. 1985. *L'homme de paroles*. Paris: Fayard.

Hall, E. T. 1959. *The Silent Language*. New York: Doubleday.

Halliday, M. A. K. 1978, *Language As Social Semiotic. The Social Interpretation of Language and Meaning*. London: Arnold.

Halliday, M. A. K. 1989. 'Context of situation' in Halliday and Hasan 1989.

Halliday, M. A. K. 1990. 'New ways of meaning: A challenge for Applied Linguistics'. *Plenary address at the* tenth AILA Congress, Thessaloniki, Greece, April 1990.

Halliday, M. A. K. and R. Hasan. 1989. *Language, Context, and Text: Aspects of Language in a Social-Semiotic Perspective*. Oxford: Oxford University Press.

Harder, P. 1980. 'The reduced personality of the foreign language learner'. *Applied Linguistics* 1/3.

Harrison, B. (ed.). 1990. *Culture in the Language Classroom. ELT Documents* 132. London: Modern English Publications.

Heath, S. B. 1983. *Ways with Words*. Cambridge: Cambridge University Press.

Heid, M. (ed.) 1983. *Kommunikation im Klassenzimmer und Fremdsprachenlernen. New Yorker Werkstattgespräch 1982*. München: Goethe Institut.

Heid, M. (ed.). 1985. *Literarische Texte im kommunikativen Fremdsprachenunterricht*. München: Goethe Institut.

Higgs, T. V. (ed.) 1984. *Teaching for Proficiency, the Organizing Principle*. Lincolnwood, IL: National Textbook.

Hildyard, A. and S. Hidi. 1985. 'Oral-written differences in the production and recall of narratives' in Olson, Torrance and Hildyard (eds.) 1985.

Hines, M. and W. Rutherford (eds.). 1981. *On TESOL '81*. Washington, D.C.: TESOL.

Hiraga, M. K. 1989. 'Snow and crow: Basho's haiku in comparison with Robert Frost's short poem in an advanced Japanese classroom'. Paper presented at Cornell University Fall 1989.

Hiraga, M. K. (forthcoming). 'Iconicity in poetry: How poetic form embodies meaning'. Unpublished manuscript.

Horiba, Y. 1990. 'Narrative comprehension processes: A study of native and non-native readers of Japanese. *Modern Language Journal* 74/2.

Hughes, G. H. 1986. 'An argument for culture analysis in the second language classroom' in Valdes (ed.) 1986.

Hunfeld, H. 1990. *Literatur als Sprachlehre. Ansätze eines*

*hermeneutisch orientierten Fremdsprachenunterrichts.* München: Langenscheidt.
**Hymes, D. H.** 1972. 'Introduction' in Cazden, John, and Hymes (eds.) 1972.
**Hymes, D. H.** 1974. *Foundations in Sociolinguistics: An Ethnographic Approach.* Philadelphia: University of Pennsylvania Press.

**Isenberg, N.** 1990. 'Literary competence: the EFL reader and the role of the teacher' *ELT Journal* 44/3.
**Iyer, P. M. Eisner, J. Lang,** and **G. de Michelis.** 1991. 'A Brave New Culture?' *New Perspectives Quarterly* 8/4.

**Jakobson, R.** 1960. 'Closing statement: Linguistics and poetics' in Sebeok (ed.) 1960.
**Jackson, Y.** 1989. 'Establishing the frame of reference. Analysis of *Snow Country.*' Term paper, Cornell University.
**Jackson, Y.** 1990. 'Negotiation of meaning and topic management in Japanese NS / American NNS conversations'. Term paper, Cornell University.
**Jarvis, G. A.** (ed.) 1974. *Responding to New Realities.* ACTFL Foreign Language Education Series, vol. 5. Skokie, Illinois: National Textbook.
**Jorden, E.** 1992. 'Culture in the Japanese language classroom: A pedagogical paradox' in Kramsch and McConnell-Ginet (eds.) 1992.
**Johnson, D. W.** and **R. T. Johnson.** 1987. *Learning Together and Alone: Cooperative, Competitive and Individualistic Learning.* Englewood Cliffs, N.J.: Prentice-Hall.
**Jurasek, R.** 1988. 'Integrating foreign languages into the college curriculum'. *Modern Language Journal* 72/1.

**Kachru, B. B.** 1986. *The Alchemy of English: The Spread, Functions, and Models of Non-Native Englishes.* Oxford: Pergamon.
**Kafka, F.** [1916] 1960. *Die Verwandlung.* New York: W.W. Norton.
**Kagan, S.** 1989. *Cooperative Learning: Resources for Teachers.* Resources for Teachers: San Juan Capistrano, California.
**Kalberg, S.** 1987. 'West-German and American interaction forms: One level of structured misunderstandings'. *Theory, Culture and Society*, Vol.4. London: SAGE.

**Kanpol, B.** 1990. 'Political applied linguistics and postmodernism: Towards an engagement of similarity within difference. A reply to Pennycook'. *Issues in Applied Linguistics* 1/2.

**Kast, B.** 1984. *Literatur im Unterricht. Deutsch als Fremdsprache. Methodisch-didaktische Vorschläge für den Lehrer.* München: Goethe-Institut.

**Kast, B.** 1985. *Jugendliteratur im kommunikativen Deutschunterricht.* München: Langenscheidt.

**Kawabata, Y.** 1947. *Yukiguni.* Tokyo, Japan: Sokansha.

**Keller, G.** 1987. 'Auto-und Heterostereotype amerikanischer und deutscher Schüler in einer neuen Kulturkunde'. *Die Neueren Sprachen* 86/1.

**Kinginger, C.** 1989. 'Task-variation and classroom learner discourse'. Unpublished PhD Thesis. Urbana-Champaign: University of Illinois.

**Koch, K.** 1970. *Wishes, Lies and Dreams. Teaching children to write poetry.* New York: Vintage Books.

**Koch, K.** 1983. *Rose, where did you get that red? Teaching great poetry to children.* New York: Vintage Books.

**Königs, F. G.** 1991. 'Sprachlehrforschung: Konturen und Perspektiven'. *Neusprachliche Mitteilungen* 2.

**Kramsch, C.** 1983. 'Culture and constructs: Communicating attitudes and values in the foreign language classroom'. *Foreign Language Annals* 16/6.

**Kramsch, C.** 1984. *Interaction et discours dans la classe de langue.* Paris: Hatier-Credif.

**Kramsch, C.** 1987a. 'Socialization and literacy in a foreign language: Learning through interaction'. *Theory into Practice* 26/4. Columbus: The Ohio State University.

**Kramsch, C.** (ed.). 1987b. Special issue on the teaching of literature. *Die Unterrichtspraxis* 2.

**Kramsch, C.** 1987c. 'Foreign language textbooks' construction of foreign reality'. *Canadian Modern Language Review* 44/1.

**Kramsch, C.** 1987d. 'Literary texts in the language classroom: A discourse perspective'. *Modern Language Journal* 69/4.

**Kramsch, C.** 1988a. 'Beyond the skill vs. content debate: The multiple discourse worlds of the foreign language curriculum' in Patrikis (ed.) 1988.

**Kramsch, C.** 1988b. 'The cultural discourse of foreign language textbooks' in Singerman (ed.) 1988.

**Kramsch, C.** 1991. 'Culture in language learning: A view from the United States' in de Boot, Ginsberg and Kramsch (eds.) 1991.

Kramsch, C. 1992. 'Foreign languages and international education in the United States' in Gnutzmann, Königs, and Pfeiffer (eds.) 1992.

Kramsch, C. and M. Mueller. 1991. *Celebrating, Understanding, Creating Poetry in the Foreign Language Class*. Lincolnwood, Illinois: National Textbook Company.

Kramsch, C. and S. McConnell-Ginet (eds.). 1992. *Text and Context: Cross-Disciplinary Perspectives on Language Study*. Lexington, MA: D.C. Heath.

Kramsch C. and S. McConnell-Ginet. 1992a. '(Con)textual knowledge in language education' in Kramsch and McConnell-Ginet (eds.) 1992.

Kramsch, C. and S. McConnell-Ginet. 1992b. 'Conversational epilogue' in Kramsch and McConnell-Ginet (eds.) 1992.

Krashen, S. [1982] 1988. *Second Language Acquisition and Second Language Learning*. New York: Prentice Hall International.

Krechel, R. 1987. *Konkrete Poesie im Unterricht des Deutschen als Fremdsprache*. Heidelberg: Julius Gross Verlag.

Krusche, D. 1985. 'Lese-Unterschiede. Zum interkulturellen Leser-Gespräch' in Wierlacher, A. *et al.* (eds.) 1989.

Krusche, D. and R. Krechel. 1984. *Anspiel*. Bonn: InterNationes.

Lach-Newinsky, P. and M. Seletzky. 1986. *Encounters. Working with Poetry*. Bochum: Ferdinand Kamp.

Lado, R. 1957. *Linguistics Across Cultures: Applied Linguistics for Language Teachers*. Ann Arbor: University of Michigan Press.

Lafayette, R. (ed.). 1975. *The Culture Revolution in Foreign Language Teaching*. Skokie, Illinois: National Textbook Company.

Lakoff, G. 1987. *Women, Fire, and Dangerous Things. What Categories Reveal About the Mind*. Chicago: University of Chicago Press.

Lakoff, G. and M. Johnson. 1980. *Metaphors We Live By*. Chicago: University of Chicago Press.

Lakoff, R. 1990. *Talking Power. The Politics of Language*. New York: Basic Books.

Lambert, R. D. 1989. *International Studies and the Under-*

*graduate*. Washington, D.C.: American Council on Education.

Larsen-Freeman, D. (ed.) 1980. *Discourse Analysis in Second Language Research*. Rowley, Mass: Newbury House.

Larsen-Freeman, D. 1990. 'On the need for a theory of language teaching' in Alatis (ed.) 1990.

Lebras, H. and E. Todd. 1981. *L'invention de la France*. Paris: Hachette.

LeGoff, J. 1978. *La Nouvelle Histoire*. Paris, Retz.

Lee, J. F. 1986. 'Background knowledge and L2 reading'. *Modern Language Journal* 70/4.

Lightbown, P. 1986. 'Great expectations: Second language research and classroom teaching. *Applied Linguistics* 6/2.

Lightbown, P. 1992. 'Getting quality input in the second/foreign language classroom' in Kramsch and McConnell-Ginet (eds.) 1992.

Little, D. G. and D. M. Singleton. 1988. 'Authentic materials and the role of fixed support in language teaching: Towards a manual for language learners. *CLCS Occasional Paper* no.20. Dublin: Trinity College Centre for Language and Communication Studies.

Liskin-Gasparro, J. 1984. 'The ACTFL proficiency guidelines: A historical perspective' in Higgs (ed.) 1984.

Long, M. 1983. 'Native speaker / non-native speaker conversation and the negotiation of comprehensible input'. *Applied Linguistics* 4/2.

Long, M. 1989. 'Task, group and task-group interactions'. *University of Hawaii Working papers in ESL*,8/2.

Long, M. 1991. 'Focus on form: A design feature in language teaching methodology' in de Boot, Ginsberg, and Kramsch (eds.) 1991.

Löschmann, M. and M. Löschmann. 1984. 'Authentisches im Fremdsprachenunterricht'. *Deutsch als Fremdsprache*, 21/1.

Lyman, P. 1988. 'The computer revolution in the classroom: A progress report. *Academic Computing*. March/April.

Lyons, J. 1977. *Semantics*, Vols. 1 and 2. Cambridge: Cambridge University Press.

Maar, P. 1973. *Summelsarium oder 13 wahre Lügengeschichten*. Hamburg: Verlag Friedrich Oetinger.

Maley, A. 1987. 'Poetry and song as language-learning activities' in Rivers (ed.) 1987.

Maley, A. and A. Duff. 1989. *The Inward Ear. Poetry in the language classroom.* Cambridge: Cambridge University Press.

Mannheim B. and D. Tedlock. (eds.). (forthcoming). *The Dialogic Emergence of Culture.* Philadelphia: University of Pennsylvania Press.

Marx, L. 1964. *The Machine in the Garden. Technology and the Pastoral Ideal in America.* Oxford: Oxford University Press.

Matsuo, Basho. [1693] 1972. *Matsuo Basho Shu.* N. Imoto, N. Hori, and T. Muramatsu (eds.). Tokyo: Shoogakkan.

Meinhof, U. H. 1990. 'Verständnisstrategien für fremdsprachige Fernsehnachrichten'. *Die Neueren Sprachen* 89/6.

Miller, J. Hillis. 1992. 'Translation as the double production of texts' in Kramsch and McConnell-Ginet (eds.) 1992.

Monaco, J. 1977. *How to Read a Film.* New York: Oxford University Press.

Morgenstern, D. 1989. 'Empowering language learners'. Presentation at ACTFL Annual Convention, November, Monterey, California.

Morson, G. S. (ed.) 1986. *Bakhtin. Essays and Dialogues on His Work.* Chicago: University of Chicago Press.

Mouchon, J. and F. Vanoye. 1982. 'Le jeu télévisé comme dispositif'. *Le Français dans le Monde* 173.

Müller-Jacquier, B.-D. 1986. 'Interkulturelle Verstehensstrategien—Vergleich und Empathie' in Neuner (ed.) 1986.

Murray, J. H., D. Morgenstern, and G. Furstenberg. 1989. 'The Athena language-learning project: Design issues for the next generation of computer-based language-learning tools' in Smith (ed.). 1989.

Neuner, G. (ed.). 1986. *Kulturkontraste im DaF-Unterricht.* München: Goethe Institut.

Ngatcha, A. 1991. *Inhalte und Methoden des Deutschunterrichts an Kameruner Sekundarschulen: Bestandsaufnahme und zukünftige Möglichkeiten der interkulturellen Kommunikation.* Hamburg: Verlag an der Lottbeck.

Noblitt, J. 1988. 'Writing, technology and secondary orality'. *Academic Computing.* February.

Noblitt, J. 1989. 'Technology and language learning'. *Academic Computing,* October.

Nold, G. 1983. 'Grundzüge eines lernfördernden Sprachverhaltens des Lehrers im Fremdsprachenunterricht' in Heid (ed.) 1983.

Nora, P. 1986. *Les lieux de mémoire.* Vol.II. La nation. Paris: Gallimard.

Nostrand, H. L. 1974. 'Empathy for a second culture: Motivations and techniques' in Jarvis (ed.) 1974.

Nostrand, H. L. 1988. 'Culture in language teaching: The next phase'. *Association of Departments of Foreign Languages (ADFL) Bulletin* 20/1.

Nostrand, H. L. 1989. 'Authentic texts—cultural authenticity: An editorial'. *Modern Language Journal* 73/1.

Nutting, P. 1987. 'Continuing the story. Poetic writing in German literature courses'. *Die Unterrichtspraxis* 2.

Nystrand, M. 1986. *The Structure of Written Communication. Studies in Reciprocity between Writers and Readers.* New York: Academic Press.

Ochs, E. and D. Taylor. 1992. 'Science at Dinner' in Kramsch and McConnell-Ginet (eds.) 1992.

Olson, D. R., N. Torrance, and A. Hildyard. (eds.). 1985. *Literacy, Language and Learning. The Nature and Consequences of Reading and Writing.* Cambridge: Cambridge University Press.

Omaggio, A. C. 1986. *Teaching Language in Context: Proficiency-Oriented Instruction.* Boston: Heinle and Heinle.

Ong, W. 1982. *Orality and Literacy.* New York: Methuen.

Ortega y Gasset, J. 1959. 'The difficulty of reading'. *Diogenes* 28.

Ozzello, Y. R. 1987. 'J'ose ou j'ose pas? Lecture plurielle d'une nouvelle de Rémy de Gourmont'. *Teaching Language Through Literature* XXVII:1.

Ozzello, Y. R. 1978. 'Contraintes et créations: pédagogie de la production poétique'. *French Review* 5.

Patrikis, P. (ed.) 1988. *Language Learning and Liberal Education.* Newhaven, CT: Consortium for Language Teaching and Learning.

Patrikis, P.C., J. H. Murray, D. A. Bantz, R. L. Jones, and J. S. Noblitt. 1990. *Multimedia and Language Learning.* Institute for Academic Technology, University of North Carolina at Chapel Hill: Academic Computing Publications Inc.

Peirce, B. L. 1989. 'Toward a pedagogy of possibility in the teaching of English internationally. People's English in South Africa'.

*TESOL Quarterly* 23/3; and Response to Betty Lou Dubois, *TESOL Quarterly* 24/1.

**Pennycook, A.** 1990. 'Towards a critical applied linguistics for the 1990s. *Issues in Applied Linguistics* 1/1.

**Perkins, J.** 1980. 'The president's commission on foreign language and international studies: Its origin and work'. *Modern Language Journal* 64/1.

**Peterson, E. E.** 1985. 'Readers Theatre: An annotated bibliography'. ERIC Clearinghouse on Reading and Communication Skills, Urbana, ILL: Speech Communication Association, Annandale, VA. (ED 289207).

**Philips, S.** 1972. 'Participant structures and communicative competence: Warm Spring children in community and classroom' in Cazden, John, and Hymes (eds.) 1972.

**Pica, T.** 1987a. 'Second language acquisition, social interaction and the classroom'. *Applied Linguistics* 8/1.

**Pica, T.** 1987b. 'Interlanguage adjustments as an outcome of NS–NNS negotiated interaction'. *Language Learning* 38/1.

**Pica, T.** 1992. 'The textual outcomes of NS–NNS negotiation: What do they reveal about second language learning?' in Kramsch and McConnell-Ginet (eds.) 1992.

**Pica, T., L. Holliday, N. Lewis, D. Berducci,** and **J. Newman.** 1991. 'Language learning through interaction: What role does gender play?' *Studies in Second Language Acquisition* 13/3.

**Pica, T., R. Kanagy,** and **J. Falodun.** (forthcoming). 'Choosing and using communication tasks for second language research and instruction' in Gass and Crookes (eds.) (forthcoming).

**Porcher, L.** 1986. *La civilisation.* Paris: CLA international.

**Prabhu, N.** 1987. *Second Language Pedagogy.* Oxford: Oxford University Press.

**Preston, D. R.** 1989. *Sociolinguistics and Second Language Acquisition.* Oxford: Basil Blackwell.

**Prévert, J.** 1972. *Paroles.* Paris: Gallimard.

**Quasthoff, U. M.** 1986. 'Nichtsprachliches und "semisprachliches" Wissen in interkultureller Kommunikation und Fremdsprachendidaktik'. *Die Neueren Sprachen* 85/3.

**Rankin, J.** 1989. 'Re-visiting *Der Besuch der alten Dame*: Strategies for interpretation and interaction at the intermediate level'. *Die Unterrichtspraxis* 22/1.

**Ratcliff, G. L.** 1985. 'Readers Theatre: A basic approach to teaching literature'. *Teaching English in the Two Year College*   12/1.

Richards, J. C. 1990. 'The dilemma of teacher education in second language teaching' in Richards and Nunan (eds.) 1990.

Richards, J. C. and R. W. Schmidt (eds.). 1983. *Language and Communication*. London: Longman.

Richards, J. C. and D. Nunan (eds.). 1990. *Second Language Teacher Education*. Cambridge: Cambridge University Press.

Richardson, C. P. and S. G. Scinicariello. 1989. 'Television technology in the foreign language classroom' in Smith (ed.) 1989.

Riesman, D. 1950. *The Lonely Crowd*. New Haven: Yale University Press.

Riley, P. 1985. *Discourse and Learning*. London: Longman.

Rilke, R. M. [1903] 1955. *Sämtliche Werke. Erster Band. Neue Gedichte*. Frankfurt: Insel-Verlag.

Rilke, R. M. 1940. *Selected Poems*. With English Translations by C. F. MacIntyre. Berkeley: University of California Press.

Rilke, R. M. 1960 *Selected Works*. Vol.II Poetry. Translated by J. B. Leishman. New York: New Direction Books.

Rilke, R. M. 1981. *Selected Poems*. Translated by Robert Bly. New York: Harper and Row.

Rilke, R. M. 1982. *The Selected Poetry of Rainer Maria Rilke*. Edited and translated by Stephen Mitchell. New York: Random House.

Rilke, R. M. 1984 [1907]. *New Poems*. Translated by Edward Snow. San Francisco, CA: North Point Press.

Rilke, R. M. 1989. *The Best of Rilke*. Selected and translated by Walter Arndt. Hanover, N.H.: University Press of New England.

Rimmon-Kenan, S. 1983. *Narrative Fiction. Contemporary Poetics*. New York: Methuen.

Rivers, W. M. (ed.) 1987. *Interactive Language Teaching*. Cambridge: Cambridge University Press.

Robinson, G. L. N. 1988. *Crosscultural Understanding*. New York: Prentice Hall.

Rogers, M. 1988. 'Here comes hypermedia'. *Newsweek*, October 3.

Rosenblatt, L. 1978. *The Reader, the Text, the Poem: The Transactional Theory of the Literary Work*. Carbondale: Southern Illinois University Press.

Ross, J. 1982a. 'Poems as holograms'. *Poetics Journal* 2.
Ross, J. 1982b. 'Hologramming in a Robert Frost poem: The still point'. *Linguistics in the Morning Calm*. Ed. Linguistic Society of Korea. Seoul: Hanshin Publ. Co.
Ross, J. 1982c. 'human linguistics' in Byrnes (ed.) 1982.
Roth, R. W. 1983. 'Teaching point of view'. *Die Neueren Sprachen* 82/3.

Santoni, G. 1983. 'Stéréotypes, contextes visuels et dimensions sociales'. *Le Français dans le Monde* 181.
Saville-Troike, M. 1989. *The Ethnography of Communication*. 2nd edn. Oxford: Basil Blackwell.
Saville-Troike, M. 1992. 'Cultural maintenance and 'vanishing' Englishes' in Kramsch and McConnell-Ginet (eds.) 1992.
Scardamalia, M. and C. Bereiter. 1985. 'Development of dialectical processes in composition' in Olson, Torrance, and Hildyard (eds.) 1985.
Schegloff, E. A. 1972. 'Notes on a conversational practice: formulating place' in Sudnow (ed.) 1972.
Schinke-Llano, L. 1989. *TIME—We the People*. Lincolnwood, Illinois: National Textbook Company.
Schofer, P. and D. Rice. 1987. *Autour de la littérature. Ecriture et lecture aux cours moyens de français*. Boston: Heinle and Heinle.
Scollon, R. and S. Scollon. 1981. *Narrative, Literacy and Face in Interethnic Communication*. Vol. VII in the series Advances in Discourse Processes, Roy O. Freedle (ed.). Norwood, N.J.: Ablex.
Sebeok, T. (ed.) 1960. *Style in Language*. Cambridge, Mass: MIT Press.
Seelye, H. N. [1974] 1984. *Teaching Culture. Strategies for Intercultural Communication*. Lincolnwood, Illinois: National Textbook Co.
Seidensticker, E. G. 1956. *Snow Country*. New York: Alfred A. Knopf.
Sheldon, A. 1992. 'Conflict talk: Sociolinguistic challenges to self-assertion and how young girls meet them'. *Merrill-Palmer Quarterly*. 38/1.
Shouno, K. 1967. *Rilke Shishuu*. Tokyo: Hakuosha.
Shweder, R. A. 1990. 'Cultural psychology: What is it?' in Stigler and Herdt (eds.) 1990.
Singerman, A. (ed.) 1988. *Toward a New Integration of Lan-*

*guage and Culture.* Northeast Conference Reports 1988. Middlebury, Vermont: Northeast Conference.

Slavin, R. E. 1983. *Cooperative Learning.* New York: Longman.

Smith, F. 1985. 'A metaphor for literacy: Creating worlds or shunting information?' in Olson, Torrance and Hildyard (eds.) 1985.

Smith, W. Flint. (ed.). 1989. *Modern Technology in Foreign Language Education: Applications and Projects.* Lincolnwood, Illinois: National Textbook.

Soulé-Susbielles, N. 1988. 'Mais que peuvent-ils donc se dire? Exploration dans le travail de "paires' ". *Les Langues Modernes 6.*

Spycher, R. 1988. 'Understanding questions in classrooms of Kantonschulen of Zürich where English is taught as a foreign language'. Unpublished manuscript.

Stevick, E. W. 1988. *Teaching and Learning Languages.* Cambridge: Cambridge University Press.

Stigler, J. W. and G. Herdt (eds.) 1990. *Cultural Psychology: Essays on Comparative Human Development.* Cambridge: Cambridge University Press.

Stockton, F. 1980. 'The lady or the tiger' in Burtow (ed.) 1980.

Sudnow, D. (ed.) 1972. *Studies in Social Interaction.* New York: Free Press.

Swaffar, J. 1992. 'Written texts and cultural readings' in Kramsch and McConnell-Ginet (eds.) 1992.

Swaffar, J. K., M. Arens, and H. Byrnes. 1991. *Reading for Meaning. An Integrated Approach to Language Learning.* Englewood Cliffs, N.J.: Prentice-Hall.

Tajfel, H. 1982. *Social Identity and Intergroup Relations.* Cambridge: Cambridge University Press.

Tannen, D. 1979. 'What's in a frame? Surface evidence for underlying expectations', in Freedle, R. O. (ed.). 1979.

Tannen, D. 1982. 'The oral/literate continuum in discourse' in Tannen (ed.) 1982.

Tannen, D. 1985. 'Relative focus on involvement in oral and written discourse' in Olson, Torrance, and Hildyard (eds.) 1985.

Tannen, D. 1990. *You Just Don't Understand. Women and Men in Conversation.* New York: Ballantine.

Tannen, D. (ed.). 1981. *Analyzing Discourse: Text and Talk.* Georgetown University Round Table on Languages and Linguistics 1981. Washington, D.C.: Georgetown University Press.

**Tannen, D.** (ed.). 1982. *Spoken and Written Language. Exploring Orality and Literacy* Vol. IX in the series Advances in Discourse Processes, Roy O. Freedle (ed.) Norwood, N.J.: Ablex.

**Tannen, D.** (ed.). 1985. *Linguistics in Context: Connecting Observation and Understanding.* Vol. XXIX in the series Advances in Discourse Processes, Roy.O.Freedle, (ed.) Norwood, N.J.: Ablex.

**Tarone, E.** and **G. Yule.** 1989. *Focus on the Learner.* Oxford: Oxford University Press.

**Torrance, N.** and **D. Olson.** 1985. 'Oral and literate competencies in the early school years' in Olson, Torrance, and Hildyard (eds.) 1985.

**Traugott, E. C.** and **M. L. Pratt.** 1980. *Linguistics for Students of Literature.* New York: Harcourt Brace.

**Treichler, P. A.** and **C. Kramarae.** 1983. 'Women's talk in the ivory tower'. *Communication Quarterly* 31/2, 118-32.

**Triandis, H. C.** 1977. 'Theoretical framework for evaluation of cross-cultural training effectiveness'. *International Journal of Intercultural Relations* 1.

**Triandis, H. C.** 1989. 'Cross-cultural studies in individualism and collectivism'. *Nebraska Symposium on Motivation.* Lincoln: University of Nebraska Press.

**Underwood, J.** 1988. 'Language learning and "hypermedia" '. *ADFL Bulletin* 19/3.

**Valdes, J.** (ed.) 1986. *Culture Bound. Bridging the Cultural Gap in Language Teaching.* Cambridge: Cambridge University Press.

**Valdman, A.** 1992. 'Authenticity and communication in the foreign language classroom' in Kramsch and McConnell-Ginet (eds.) 1992.

**van Eunen, K.** 1987. 'Phantasie in Germany: Fiktionale Kurztexte im Deutschunterricht'. *Die Unterrichtspraxis* 2.

**VanLier, L.** 1989. 'Reeling, writhing, drawling, stretching, and fainting in coils: Oral proficiency interviews as conversation'. *TESOL Quarterly* 23/3.

**VanPatten, B.** and **J. F. Lee.** (eds.). 1990. *Second Language Acquisition—Foreign Language Learning.* Clevedon, England: Multilingual Matters.

**Vigner, G.** 1991. 'Ecole et choix linguistique: Le cas du Cameroun' in Coste and Hébrard (eds.) 1991.

**Wardaugh, R.** 1986. *An Introduction to Sociolinguistics.* Oxford: Basil Blackwell.
**Weinrich, H.** 1983. 'Literatur im Fremdsprachenunterricht. Ja, aber mit Phantasie'. *Die Neueren Sprachen* 82/3.
**Wells, G.** 1981. *Learning through Interaction.* Cambridge: Cambridge University Press.
**Widdowson, H. G.** 1975. *Stylistics and the Teaching of Literature.* Oxford: Oxford University Press.
**Widdowson, H. G.** 1979. *Explorations in Applied Linguistics.* Oxford: Oxford University Press.
**Widdowson, H. G.** 1981. 'The use of literature' in Hines and Rutherford (ed.) 1981.
**Widdowson, H. G.** 1990. *Aspects of Language Teaching.* Oxford: Oxford University Press.
**Widdowson, H. G.** 1991. 'Aspects of the relationship between culture and language'. *Triangle 7.* Paris: Didier-Erudition.
**Widdowson, H. G.** 1992a. *Practical Stylistics.* Oxford: Oxford University Press.
**Widdowson, H. G.** 1992b. 'Types of equivalence', in *The Role of Translation in Foreign Language Teaching.* Triangle 10. Paris: Didier–Erudition.
**Wierlacher, A.** (ed.) 1985. *Das Fremde und das Eigene. Prolegomena zu einer interkulturellen Germanistik.* München: iudicium.
**Wierlacher, A.** 1989. 'Magisterstudium Interkulturelle Germanistik an der Universität Bayreuth. Zur Architektur eines neuen grundständigen Faches' in Wierlacher *et al.* (eds.) 1989.
**Wierlacher, A., D. Eggers, U. Engle, H.-J. Krumm, D. Krusche, R. Picht,** and **K.-F. Bohrer** (eds.) 1989. *Jahrbuch Deutsch als Fremdsprache.* Vol. 15. München: iudicium.
**Wildner-Bassett, M. E.** 1990. 'Coexisting discourse worlds: The development of pragmatic competence inside and outside the classroom' in VanPatten and Lee (eds.) 1990.
**Woken, M.** and **J. Swales.** 1989. 'Expertise and authority in native-non-native conversations: The need for a variable account' in Gass *et al.* (eds.) 1989.
**Wolfson, N.** 1983. 'Rules of speaking' in Richards and Schmidt (eds.).

**Yule, G.** and **D. Macdonald.** 1991. 'Resolving referential conflicts in L2 interaction: The effect of proficiency and interactive role'. *Language Learning* 40/4.

**Zarate, G.** 1982. 'Du dialogue des cultures à la démarche interculturelle'. *Le Français dans le Monde* 170.

**Zarate, G.** 1983. 'Objectiver le rapport culture maternelle / culture étrangère'. *Le Français dans le Monde* 181.

**Zarate, G.** 1986. *Enseigner une culture étrangère.* Paris: Hachette.

**Zarate, G.** 1990. 'Pédagogies des échanges'. *Le Français dans le Monde* 237.

# Index

Entries relate to the Introduction and Chapters 1 to 8, including chapter notes. References to the notes are indicated by 'n'.